John Patrick's Advanced Craps

John Patrick's Advanced Craps

The Advanced Player's

Guide to Winning

by John Patrick

A LYLE STUART BOOK
Published by Carol Publishing Group

A Lyle Stuart Book
Published by Carol Publishing Group
Lyle Stuart is a registered trademark of Carol Communications, Inc.

Editorial, sales and distribution, rights and permissions inquiries should be addressed to Carol Publishing Group, 120 Enterprise Avenue, Secaucus, N.J. 07094

In Canada: Canadian Manda Group, One Atlantic Avenue, Suite 105, Toronto, Ontario M6K 3E7

Carol Publishing Group books may be purchased in bulk at special discounts for sales promotions, fund-raising, or educational purposes. Special editions can be created to specifications. For details, contact Special Sales Department, Carol Publishing Group, 120 Enterprise Avenue, Secaucus, N.J. 07094

Manufactured in the United States of America
10 9 8 7 6 5 4 3 2

Library of Congress Cataloging-in-Publication Data

Patrick, John, 1932-
    [Advanced craps]
    John Patrick's advanced craps : the advanced player's guide to winning / John Patrick.
        p.   cm.
    "A Lyle Stuart book."
    ISBN 0-8184-0577-5 (pbk.)
    1. Craps (Game) 2. Gambling. I. Title.
    GV1303.P36 1995
    795.1'2—dc20   95-4842
                                                          CIP

I've written six previous books and dedicated them all to my family. No reason to change now, 'cause they represent everything I love.

*To My Mom and Dad
and to my daughters
Lori and Colleen.*

All my love.

Contents

Preface

This book is on craps and gets pretty deep into the art of money management and discipline, something that is lacking in about 90 percent of the people who gamble.

The approaches are conservative but effective. Maybe you'll like the methods or maybe you won't. I really don't give a rat's tail if you think you're above a Disciplined approach to gambling and will laugh at these conservative methods.

If that's the case then don't read the book. These methods are geared to show you how to grind out small returns and maybe that's not your bag.

But if you're tired of playing like a dork and wanna learn how to win, read on.

But if you do read on, be sure you heed the advice and give the moves a good shot.

You won't be disappointed.

Acknowledgments

I didn't get borned smart and I ain't smart today. But I do know gambling, and there are several people who have helped me in conveying the art of winning to interested parties.

These guys are all experts in their respective games and I thank them for their contributions: Fred Ost, Dwight Davis, Carl Bajor, Joe Abrams, Ralph Ferrara, Gary Grezner, Mark Zimmer, Austin Kosik, Les Scally, Charley Zimmerman, Barry Urban, Jim Gilrain, Bob Nash, and of course the Vegas expert Howie Goldstein.

These guys are tremendous players and great friends, and help me constantly. It is my privilege to know and work with them.

John Patrick's Advanced Craps

Introduction

1

The Beginning

It's time to move up the ladder of craps play, but first you must understand where you stand as a player, before you get too deep into this game.

This book covers advanced methods of playing and especially a progressive money management approach. We'll be going over variations of wagering from the $5 bettor to the $500 a pop plunger.

Usually I keep the examples of play in tune with the average gambler who brings anywhere from $100 to $500 to the casino, but little by little you'll see these examples alluding to the higher-heeled people.

That doesn't mean I condone the fact that you wanna bet bigger amounts. You'll see in the Bankroll section that you don't have diddely beans to say about what you bet. The total amount of money that you bring to the casino dictates your bets.

But I don't wanna start jumping ahead, as we'll get to all of that in due time. What this section is designed to do is make you aware of what it takes to be a successful player.

It's also important that you realize it doesn't take a bloody genius to learn the game of craps. Everything about the game is very basic, except when it comes to money management.

If you won't follow the strict money management rules that are laid out for you, then you'll never be a consistent winner. But you should know that already.

As we breeze through these chapters, you'll see that the majority of moves are designed to make you a conservative player. That means I want you to be aware that the object of gambling is to win—not to gamble.

A lot of methods will be new to you lifetime craps players but before condemning this approach, I'd like you to grasp the theory and then make your decision as to whether you would want to play this way.

One thing is for sure, it'll provide an insight into gambling that will reduce your losses—if you follow the rules.

If you decide to revert back to your regular way of playing craps, that's your choice. But methinks you'll pick up some disciplined methods that will positively change your way of playing craps.

2

Who Gambles

I don't give a rat's tail if you gamble $500 a day, seven days a week at the plushest casino in the world or play penny-ante poker one night a month at your brother-in-law's house. If you put money at risk—and the amount of that bet is irrelevant—you are gambling.

Don't try to con yourself into saying you are not gambling when the size of the bets are just small amounts! Gambling is risking money to win money.

A person I know, G. I. Empure, is a pain in the neck, along with being a bore, along with being a self-proclaimed purist. He thinks gambling is evil and anyone involved with it must be a dangerous member of the mafia. When he learned that I had written books on gambling, he ruled my yard "off-limits" to his kids, branded me a "probable criminal" and a menace to the town.

Years ago, a woman with a similar feeling toward gambling told me she knows that all gamblers wear black clothes, turned-up collars, hats pulled down over their eyes, and probably crawl out from under a rock after dark.

I don't know if my acquaintance's words are a step up or a step down, but I do know that many people believe that gambling is one of the lowest forms of endeavors, ranking right up there (or down there, if you will) with drug dealing, killing, rape, and politics.

I don't mind the other comparisons, but it hurts to be compared to political shenanigans, however, that's another story.

The point I'm trying to make is that gambling is not looked upon favorably. It still ranks up there as one of the most popular pasttimes for millions of people, and I mean millions.

For just a minute, think about the people you know or work with or associate with. Write down each one of them who does not gamble at all during the course of the year.

This includes casino games, sports, cards, horse racing, pot bowling, bingo, lottery, even penny-ante gin rummy games in the afternoon senior citizens' get together.

The world loves to gamble, and the reasons will be stated later on. But the thrill of the chase, the anticipation of winning, makes for a lot of excitement, and that's why gambling is so popular.

How many people did you write on that sheet of paper who never risk even one dime during the course of a year? Not many, I'll bet.

My mother, bless her eighty-two-year-old heart, loves to gamble. The girls at her four senior citizen clubs tease the heck out of her, but that doesn't stop her one bit.

She still goes to bingo four nights a week, plays gin rummy, poker (penny-ante), the lottery, and goes to Atlantic City five to six times a month. I personally take her to Atlantic City at least one day a week—every single week.

Should she be burled in erl cause she gambles to much?

It don't mean a ding-dong to me if you wanna gamble—but if that is what you wanna do, then be a perfect player, not a dope.

I know for a fact that my acquaintance plays the lottery, goes to the track three to four times a year, makes an occasional bet on a football game and the World Series and plays poker every second week of the month—just for fun. Hey, baby, that's gambling.

Same goes for you. You wanna gamble, go for it. But learn to play the game you invest your money in. Take the time to become so perfect that you have a 50–50 chance of winning.

So you wanna be a gambler? Right on! But be the best you can be.

3

50–50 Chance

Let's get you aware of what your chances of winning in gambling are. Even if you are a perfect player, an absolute genius in the game you play, your chances of winning are never better than 50–50.

Naturally, the house has a vig or edge attached to every game, but even if there was no edge your chances would always be no better than 50–50.

Rollin Ball is a died-in-the-wool roulette fanatic. He goes to the casino with seventy-eight systems on how to beat the outside bets of Black/Red, High/Low and Odd/Even.

Now let's suppose the house told Rollin that he wouldn't have to worry about the 0 and 00. They would remove those house numbers from the layout. Since Rollins only plays the color black, all he has to worry about is that ball rolling into the red.

Even with the elimination of the 0 and 00, he still has no better than a 50–50 chance of winning, since there are eighteen black numbers and eighteen red.

The same goes for every other game you play. Let's suppose it's sports betting that turns you on. Even if your local bookie told you that he wasn't gonna charge you any vig to make that bet, you chance of winning is still no better than 50–50.

The card counter in blackjack can get about a 2 percent edge on the house if he's a perfect player, but that doesn't mean he has the casino backed against the wall. In reality, he has a little bit over a 50–50 pop at winning.

The reason I'm telling you this right now is to get any illusions out of your head about making the big kill in gambling.

That's why it never ceases to amaze me why some ding-dong, with $150 in his pocket and a sprinkling of knowledge about a particular game, thinks he's gonna go to that casino and double and triple his stake.

He's a dreamer—and so are the millions of people like him that think gambling means big returns. How can it, when you're taking on an opponent that has as much chance of winning as you do?

The only way to win an gambling consistently is with a strict disciplined approach. That's what you'll find in these pages.

There will be days when everything is going well and the money management moves will show you how to maximize those streaks. There will be days when all the knowledge in the world won't help you offset cold streaks or chopping tables.

But the loss limit rules will help you minimize those losses and get you out of the casino before you go broke.

So just keep in mind that the perfect player has no better than a 50–50 chance of winning, but he does know how to control his money.

Maybe some of you aggressive players will begin to realize that there is another way to play. It's conservative, but effective. I'd just like to have the interest on the money I blew back to the casinos after getting ahead and deciding to go for bigger returns.

One more point about your 50–50 chance of gambling. That's only if you're a perfect player. There are guys running around the casino playing Blakjack, Rulette and Bakarat with not even the foggiest notion as to how to spell the name of the game, let alone know how to play it.

Their chances aren't even close to 50–50. They're plodding along at about a 30–70 chance. Are you a player who doesn't know everything about the game you're risking your money on? Tsk! Tsk!

4

Vigorish

If you're not aware of it yet, you might as well be informed that I have written six other books on casino games and one of them was on craps. In that book I explained about Vigorish and a lot of basic things that will be only touched on in this book.

If you wanna get deeper into Vigorish, read that book before you get into this one, because the intent on these pages is to get heavy into money management moves and advanced systems. To do that you should already be versed on the preliminary aspects of the game.

However, for clarification, I will again list the House Vig for the different parts of the table.

Casino's Advantage on Craps Bets

Bet	Casino Pays	Casino Advantage
Pass Line	Even Money	1.41
Pass Line & Single Odds	Even Money & Odds	0.84
Pass Line & Double Odds	Even Money & Odds	0.60
Don't Pass (Bar 12)	Even Money	1.40
Don't Pass & Single Odds	Even Money & Odds	0.83

Don't Pass &	Even Money &	
Double Odds	Odds	0.59
Come	Even Money	1.41
Don't Come (Bar 12)	Even Money	1.40
Place Bet on 4 or 10	9–5	6.67
Place Bet 5 or 9	7–5	4.00
Place Bet on 6 or 8	7–6	1.52
Buy the 4 or 10	2–1 (5% commission)	4.76
Lay Bet vs. 4 or 10	1–2	3.03
Lay Bet vs. 5 or 9	2–3	2.50
Lay Bet vs. 6 or 8	5–6	1.818
Field* (2–1 on 2 and 12)	Even Money	5.56
Field* (3–1 on 12; 2–1 on 2)	Even Money	2.70
Any Seven	4–1	16.67
Any Craps	7–1	11.10
Eleven	15–1	11.10
Hardway 4 or 10	7–1	11.10
Hardway 6 or 8	9–1	9.09

You're gonna find that a lot of my systems in craps have to do with how you handle the place bets. In many instances I'll be having you bypass the Come-Out roll and go right to place betting.

Bida Nummers just had a fit. He is a mathematical genius and does everything by the numbers. He can't believe that I would have you give up a bet with a house edge of eight-tenths of 1 percent (Pass Line with odds) to take a place bet that has a house edge of 1.51 percent (placing the 6 and 8).

There are reasons for these moves and they will be elaborated on in great depth later on. Just understand that the difference of seven-tenths of 1 percent that I am asking you to give up has plus factors in other areas.

Bida Nummers will never accept my explanation. He is too wrapped up in his statistical approach that logic takes a back seat.

All of the books written on gambling harp over and over on Vigorish, but it's time you realized that the subject is getting so beat to death that they have people scared to make hedge bets.

If I have a $10 bet on the Don't Pass and 6 or 8 becomes the point, I immediately hedge my play, by placing the 6 or 8. Another example is a $10 bet on Don't Pass and 6 or 8 again becomes the point.

There are five ways for me to lose (5 and 1, 1 and 5, 4 and 2, 2 and 4, 3 and 3). By placing a dollar on the Hard 6, I have reduced my chances of losing from five ways to four. But since the house vig is 11 percent on the hard way bet, Bida Nummers immediately condemns that action.

Yet it is a strong move and should always be done.

Just be aware of the House vig in the games you play. Understand that I'll be suggesting moves that may seem to favor the house, but they are strictly intended to reduce your losses.

It's time some of the antiquated nonsense that has been handed down through the years finally gets put in its proper place: Out of your mind.

Vigorish will always be there. My hedging methods attack it from a different direction: minimizing dollar losses.

5

The Big Four

I know you've heard it before. I know you're bored with my bringing it up. I know it's on the front cover. I know each section refers to a part of the Big Four. I know you wanna skip over this chapter. I know that you know that I know that you know that I know that you know all of these things.

Don't skip over it. The power of these four things will determine whether you win or lose on a given day. These four things are what gambling is all about.

1. Bankroll
2. Knowledge of the game
3. Money management
4. Discipline

Bankroll: Based on thousands of discussions with people over the past few years, it is evident that I spent too little time in my videos and other books emphasizing bankroll. Too many people tend to play with small starting amounts and this forces them to curtail their play. I've said it before, but read it again: bankroll is the money you bring to battle and the amount of your wins and losses that day is based strictly on that bankroll.

Knowledge of the game: You should be perfect at the game you play, in this case craps. Just because you're a "wrong" bettor doesn't mean you shouldn't have complete awareness of the other bets on the table and vice versa. Being perfect at the game you play ain't no sin. But it's a crime to see people playing games where they are not perfect and I don't wanna hear any silly excuses as to why you do not have a complete grasp of the game you play.

Money Management: You're gonna get a bellyful of this subject in its proper section, so there's no need to elaborate on it right now. In a nutshell, money management is knowing exactly what bet you will make after a win and exactly what bet you will make after a loss and these amounts are set up, based on your bankroll.

Discipline: Most of you know what this is because you ain't got it. Most of you will never win consistently because you don't have discipline. Discipline is control. If you don't got it, you'll absolutely *never* win consistently.

There you have the Big Four, the key to gambling successfully. Even though you know what it is, I wonder how many of you will follow every rule to give yourself that 50–50 chance of winning.

You know, I don't want you thinking that if you adhere to every part of the Big Four that you have the casino bobbing and weaving. Not a chance.

If you follow every single solitary discipline suggestion I lay out for you and you pack the Big Four stipulations into your gambling days, your chances of winning will still only be about 50–50.

So if you don't think you can become a tight player and do what it requires, just close the book now and turn your attention to an easier endeavor, like sky-diving—without a parachute.

You think that's a silly statement? No sillier than watching some dork go to a table and get wiped out because he had no discipline.

Matching the two activities, deciding which one gives you a better chance to land on your feet—I'd say skydiving without a parachute.

6

Need

You ain't gonna like to read this chapter cause it strikes too close to home. It covers the reasons people gamble, yet they don't wanna hear it.

Even though you'll disagree with the theory, you'll end up reading these words and shake your head that it doesn't apply to you. But it does!

See if you can find yourself in at least one of these categories. It ain't a crime if the shoe fits you, but it is a crime if you refuse to correct your gambling bad habits. Maybe it's a form of self-evaluation.

People gamble out of need. They need this escape into the land of fantasy. That's what gambling is, you know. Fantasy. A lot of people think gambling is gonna give them the big returns that'll turn their whole life around.

Gambling offers people a chance to step into a land where things are different, wild, intimidating, romantic, promising. Many of these things cause the average citizen to look for escape in the world of gambling.

Let's list a couple of "needs" that may draw the average player to a casino.

a. Need for money
b. Need for excitement
c. Need for entertainment

d. Need an outlet from everyday job

e. Need the thrill of anticipation

Somewhere in that list we all figure. My humble opinion is that the underlying factor is *e* because it does offer the dream of eventually "breaking the bank."

I personally don't think that gambling in itself should hold out the facet of excitement or entertainment. The shows and restaurants should be able to cover your thrills, but the gambling part should be strictly an exercise in trying to win money.

I gamble to win money. Period. My need falls into that category.

I don't believe that gambling itself should provide the excitement. I find nothing exciting about playing craps for three hours, losing $400 and walking away saying I had a bellyful of thrills.

My gut is wrenched when I get beat. I hate to lose. That doesn't mean I go looking for a gun to blow my head off on losing days. But losing days leave a rotten feeling.

However, there are millions of ding-dongs like Watt Da Hek. He plays craps in the casinos twice a month, after he puts together a bankroll of $500 by scrimping and saving every dime he can.

He plays like a fool, making crazy illogical bets, acts likes a dope by making a pest of himself at the table, loses his $500 after being ahead $800 and finally drags his motley body away from the game.

He trudges into the bar, grabs a drink and announces to anyone who'll listen that he just blew a wad at the table.

Somebody will ask Watt Da Hek if it bothers him to lose the money. You know what his answer is?

"What the heck, it's only money and I really had a great time." Then he'll go home and cut coupons from magazines for two weeks trying to save fourteen cents on a can of peas, getting ready for his next suicide mission at the table.

They got pens for quacks like this, but if you tell them they're crazy they look at you like you don't understand where they're coming from.

Their constant comment is: "Hey man, that money was just chicken feed. I'm going for the kill. Anyhow, everybody losses at gambling, so what the heck difference does it make? Money means nothing to me!"

Then he'll out-fumble you when it comes time to pick up the check for a lousy hamburger and coffee.

Maybe this guy needs excitement, but the gambling table should not be the place to find it.

You want excitement? Walk down the street some day, find the biggest guy on the block and start making a play for his wife by sending her flowers, making small talk, stopping in for coffee (when gargantua isn't around).

When he finds out, you'll have all the excitement you can handle!

But if you gamble, make it like a job, not a need to be fulfilled. If you can't do that, if you still persist in blowing money at the tables, then your need is something only a special doctor can help you with.

A lot of you reading this page will scoff at this analysis. You'll say I don't understand.

I understand alright. Gambling should not fill a *need*. It should be something that is attempted only when you're a perfect player and I mean perfect!

Are you?

7

Expert or Dope

It really doesn't bother me to write this chapter, but if it bothers you to read it then perhaps it's because the message is so close to home.

I look upon gambling as an exercise that could frustrate even the calmest, coolest cat in the county. It has bankrupted thousands of people, destroyed lives and busted up families.

It has cost people their jobs, their homes, their sanity, even their lives. In other words, gambling is a potential danger to your health, to your family and to your own well being.

Some people reach the breaking point without being able to stop themselves. Some are fortunate enough to get to G.A. (Gamblers' Anonymous) and manage to salvage their lives.

Gambling ain't gonna go away and people ain't gonna stop gambling, so let's look at the alternative.

It's handling the situation, dealing with it in an intelligent way. So you wanna gamble—then back off, find the correct way to handle it, and then approach it intelligently.

Which brings us to the title of this chapter: "Expert or Dope." You're either one or the other.

Lotta Gaul is a successful business woman. She finished four years of college, then went for her masters. She is a computer genius, going for her doctorate, while pulling in a decent $65,000 per year salary. She is an expert in her chosen field.

However, Lotta Gaul has a little sideline that sparks her interest. She loves to play blackjack. Every week she bustles down to AC, grabs a room for two days and delights in banging away at the tables.

So far this year she has dropped $37,000 and has taken to using credit cards and credit lines to "soften the blow." Her losses have eaten into her savings, started to drain her cash flow and most of all, have begun to encompass most of her thinking time.

She is constantly reliving the sessions at the tables and rehashing the moves she should have done or would have done or could have done. In other words, the gambling fever is beginning to get to her.

Lotta Gaul has a lot of gall. What right does she have to blow $37,000 on a game where she obviously is over-matched? Lotta is an expert in her chosen profession. Good!

Lotta is a dope when it comes to gambling. She is coming into, or trying to come into, a world where she is out of her class.

To succeed in gambling you must be perfect in order to compete, or else you're too stupid to realize the dangers that are sitting there waiting for you.

There are a lotta dopes in the casinos and very few experts.

Examine your own playing techniques and see which label fits your play. I can walk through a section of the casino and pick out the winners and losers, and the experts and dopes.

They wear the tag on their faces and show their intelligence in the way they play and bet.

I want you to be a winner. In order to do that you gotta be an expert in the game you play.

Like I've said before, there are a lotta Lotta Gauls who have the gall to gamble. Don't you be one.

The choice is yours—be an expert or be a dope!

8

The Little Three

You veterans of my teachings are again nodding your heads as you glance at the title of this chapter. You're both right and wrong in your analysis.

You know what I'm gonna say, but how many of you will really devour the message.

I give seminars and people go out of their way to tell me they've watched my videos until their eyes begin to bulge.

"What's the Little Three?" I ask. The silence is deafening. So once and for all, get to realize what they are and how they can benefit you.

1. Theory
2. Logic
3. Trends

Theory: You've heard me allude to theory in the past four chapters, but in layman's terms it is simply: opinion. My opinion on how to gamble to win is to adopt a conservative approach. This works for me, so naturally I preach it. There are different stages of conservative play, so you can apply your own brand of moves. Same goes for the aggressive player. If that style is your bag, I hope you handle it with enough discipline to make your sessions profitable. Theory! It's opinion on how to win. Have one and stick with it.

Logic: Did you ever try to talk logically to a two year old, or reason with a six week old kitten? How about trying to intelligently make a point with a tree? Pretty difficult isn't it? Yet all I want to do is make a logical point when it comes to gambling. Suppose you get ahead a sum of money, let's say you're up $100, with a starting bankroll of $500. Isn't it logical to put the $500 in your pocket and rat-hole at least half of that $100! Logically, that beats giving the whole $100 and a portion of the $500 back to the house. Yet logic seems to leave most people when it comes to gambling. Logic means approaching something with an intelligent plan. I try to get people to use logic in their approach. Do they listen? Let me put it this way: I've had more success talking with the trees.

Trends: Trends are streaks. Streaks are patterns. Patterns tend to dominate in gambling and I can't give a smart answer as to why that happens. But it does. Trends are what we look for in any type of gambling and to give you an idea as to how important it is, a whole chapter is dedicated to trends.

There you have the Little Three. They will make an impact on your gambling forays. Maybe not as much as the Big Four, but enough to warrant a second look. Will you remember them? Not a chance, and that's a pity.

9

Self Analysis

We'll be swinging into the Big Four in the next section, but just a word to the wise at this time.

Many of you will scoff at the conservative approach and insist that you need the big returns to make gambling worth while. You're wrong!

There are days when guys make a giant kill at the tables, but chasing a repeat of that day will ultimately cost them a lot of rotten experiences.

Sure it feels good to triple your starting bankroll. But get to realize how rough it is. You wanna win a lot? Bring a lot!

Many years ago there was a very successful player from New Jersey who won consistently at poker, the races, sports, almost everything he tried. He didn't bet big, but he bet often and won a lot more times than he lost.

Soon the lure of bigger game crept into his thinking and he mapped out plans to take on Vegas. For one year he put aside parts of his winnings for the eventual pop into the big leagues.

His reasoning was that as long as he was so successful in the small pond, he might as well go for the big fish.

Pretty soon a sizeable bankroll was put together and he headed towards the desert, confident that his luck and success in New Jersey would carry over to the new frontier.

He envisioned killings at the table that would make him

super-rich in a matter of months. His main games were Poker and Blackjack, where he had been tremendously successful over the years. But he had also put together a type of Martingale system in Roulette, which would be the icing on the cake.

He arrived in Las Vegas at 2:00 P.M. on a Wednesday afternoon in 1959. The world was his oyster. His multi-thousand-dollar bankroll would be a springboard to riches untold.

He swung into action immediately, fully confident that the town would be buzzing in no time about the new king of the tables.

I was dead broke on Friday!

To be continued...

Bankroll

10

What is Bankroll?

Here is the first step in the Big Four of gambling that you *must* know in order to even have a 50–50 chance of winning. The amount of this bankroll is the catalyst for your whole day.

There are amounts you should bring to the casino in order to play intelligently and comfortably, but let me explain why the bankroll is so important.

Paye D. Bills is a typical visitor to the casino. Just like many of his cohorts, he looks upon gambling as a quick fix, an easy way to put together a lot of bread from a hot run.

Paye D. Bills looks upon gambling as a way to settle his bills at the end of the month. As the weeks wind down, Pate D. Bills slips closer to brokeville and looks for a way to recoup some money. He'll put together $300 and head for the tables, looking to turn it into $3,000.

Ninety percent of the time he'll lose and the reasons are all easy to see. He approaches a table with dreams of big bucks and immediately starts betting like money's going out of style by noon. In his case, it might as well go out of style, cause he's broke in a matter of hours.

This guy isn't looking for the intelligent return. His need for

23

money is so pressing that nothing less than a windfall will keep him from falling deeper in debt. But he goes deeper, all because of the lack of awareness as to what to expect from the money he brings to action.

Again I tell you, and please swallow this statement 'cause you cannot deviate from it: *Bankroll is the amount of money you bring to battle and predetermines the amount you will bet, the amount you will win and the amount you will lose that day!*

That in a nutshell explains what it is and upcoming chapters will bang out the theories that will show you how to best handle that money.

There's nothing wrong with wanting you to pay your bills with your winnings, but like guys like Paye D. Bills think they can satisfy all their debts with one day at the tables. Nice thought, but rarely apt to happen.

It's like asking congress to pay off the national debt with the taxes they receive one month from the town of Mission, Kansas.

Bankroll does not have to be $10,000 or $5,000, or even $1,000. Actually it could be the $300 mentioned above. There's no crime in bringing $300. The crime is expecting too much from the amount you do bring.

Whatever you bring is your Bankroll and don't feel bad 'cause you're sitting at a table making $5 wagers when the guy sitting next to you is betting hundreds. You'll get to that point, but only if you diligently work at increasing your Bankroll to the point where you can make these bets.

What is Bankroll? It's the amount you-you-you yourself bring to the casino. That's *your* bankroll!

11

Scared Money

Here's another description of the typical bankroll that a player will bring to the casinos. It's in the same family as the short bankroll and causes the same amount of anxiety pangs.

These people bring money that is not only usually short of the necessary minimum, but past performances at the tables cause these bettors to always fear the worst.

Frett A. Lott has been to the tables eleven times in the past six months. Every trip has resulted in a loss. The guy is a novice when it comes to gambling, but several of these trips had him ahead a sizeable amount. But he wouldn't quit and eventually left the casinos broke.

Now he is a bit shell-shocked and frets about the fact that he may lose again. Hence every bet is made with trepidation and he is almost resigned to the fact that he is destined to lose.

Now everytime he enters a casino, he plays scared. He won't double a Blackjack hand of A/3 vs. a dealer's five, as he feels he'll lose. He never takes odds in craps when point is 4, 5, 9, or 10. He figures it's not worth the possible loss potential.

When he loses he states: "See, I always lose."

When he wins, the words come out: "Can't believe I won, but that just means I'll lose the next three hands."

If he loses two hands in a row, his palms start to sweat, his foot twitches, he gets a headache, and his throat turns to gravel. He immediately thinks: "Here it comes, the old losing streak. I'll probably drop seven in a row. I wish I didn't come today."

Frett A. Lott is a bundle of nerves and a worry wart. He brings small amounts of money cause he's scared that if he brought more, he'd lose more.

There's no place in the casino for a guy like this. If you fall into the category of a person who plays with scared or short money, you're eventually gonna get whacked at the tables. It's inevitable.

Don't play scared. Better you didn't play at all. It's not a crime to be unable to put together a smashing amount of money that will allow you to take a big shot.

The crime is the punishment you put upon yourself by leaving yourself in a position to lose money at gambling.

For an instant, think back to the Big Four and about the first step. Ask yourself these questions:

1. Do I honestly have enough money to gamble sensibly, with a decent bankroll?
2. Do I play with money that is needed for more important things?
3. Is it really worth the rotten feelings that crawl through my mind when I lose money I can hardly afford to lose?

If the answer to even one of these questions leaves you in a quandry, then be sharp enough to get yourself to quit.

The next chapter tells you what you should have. You won't like it, but read it!

12

Proper Bankroll

Not many of you are gonna like this chapter. Not many of you are gonna agree with this chapter. Not many of you are gonna abide by these guidelines.

I guess that about covers everybody reading this book, but if one or two of you would like to abide by this strict rule, I think you'll see the power in it.

When you buy in at a table the amount you play with should be based on what the table's minimum is. It differs with the game you play, but in all instances it is done with one thought in mind: Be able to play comfortably and long enough for a trend to develop.

Following is the basic minimum amount you should take to a table:

a. **Blackjack:** Thirty times the amount of the minimum.
b. **Roulette:** Twenty times the amount of your inside bets and thirty times the amount of your outside bets.
c. **Craps:** Ten times the amount of your first bet, or enough money to cover ten shooters at that session.
d. **Baccarat:** Thirty times the amount of the minimum.

Now be honest with yourself. How many of you bring this much to the tables as outlined for each game?

It is my humble opinion that most people play with only a

27

handful of chips, leaving themselves prey for a table going against the way they are betting.

Since we're talking about craps in this book, let's go over the amount laid out for this game.

You'll find different methods of play in the latter pages, but whatever system you choose, the total of the first bet signals the total amount for that session.

Let's say you are betting the Pass Line for $5, taking single odds and placing two numbers. Five becomes the point and you take odds and place the 6 and 8 for $6 each.

Your total outlay for that bet is $23. You should have enough money to cover ten players at that table, at an amount equal to that $23. That means $230 should be your buy-in.

That does not mean you're gonna lose the whole $230 as you'll see in the Loss Limits chapter, but you must have this starting amount.

Naturally, if you lose on the first four shooters, you wrap up that session. Suppose this method was the one you chose and after you bought in, the first four shooters established a point and on the next roll sevened out. Not once did they make a point or even a place number.

Wrap up your session with the four straight losses. The balance goes in your pocket.

The first question that comes to your mind is: "If I'm not gonna lose the whole $230, why not just bring about $92 to the game?"

Here's the logical answer to that and it takes a little bit of understanding the human mind to fully grasp the theory:

If you go to a table and lost $92 out of $92 you're gonna leave that table feeling downright rotten—completely wiped out. But if you take $230 to the game and lose $92, at least you still have money when you walk.

It's a type of psychological warfare, but it does have its good points.

Setting ten players as your guide allows you to keep a handle on the money you will buy-in for.

If you use a system that calls for you to bypass the come out and then place the 6 and 8 for $18 each, then your risk factor is $36 on that first shooter and $360 should be the amount of your session money.

Think about the number of times you broke this rule. Now think about the number of times you'll obey it. I think the figures will change very little. Yet it is soooooooo important to follow these discipline rules.

Next time and every time you play craps, do this:

a. Set up your method of play.

b. Divide bankroll into sessions.

c. Predetermine betting amount per shooter, based on session money.

d. Be sure you have 10 times the amount you lay on the first shooter.

Simple ain't it? Then do it!

13

Sessions

Most of you know what this is already, so the explanation will be geared towards multiple sessions, instead of just three.

A sorry sight is to watch some guy race into a casino, grab the first spot at a table and whip out his entire wad. The poor guy can't wait to get into action.

He pulls out the entire $600 he brought to town and plops it on the table. Naturally he doesn't take time to chart the table. His whole cash fund for the day is at risk at a table where he has no idea whether it is with or against the way he chooses to play.

I want you to divide your starting bankroll into equal sessions. Each session will consist of a different table and will have its own set of win goals and loss limits.

The bankroll will determine the amount of each session, and it must stay within the guidelines of the previous chapter.

Let's suppose your method of play was $5 Pass Line, single odds and placing two numbers, the same one discussed in the prior chapter. Your total outlay of $23 calls for a session amount of $230.

Your bankroll now determines the number of sessions. If you have $1,000 as your start, then you can go to four sessions of $250 each, or three sessions of $333 each.

No, you cannot go to five sessions of $200 each. Bang, here comes the flurry of objections.

Most of you are screaming that the difference is negligible and since you won't lose the whole amount, what difference does it make?

It makes a lot of difference. If some of you people are allowed to bend and stretch these rules, you'd find a reason to go to a session with a roll of dimes, three five dollar bills, a gift certificate from Sears, two unused three-cent stamps and a letter from your mother.

And don't tell me I'm wrong, 'cause it happens every day.

You wanna play five sessions with this system, then bring the extra $150 to the casinos for a bankroll of $1,150. There is no room for bending. It only leads to breaking.

If you want seven different sessions with this system, then you must have a total bankroll of $1,610.

For you people who have short bankrolls, play at smaller minimum tables, or wait until you're properly set with the right amount of money.

A system we'll go over later calls for you to bypass the come-out and then place the 6 and 8 for $6 each, which is an outlay of $12. The session amount would be $120 and the total bankroll $360.

If you play this method for ten sessions, you must have $1,200 to start. Just remember: You can start a session with more than ten times the amount of the first bet, but never less.

In other words, if you bring $1,200 to the casino, you can play this system for ten sessions at $120 each, or you could play five Sessions at $240 each, or any number of sessions with at least $120.

But no cheating and bringing less that $120. You'll then play short, which leads to scared, which leads to...oh man, you've heard it before, there's no need to repeat it.

Sessions are easy to understand but must be laid out beforehand as to how you will play and how you will bet.

One more thing. If you plan to play "right" at a table, do all the charting required and then buy in. You are committed to stay betting right.

If the table turns cold, you cannot switch to the "Don't" side. You must leave that table and head out to chart another game.

If you start switching at a table, you'll drive yourself crazy going back and forth, trying to get reads on the flow.

The only aside to this message is if you had predetermined to bet "Follow the Trend" before you bought in. Then you would merely bet on whatever the previous shooter did.

But we'll get into that later. Just get to understand and plan your sessions and no cheating on the amounts.

14

Charting a Table

Remember the old TV series: *Naked City?* It always ended with, "There are eight million stories in the Naked City—this has been one of them!"

Well, there are three chapters in this Bankroll section that I want you to absorb. This is one of them! Charting a Table!

Ken Knot Wate is a degenerate weekend gambler. He works in an office all week, but longs for the Saturdays and Sundays when he can stand at a crap table and yell himself hoarse.

He can't wait to jiggle those bones in his hands and get involved in the multi-exciting game of Bank Craps. There isn't a thing about the game he doesn't know.

He is familiar with all bets on the table and has memorized the odds and payoffs of every possible betting denomination.

But Ken Knot Wate has one drawback that is a curse to thousands of people like him. He just can't wait until he finds a table that is showing in the direction he decided to bet that day.

Earlier in the first section there was a chapter dedicated to trends. It is an unexplainable trait that is as synonymous with gambling as Loni Anderson is to mountains and hills. Well, you get the point.

These patterns have a way of popping up and lingering for periods of time. Some hours of the day, you'll find shooter after shooter establishing a point and immediately sevening out.

That's a cold table and the Don't bettors long for these streaks. They should be able to capitalize on them. But both the "right" and "wrong" bettors are too stupid or too stubborn or too lazy to leave a table when a streak goes against them.

You'll always hear them spit out the ridiculous statement: "Hey, this table can't stay cold forever. It's due to change."

Sure, and Little Orphan Annie will someday develop so well, she'll make Loni Anderson look like a boy.

How anyone can be so stupid as to think they can ride out losing streaks by just staying in there is foreign to me.

By the time that bad streak ends, you need a monstrous hot run just to recoup the losses you incurred waiting for the table to change.

What is so hard about leaving a table when you're getting whacked?

On the other side of the coin, why even go to a table that is running against your desired mode of play?

Yet it goes on hour after hour. People won't take the time to chart the tables and that is a prime reason for the defeats they eventually suffer.

When a certain shooter gets red hot, he seems to bang out every number over and over. If you would chart the table and see this pattern developing, you would catch this streak. You have to, if you want to win on the "right" side. You gotta get these streaks at least once a day, but you gotta have the patience to chart.

All craps players admit that these trends occur every time they play. They out-and-out admit that they're aware of them.

Well, if you're so aware of the fact that these patterns have a way of occurring, why not chart the tables and play only in the games where the shooters are hot?

Can you give me one solid, intelligent reason why you won't, or can't, follow these trends? Of course you can't.

Oh, there'll be the usual stupid explanations such as:

a. I like this table.

b. It's due to go my way.

    c. I ordered a drink and am waiting for the cocktail waitress
to get back.

    d. The female dealer at this table called me by my first name,
I think I'm gonna get lucky.

    e. My wife is gonna meet me at this table so I don't want her
to miss me.

    f. The other tables are crowded.

    g. I don't know why I stay here.

Of all of the above answers, I think the last one is the most
intelligent and that was uttered by Whack O. Ruesky, who can't
tell the difference between a set of crap dice and roulette wheel.
But he's still smarter than the other dorks.

He doesn't know why he's there, but admits it. The others
don't belong there, but try to con themselves into thinking
they're right.

Charting a table is a powerful necessity for playing any game.
The next chapter shows you how to chart.

Ken Knot Wate, who started to read this chapter, ran out of
patience. He could not wait to get to a table. He's over there
involved in a game right now, beads of sweat pouring down his
motley brow.

He curses the various players who have the audacity to
establish a number and seven out.

To avoid all this stress and strain, all he had to do was wait and
chart the game to see which way it was going.

But Wate wouldn't wait and now carries the weight of an ice
cold run down the long road of frustration.

Typical craps player. If you are one of those people who won't
or can't chart a table—blink once within the next five minutes.

If you're guilty you'll blink, so don't try to hold it.

15

How to Chart

I thought you'd never ask. It is so easy to do, but the reason most people won't chart—and this includes most of you reading this page right now—is because it is time consuming and tedious.

Most people enter a casino, can't wait to get into action and will hop to the first table that has a seat, or in the case of an empty casino, but into a game and go head to head with the best looking dealer on the floor.

I'm writing this page on a Wednesday night in the Claridge Casino in Atlantic City. It's about 4:00 A.M. and I've just come up to my room after a day and night at the tables.

My day started at 2:15 P.M., when I pulled into the parking lot. Most of the afternoon and night was spent charting tables and playing craps. Approximately three hours was spent eating and relaxing in the lounge.

That left about ten solid hours on the floor for a return of $645. Now you may scoff that the return wasn't worth the effort. That's your opinion. To me it was a day's pay.

I was playing the Patrick system, a method you're aware of and will be explained later, but the point I want to make is that most of my time was spent charting.

The trick was finding a table that was condusive to the way I wanted to play this day.

Sure, it was tedious and tiring and boring and frustrating. Sometimes a table would be charted for three players and just as I was about to buy-in, the trend would change.

Off I would go to another game. After awhile you get gun-shy, even overly cautious. But it's all part of the overall scheme to play this conservatively.

The trick in gambling is to hold losses down. Make sure when you enter a game that the flow is in your favor.

There will be times that the flow will switch after you get there, so you just walk again.

But most of the time you'll be able to ride the trends at a table to strong, decent returns.

Let's get to the actual charting of a table and you'll see how very simple it is.

First you decide whether you will bet Right or Wrong. Next, you pick a system for the side you choose. There are many such methods in the Money Management section, so don't worry about that right now.

Let's assume you decide to bet Right. The method you choose includes bets on the Pass Line and placing of two numbers after the point is established.

Naturally you want a hot table, but there are different types of that nature.

Since you have included a Pass Line bet with your method, you must find a table where points are being made.

You've seen hot tables where a shooter establishes a point, then throws fourteen numbers before sevening out.

The next shooter establishes a point, bangs out seventeen numbers and sevens out. Then a lady picks up the dice, establishes a six as the point and proceeds to hold the dice for forty-five minutes.

She sevens out before making her point, but all the numbers bettors at the table made a fortune.

The poor guy who was just betting the point, never placing a bet, ended up losing, yet that was a "hot" table. Just realize that there are different degrees of "hot."

Since the system you chose included the Pass Line, you want a table showing both wins on the point and on the Place bets.

There are rules of thumb for this method, so you pick the one that suits you best.

First of all, you chart tables where there is room for you to play. Why the deuce would you chart a table, then find there is no place to get in?

When you get to a table, it's a good idea to see if there are many place bets on the layout. At least you get an idea as to whether the other players are in on any previous trend.

If there are a lot of Don't bettors at the table, it is probably a cold table. Don't bettors tend to play more cautiously than their "Let it all hang out" brothers on the Do side.

So when you see a table loaded with Don't Pass bets, you know the buzzards are circling and the prey is that particular game.

To bet Right, I want at least two players to make a minimum of one point each, plus throw three "inside" numbers before a decision.

Let's start with that rule and clarify it, 'cause there must be complete understanding.

When you reach a table, the next two shooters must each make at least one of their Pass Line bets and also throw at least three numbers which will include the 5, 6, 8, 9, 'cause they are the Place numbers you will be using.

Suppose the first shooter establishes a 5, then throws seven numbers, which include six inside ones, then makes his point. You've got your attention focused on that game.

He establishes a 6, throws five numbers and makes the 6. He comes out again, establishes a 10, throws five numbers and sevens out.

The dice pass to the next shooter who establishes a 5, throws two numbers and sevens out.

You do not buy in, but you can continue charting that table, waiting for two successive shooters to make at least one point number, plus three of the inside numbers.

You conservative players can make it that each of two successive shooters make two points each, plus two inside numbers each and you wouldn't be wrong.

Are you gonna like this rule? No, you're not! But I don't give a rat's tail whether it stirs your juices or not, it's the way to chart.

Sometimes it'll take an hour or even two, to find the run you want. But at least you know you're getting in on a trend.

The method proposed in this chapter is aimed at you people who include a Pass Line bet in your game, so you gotta include the making of the point to coincide with a shooter throwing a lot of inside numbers.

Hold this thought and go right to the next chapter.

16

Charting Place Numbers

Since the Inside numbers can be made a total of eighteen ways, you've got a 50–50 pop of catching these hits, but you still wanna make sure you don't have a paper champion throwing the dice.

That means a table where everyone establishes the point and throws a dozen other numbers and then sevens out. They're pulling down your basic bet with odds everytime. Again, the Money Management section will cover this, but for charting purposes you better realize this fact.

By now you should have an idea of how to chart a game when you include the Pass Line bet. If you don't like the method I suggested, make some adjustments. But don't water it down.

A. Jusment doesn't like my theory, cause it'll take too much time. He wants to go to a table and if a guy 'looks' like he's gonna make a long run, then A. Jusment will adjust his thinking to where he will jump all over that player—only because he has this silly feeling that something's gonna happen.

To me, a gut feeling is a pain in the stomach—nothing more. But to ding-dongs like A. Jusment they are the signal that such and such a player is gonna do such and such with the dice.

He'll see some six-foot-four macho type dude, with muscles bigger than Dolly Parton's trademarks, pick up the dice and A. Jusment will swing over and bet right because the guy 'looks' like he's a player.

The guy throws four successive craps on the come-out, finally establishes a 10 and bangs the whole table with a 7.

Up pops Gran E. Shortsocks, an eighty-eight-year-old grandmother who looks like she has an hour and a half to live. There are side bets as to whether she has the strength to life the dice, let alone throw them. She has to stand on a chair to reach the table and A. Jusment now bets wrong, because he reads her as being a wash-out.

She holds the dice for two hours, and our hero curses everything that lives—animal, vegetable or mineral—except his own stagnant brain, which probably has been dead for years anyway.

Don't bet on hunches, feelings or wishes. Only bet on trends and you find trends by charting.

Let's chart the Place numbers. In this method of play, you have no Pass Line bet and make your wagers after the point is established.

I want a minimum of two players to throw at least three inside numbers each, before you enter the game.

Whether they make their point or not is of no concern to you, cause you're not playing the Pass Line.

Suppose the first shooter establishes the 9 then bangs out 11, 10, 5, 3, 3, 12, 4, 10, 11, then makes the 9. He does not count as a hot roller. The ten rolls he made consisted of only two that would have done you any good (5 to 9) and that's if you had been placing them, which is highly unlikely, without first getting a 6 or 8 (explained later).

So that shooter's efforts are ignored.

The next guy establishes an 8, then throws 4, 10, 6, 6, 11, 3, 4, 8. That counts as a plus.

He comes out and sets the 10 and follows up with 5, 2, 3, 4, 3, 11, 4, 10. No good, the streak is stopped and you must start over waiting for two successive shooters to bang out three live inside numbers.

A hot roll does not consist of one shooter making six straight points and converting at least three inside numbers before each decision.

You must wait for him to seven out and then the next shooter must also throw at least three inside numbers after he establishes his point. If he does, now you can join him after next come-out is set, or when the following shooter starts his roll.

Since the average amount of place numbers that are thrown after a point is established, until a decision is reached is three, then you want to use that number as your mean.

You are defining it even further by not counting the 4 or 10 as pluses for your charting, but that is because I don't believe in these numbers in the first place.

Perhaps you would like to come up with your own theory of charting Place numbers. That is perfect with me, as long as it has validity.

For instance, you might want just the 6 and 8 to be your dominants. You could set the mean at two numbers after the point is established, but the two hits would have to be a combination of the 6 and 8.

Let's say you want three straight shooters to throw at least two sixes and/or eights.

First player establishes a 10 then throws 6, 5, 8, 3, 11, 6, 10. He counts. Then he follows up with 6 as the point and throws 4, 8, 8, 12, 2, seven out. He counts.

Next shooter establishes a 4, then bangs out 5, 5, 9, 3, 6, 4, 9, seven out. He doesn't count cause only one 6 was thrown and the fives and nines were deemed meaningless.

You must start over, waiting for three straight shooters to give you at least two sixes and/or eights. If you want, you could use two shooters making at least two sixes and/or eights, but no less than that.

I'll give you one more example to a pattern that does pop up quite often. If you adopt a method whereby you incorporate the Regression system on the 6 and/or 8, or a method which calls for an immediate "off" on your 6 and 8 after one score, then this charting method could be used.

Wait for two consecutive shooters to throw at least one 6 or 8 after the point is established and then you may play.

The reason is that the Regression system or immediate "off" theory will lock up a profit after one hit.

So a table showing at least one 6 or 8 would tie in with your plan of attack and you could utilize the particular pattern that is showing.

You'll come up with different ways to play when you get to the systems and then you can set up your charting scheme.

The ones I've laid out for you are effective and many of you will adopt them or even improve upon them.

Remember this about charting: It is a necessary part of your game plan. Sure, there's gonna be times when you'll chart for hours and after the buy-in find the trend has ceased.

That's part of gambling and it's gonna happen. But in the long run, you'll find it a powerful tool. I've said this a few chapters back, but you must grasp it. Charting is one of the most important parts of your day.

Charting is essential to gambling, just like it is to girl chasing. Or didn't you degenerate, girl-chasing, self-styled romeos check out many girls before you made your big move? Some of you would evaluate thirty females before you swung into second gear.

Many times it was a lack of guts to do anything, but most times it was to be sure you had a decent shot at scoring.

Well, gambling's the same thing or didn't you know that? And it's just as tough.

1. Pick your game (or girl)
2. Check it out (or her)
3. Make sure you make your move when the time is ripe
4. Enjoy the fruits of victory.

Based on the stupid lines that some guys give to girls—stick to gambling.

17

Win Goals

How much do you want to win? It's amazing the number of people that give me a blank stare when this question is put to them. It's like you were picking their wallet. They stare at you and answer with an almost incredulously adamant air. "All I can," is the stock reply.

I admire their positive thinking. I question their impractical dreaming. Sure, we all want to win alot of money, but this is seldom the case in the world of gambling.

Very few people realize that the setting of a win goal does not restrict the amount they will win that day, but gives them a figure to aim at.

As you probably already know about my theory of gambling, I believe it is more important and a lot easier to win small amounts consistently, than to shoot for the moon.

Now before you split your over-taxed gut in indignation, just realize what I am asking you to do.

Set a win goal! That is an amount of money you will win that day, based on your starting bankroll. It does not necessarily mean the day ends when the goal is reached, but it does mean you will leave the casino that day with a profit in your jeans, and isn't that what the exercise was all about in the first place?

Later on you will read all about guarantees and excesses and the handling of the win goal. That's when we get deep into the theory of discipline.

But each and every person who puts down a bet should have a predetermined amount that he or she wants to reach that day, and the amount is 20 percent.

Now you can shake your head in total objection and fly into tantrums about this being beneath your level of acceptance and all the other ways you have of showing your disagreement, but that's the figure.

In all reality, it is higher than I want you to set. But giving you anything lower will have you stamping your foot in anger and I wouldn't be heard over the noise of thousands of feet being banged on wood.

When reality reaches a player, which sometimes takes a long time, he realizes this is a fair percentage. It's just hard to accept in the beginning.

Think how many times you entered a casino and did not set that goal, that amount of money that you would like to win that day. Still using 20 percent as the figure, I'll bet there were many times you were ahead that amount. Did you quit? Nope!

And when the winning streak ended and you lost everything back, did you quit? Nope! Did you feel rotten when you got home and ended up a loser instead of a winner? Didn't you feel rotten? Yup!

On your next trip, did you change your approach and use Discipline? Nope!

The previous conversation could be held with thousands of people who go to a casino. These people all have the following in common:

1. They love to gamble.
2. They love the thrill of the action.
3. They have an idea of how to play.
4. They all have a decent bankroll.
5. They all usually get ahead a few dollars.
6. None of them quit when they get ahead.

7. They all put back their winnings.
8. They then kick back the bankroll they brought.
9. They usually end up losing.
10. They always feel rotten that they never quit when they were ahead.
11. They all swear to change.
12. None of them ever do.
13. They're all dorks.

If you qualify for even one of the aforementioned negatories, you're in category thirteen—the low point of gamblers.

All I'm asking you to do is grasp what it takes to be successful in the casino.

I want you to set win goals. This goal will give you something to shoot for, provide a direction, a level at the table where you will guarantee yourself a profit for that particular session.

I'm not asking you to swallow poison, cut your throat, slash your wrists, cut the grass or talk nice to your wife—all the things that you don't like to do.

I'm trying to get you to do things you would like to do: Win at gambling. And one of the biggest steps is setting win goals.

You don't have to go back and memorize anything in this chapter, only be aware of the stupendous importance of its message.

There will be numerous references to the win goal. It's a basic percentage of 20 percent, with various offshoot decisions when we reach the Money Management and Discipline sections.

But you get an idea of how strongly I feel about this part of your day's preparation. Maybe Ken Knott cannot see it's importance, but he probably couldn't see the forest for the trees; the ocean for the water; the lawn for the grass or his stupidity for his ignorance.

Win goals: spelled backwards it means niw slaog, which means mandatory in Irish!

18

Loss Limit

Here's the second level of the two-headed monster that destroys most gamblers. It's the loss limit that everyone must place on the money they bring to battle.

It's the refusal of people to place this limit on their money that leads to total wipe-out: a devastating, sickening, rotten, empty feeling when you leave a casino broke.

I know most of you are saying that you only bring an amount of money you can "afford" to lose. That's crap and you know it. I don't give a pig's eye who blabbers out nonsense like this, it always comes out like the words of a fool.

It doesn't matter if you're Mary Wittow, living on a fixed income of $200 a month of Ken A. Ford, a super rich cat pulling in 5,000 G's a week. If you play to lose—you will lose.

Naturally Mary Wittow is in a lousy position because the small bankroll probably makes her play scared. But you can be sure when she left her house in the morning she had dreams of big returns, because she honestly needs the money. The $200 is money she has scrimped and saved for two months to allow herself a "shot" at some extra money.

She tells herself that it is extra money and cash that is put aside and won't affect her life. But deep down inside she is conning herself.

When she loses that whole $200, the reality of that loss

47

engulfs her and the ride home is total dejection. She curses herself for blowing the whole amount and wishes she had saved a little of it.

Ken A. Ford can afford to lose the $5,000 he brings, but his 'need' is more of a macho thing. He wants to prove to himself, his friends and the casino people that he can beat the table.

On the way down he tells himself that he's really gonna give it a big shot that day. He does, but catches some bad runs and loses the whole stake 'cause he starts to bet higher and higher.

He also leaves the casino in frustration, but his is more of a rage. He, to, is disgusted cause he gave them his whole stake. The reality also hits him after he leaves and gnaws at him all the way home.

Both of these people played to their last chip. Both went broke and the rotten empty feelings hit both of them.

Maybe you're in the same boat and have that same stupid illogical reasoning that you'll bet until you're cleaned out.

Do you think betting that last chip—or set of chips—will suddenly allow you to recoup all the day's losses? Do you think all of a sudden that the sweet smile of Lady Luck is gonna grace your series?

The answer is no, and if you stop and go over that previous paragraph six or seven times you'll see how dumb it is to chase an elephant with a water gun. Maybe you'll win a few hands, but ninety percent of the time you'll lose that back too. Make that 99 percent.

What I wanna do is put a limit on your losses on the days that things go bad, and this is for all the Mary Wittows with small bankrolls, all the Ken A. Fords with heavy bread, and every single person who bets more or less than these two.

I want a limit on your losses and when that limit is reached you are donerooski for that day.

It's gonna be the roughest thing you have to do—walk away from the tables while you still have chips burning a hole in your pocket. But when things are going bad, you gotta have the guts to quit!

The loss limit in craps is 50 percent. That's the absolute maximum amount of money you can lose at a session or for your whole bankroll. You can set any loss limit you desire, but it cannot exceed the max.

Mary Wittow could set 30 percent and Ken A. Ford can set 40 percent. Neither one is wrong. If Mary breaks her $200 into two sessions of $100 each, she has a limit of $30 that she can lose per session and $60 of her total bankroll. She'll still bring home $140. Now you're gonna laugh and say, "Well, if she's only gonna lose $60, then just bring $60 to the game!"

No! Then she's still going home broke. You see, psychologically, the idea of taking $60 and losing the whole $60 gives off a more rotten feeling than if you brought $200, lost $60 and at least brought $140 home.

There is not that total feeling of wipeout. It's a little thing, but actually a big thing if you know what I mean. If you don't, then you're a little denser than even I thought you were.

Same is true of our friend Ken A. Ford, who sets a 40 percent loss limit on his $1,000 session money. I know he's gonna feel itchy about leaving the table with $600 in his pockets. But if he didn't do anything with $400, who's to say the other $600 will turn that table around? Let him go chart out another game.

I do not expect 100 percent agreement from people on this seemingly curtailing endeavor, but until you realize its importance, you cannot win at gambling. That's because the number of days when you suffer total wipeouts will more than offset the several times when you'll win 20 percent or 30 percent of your bankroll.

Following is the loss limit for each game in the casino:

Blackjack	40%
Roulette	50%
Craps	50%
Baccarat	60%
Slots	60% of 30% of your bankroll
Video poker	70%

The differences are self-explanatory. Blackjack is the roughest game in the house, so you must drop your potential loss limit. Baccarat gets a lot of streaks and you can allow longer sessions. Slots should have about 30 percent of your total bankroll allocated to these one-armed bandits and then your loss limit is 60 percent of that 30 percent.

Video poker has a low vig at certain machines and this again allows for longer sessions, so the loss limit is raised.

Naturally you can set any loss percentage that you want on your sessions, but you must adhere to the maximums.

You're gonna hear about these again, so don't think you're getting away with just a few pages of me yelling at you to set these limits.

The last two chapters will determine just how successful you're gonna be. Either you put the win goal/loss limit theory very high on your priority list or you're honestly wasting your time reading the rest of the book.

Harsh words, maybe, but true, even though only a few of you are nodding in agreement.

I still haven't fully convinced Ken A. Ford, cause he views gambling as a lark and a place to get his jollies. But maybe a few more chapters and even he will begin to come around.

Loss limits—set 'em and abide by 'em.

19

Minimum Bets

This chapter is gonna hit home to a lot of people and others will just pooh-pooh it away, as though any mention of it is beneath them to even consider it to be a factor in their play.

Well, if it's such a small factor, why does every single gambling table in the world make mention of this fact: minimum bet!

It's because it's a big thing that should be considered as part of your trip to the tables. In fact the table minimums have a big say in the breaking of your bankroll into sessions and controlling your betting series.

Minimum bets are put there for a purpose. They tell the player what the lowest amount he or she may make on the outcome of a hand or roll of the dice.

The minimums are controlled by the individual casinos and adjusted as per the number of people in the casino.

If the place is empty, you're gonna see a lot of low minimums. If it's busy, they bang up the cost per roll.

It's called economics and smart moves by the casino. If a person with $40 in his pocket goes up to a $25 table, it's obvious his elevator doesn't stop at every floor. But tell that boob that he only has enough for one bet and he looks at you like you just short-circuited.

Let's divide the comments on minimums into sections of the

country, starting first with Atlantic City.

As of this writing there are twelve casinos and on weekends, holiday, and summer times, the crowds flock to their tables. The casinos raise the minimums to take advantage of this situation.

That's their privilege and their right, and who can blame them? They don't put a gun to your head forcing you to play.

During the week and on slow days, there are many $5 tables and even $3 tables in craps. Based on the fact that I want you to have ten times the amount of your first bet in order to play, these tables will be suitable for most players.

If your outlay on the first shooter is $22, you should have $220 per session and $660 bankroll for action at a $5 table.

If the table minimum is $10 and you have $220, then you cannot play $44 per shooter. Your options are as follows:

    a. Bypass Come-Out and place $12 six and $12 eight
    b. $10 bet on Pass Line with single odds (no place bets)
    c. $10 Don't Pass, single odds and $10 Don't Come bet (this is
       OK!)
    d. Don't play

Either you have the money to play the way you should or you pass until you have the bread. Or you can visit the casinos when the table minimum is in your financial realm.

In Vegas, Reno, and Tahoe, a number of casinos allow a more liberal approach to the minimums. You can find dollar tables, fifty cent tables, quarter tables—even ten cent tables.

Once a friend of mine, G.I. Mabroke, was going through a run of bad luck. In fact, it was so bad that he didn't have a dime to put in the slot machines.

Walking through the roulette section, his wife suddenly got a stone in her shoe. He lifter her onto a table to remove the pebble.

The croupier spun the wheel and number 10 showed. Unbelievably, G.I. Mabroke had placed his wife squarely on that number (she had a small dumper).

Bank, he had a winner! They paid him thirty-five wives. He continued to play and lost several of them back, but still left with a couple of handfuls, but that's another story.

The thing is, in Vegas you have the opportunity of playing with tables where the minimums are not as high. This is not to say that Mabroke's wife was worth less than $5, but you get the point.

Minimum bets play a big part in controlling your bankroll. Don't play at games where these minimums put a strain on your money.

Play only where the minimums are the lowest, if you can. It's always easy to bet higher at a table. The smart player always leaves the door open to where he can bet the lowest when things are going lukewarm for him.

And for you guys that are broke, just like G.I. Mabroke, go find a roulette table like he did. What have you got to lose?

20

Various Bets

Some of you won't take the time to set up your series bets, based on the amount of your session money, so I'll give you a couple to get you started.

Realize however, that this is simply the initial bet, not the continuing bet in a series based on wins and losses. That'll be covered in the Money Management section. This is to pound into your head the importance of the minimum bet.

RIGHT BETTORS

SESSION MONEY:	$200
PASS LINE:	$5
ODDS:	SINGLE
SIX & EIGHT	$6 EACH
SESSION MONEY:	$200
PASS LINE:	NIL
SIX & EIGHT:	$12 EACH
SESSION MONEY:	$400
PASS LINE:	$5

ODDS: SINGLE
SIX & EIGHT $12 EACH

SESSION MONEY: $400
PASS LINE: $10
ODDS: SINGLE
SIX & EIGHT: $12 EACH

SESSION MONEY: $600
PASS LINE: $10
ODDS: SINGLE
SIX & EIGHT $18 EACH

SESSION MONEY: $600
PASS LINE: NIL
SIX & EIGHT $24
SIX & EIGHT (option): $30 EACH

WRONG BETTORS

SESSION MONEY: $200
DON'T PASS: $5
ODDS: SINGLE:
DON'T COME: TWO BETS
ODDS: NONE
                    (After Don't come established)

SESSION MONEY: $200
DON'T PASS: $10
ODDS: NONE
DON'T COME: TWO FOR $5 EACH

SESSION MONEY: $400
DON'T PASS: $10
ODDS: SINGLE

DON'T COME:	TWO FOR $10 EACH
ODDS:	NONE
	(After Don't Come established)

SESSION MONEY:	$600
DON'T PASS:	$10
ODDS:	SINGLE
DON'T COME:	TWO FOR $10 EACH
SIX & EIGHT:	$12 EACH

There are so many combinations, it is impossible to list them all. Get an idea and apply to your own individual bankroll.

Bett D. Maxx is starting to agree with the theory but one thing is haunting him:

"I feel a little cheap betting smaller amounts. They'll look at me like I'm not important."

I was waiting for him to say that, and maybe his statement strikes a sore spot with a lot of you guys that think you're supposed to lay out heavy plays cause you wanna impress people.

Many years ago I had that same thought. In effect I was subconsciously playing to make myself accepted by the dealers. It took em a long time to realize this was one of the problems with my game. Actually there were a lot of problems with my overall approach to gambling, but that's another story.

Today I can walk up to a table, bypass the Come-Out, place the 6 and 8 for $6 each and not even blink. After one hit I'll take them both down and I don't give a diddedly dang what anybody says or thinks. And you shouldn't either.

Get into the habit of reducing the amount of your first bet to realistic figures. As you win, you can always start socking it in.

Set up the amounts of your initial bets, so that when you get to the tables you don't have to fumble through your notes to decide how much you'll wager.

As a start, just cut in half the amount of your present outlay on both the line and place bets. Here's a start:

PRESENT LINE BET	ADJUSTMENT	PRESENT 6 & 8 PLACE BETS	ADJUSTMENT
$5	$5	$12	$6
$10	$5	$18	$12
$20	$10	$18	$12
$25	$15	$24	$12
$50	$25	$36	$18
$100	$50	$60	$30

That's not so hard is it? Don't worry, as you hit various plateaus of winning, you can begin to lay it out.

Is that a smile of relief I see on Bett D. Maxx's face? Glory be, and I didn't know mountains could bend.

Knowledge of
the Game

21

Smarts

For you people who can't comprehend a nine letter word like knowledge, we'll break it down to a six letter word: smarts! You should all know what that means. But there's a lot of you that know the meaning of smarts, but check it at the entrance of the casino.

So many people walk through the doors of a casino and for some reason, leave years and years of knowledge on the back seat of the car. Why?

Is the intimidation factor of the tables so great that you turn into a dingbat at the games? I sure as heck don't understand why people play so stupid, but they do.

Knowledge of the game is the second leg of the Big Four and calls upon you to be a perfect player. The games are not hard to learn. In fact it's downright snap city to grasp both the object of the game and the correct payouts.

But you gotta wanna learn about the game you're playing. You gotta know every single, solitary facet of the table or maybe you got a good reason as to why you play without being a perfect player.

Go ahead; each one of you examine your own knowledge of the game you play and see if you're perfect. See if you know everything there is to know about it.

Since we're talking about craps right now and since we're into the advanced book, every one of you should know the answers to these few questions I'll throw out to you:

1. How many different combinations are there on a set of dice?
2. What is the house vig when you place the 9?
3. What's the charge for buying the 4?
4. How many ways can you make a hard 5?
5. What should the true payoff be for the hard 8?
6. What is the worst bet on the craps table?

You should have zipped through these questions and recited the correct answers. If you didn't, you don't know the game. If you don't know the game, you shouldn't play.

How many of you had at least one wrong, yet played craps in the past few months. (Answers at end of chapter.)

How many of you got at least one wrong, still played, and disagreed with me that you should be perfect, go ahead, write me a sensible reason why you play craps and yet you're not a perfect player.

The horror of it is that there will be people who are not perfect, continue to play and will take the time to write to me and condone the fact that they play and condemn me for chastising them. What a joke.

Bill A. Kingdem is a financial genius. He has built a private kingdom and become a multi-millionaire. He doesn't waste a dime in his business, cuts corners unmercifully with his employees, brown-bags his lunch to save money, uses his wife as a secretary to save money, and his mother is the cleaning lady for six of his hotels.

He pays her salary by letting her live rent-free over his chauffeur's garage. He hasn't wasted a penny in years, in fact his running a business has caused him to receive the "Genius of the Business World Award" nine straight times.

Yet he'll walk into a casino, saunter up to a craps table, proceed to ask the dealer twenty-seven questions on how to play, blow $7,800 in twenty minutes, and walk away smiling because he was comped and received a free lunch.

Another case of a cool cat losing his cool and his cash, as soon as he ventures into something he knows nothing about.

Why? Why do people treat gambling like they're supposed to lose? I'll never understand it.

Bill A. Kingdem can go out and build all the fortunes he wants cause he knows what he's doing in the business world. But he should stay away from the tables.

So should you if you're not perfect. Are you perfect?

Knowledge of the game is a necessity and mandatory if you expect to have successful days.

Get some smarts before you get involved. Here's the answers to the quiz that I hope you all passed perfectly:

1. 36
2. 4 percent
3. 5 percent
4. No such animal.
5. 10 to 1. (They pay 9 to 1.)
6. Any Seven.

Don't go twisting your elbow and patting yourself on the back if you had them right. You're supposed to.

22

The Table

We're into the second part of the Big Four, which is Knowledge of the Game and that means the part where I explain all of the different sections of the game. But this is an advanced book and the purpose is to go deeper into the money management part coming up in the next section.

To save time, I'm telling you to refer back to my first book on craps which goes deeper into the table explanation. By this time you should have the whole layout memorized anyway.

An earlier chapter went over the Vigorish and payoffs so you don't need long, drawn out explanations of that.

However, for the benefit of those people who need a little reminder, I'll touch each part of the table. But it'll be brief, so be sure you catch it this time.

All crap tables are the same in every casino, except some have different wording as to the payoffs of bets (explained in the next chapter).

Also, the tables in Las Vegas employ the Big 6 and Big 8 bet, which Atlantic City does not.

You should know all of these things by now, but if you don't, devour it, as every little thing might save you a couple of bucks down the line.

The game of craps moves so fast that the novice has a hard time keeping up with the flow of action. Even the layout looks complicated. But in reality, it is a very simple game.

Both sides of the table are identical. In this way, more people are able to play at the same time. The next page shows a typical layout. Check the description below with the corresponding letter:

A. Pass Line . . . . Bet is made before dice come out.

B. Come . . . . Bets are made after the original point is established, and allows you to have additional bets working.

C. Don't Pass . . . . Bet is made before point is established. Opposite of pass.

D. Don't Come . . . . . . Bet made after point is established. Looking for additional numbers to have working for you.

E. Place Bets . . . . Numbers 4, 5, 6, 7, 8, 9, 10, may be placed, or taken down any time you wish.

F. Big 6 and Big 8 . . . Available in Las Vegas Casinos. *Never* never bet it!

G. Field . . . . One roll bet can be made any time.

H. Hard Way Bet . . . . Proposition bet that number will appear 'hard', before a seven or an 'easy' combination of same number. Covers 4, 6, 8, or 10's.

I. Any Seven . . . . Bet that a combination of seven will show on next roll. Worst bet on the table, in fact, worst bet in the casino, tied with the Big Wheel, and the blackjack player that doesn't have complete knowledge of Basic Strategy.

J. C or E . . . . One roll bet on either designation (C) stands for craps (E) stand for eleven.

K. Any Craps . . . . Could be 2, 3, or 12. It is a one roll bet, paying 7-1.

L. Horn . . . . Combination of the three craps bets, and also the eleven.

M. Dealer . . . . His position at the table.

N. Stickman . . . . His position at the table.

O. Box man . . . . His position at the table.

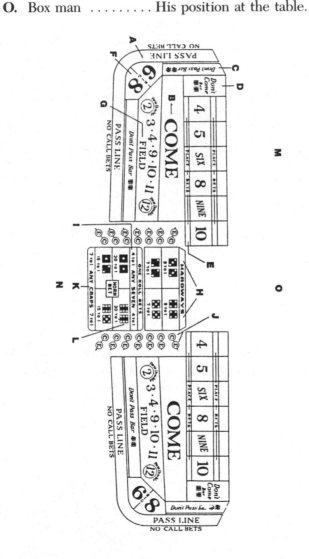

23

Right Bettor

There is no surefire, absolute positive way to play craps. But every book written on the subject alludes to a subscribed method of play:

1. Bet Pass Line.
2. Take as much odds as allowed.
3. Take two Come Bets.

I am going to say the same thing many times over in this book, so don't get irritated if it is repetitious: "Money management and discipline are more important than how you play."

My theories differ tremendously with a lot of hogwash that is handed down, although I agree that you should have three numbers working for you when you do bet Right.

Incidentally, since this chapter is on Right betting, let's define the topic. There are two types of players at the table:

1. Right, Do, or Pass Line Players
2. Wrong, Don't, or Don't Pass Players

If you follow the flow of the dice and bet that numbers will come, you're classified as a "right" bettor. It does not mean it is the right or correct way to play—it is strictly a term.

If you bet against the dice, you're called a Wrong or Don't bettor. But there's a right way to bet Wrong, a wrong way to bet Wrong, a right way to bet Right, and a wrong way to bet Right.

Got that? You better my friend, 'cause if you don't know how to bet correctly—whether it be Right or Wrong—you're gonna get whacked.

You're gonna see ways for you to handle the Right betting methods, and many of them don't even call for Pass Line betting.

So go all the way back to the beginning of this chapter and look over the subscribed method of play and then put it out of your head.

1. You do not necessarily have to bet the Pass Line.
2. You should always take odds when you bet the Pass Line, but not always the maximum allowed. (Your bankroll prescribes the amount of your odds.)
3. Never bet the Come—never, ever, never, never, ever.

I want you entering your craps schooling with an open mind, as you'll be seeing different theories of play opening up, and many of these will differ with old school teachings. Just remember that the Right bettor is going with the flow and looking for hot rolls.

M.T. Hedd qualifies for the previous paragraph, as to playing with an open mind. Fact is, he has nothing in there at all.

His sessions consist of pouring money all over the table, putting maximum bets on the Pass Line, full odds, all the Hard Ways, 3 Come bets and a couple of buys on the 4 and 10.

His empty headed, high-powered method of gambling— where he thinks each shooter is gonna hold the dice for two hours—has resulted in his leaving the casino with empty pockets more times than not.

But has this changed M.T. Hedd's mindless, stupid approach? Is he gonna learn to bet properly? Is he gonna manage his money and cut down his losses? Is he gonna correct his mistakes and make only intelligent moves? Is Loni Anderson gonna be accused of promoting the flat look? NO! to all questions.

M.T. Hedd cannot change and won't even acknowledge that he is doing things wrong.

If you're a Right bettor, that's your choice—but there are sensible ways to bet Right, so approach it with an open mind.

24

Wrong Bettor

Naturally the Wrong bettor is opposite of the Right bettor and he tends to be a little more conservative. His theory is that the seven is so powerful that he wants it working for him.

But one thing I wanna clarify right now. You'll hear people say: "I'm going with the house, I'm gonna bet Wrong."

Get this into your head and keep it there: The house is not a Wrong bettor. The house is simple opposite of whatever you are.

If you bet Right, the house is naturally betting Wrong. But if you bet Wrong, the house now becomes a Right bettor.

People misconstrue their evaluation of this motive. It just so happens that approximately 90 percent of all craps shooters are Right bettors. This makes the house an automatic Wrong bettor, because it is booking the game.

If five people walked up to a craps table and everyone bet Wrong and each took a turn throwing the dice, while betting on the Don't Pass Line, the house is now a Right bettor.

Just remember the house is always opposite you. The reason they win is not because Right bettors always lose. The house wins because players have no money management or discipline.

Just as in Right betting, there are ways to bet Wrong. I don't give a pig's ear which way you play, just as long as you play smart.

I'll give you systems for both sides of the table and you pick the ones you like best.

If Don't betting is your bag, good! Play that way. As you go deep, deeper, deepest into this game you will also come up with your own spinoffs of all of the systems.

The Don't bettor is betting against the flow of the dice. He should always be at a cold table—where the 7 is showing with alarming consistency.

One final thought on the decision of which side you choose. Neither one has an edge, as it all comes down to the trend which is showing at that time.

You do not have to brand yourself as a positive Right or Wrong bettor. There will be sessions when you'll bet Right and other sessions when you'll bet Wrong.

But you will never switch back and forth between Right and Wrong at the same table—as the trend switches—unless, and I repeat *unless*, your method of play was predetermined to "follow the trend" at that particular session.

If M.T. Hedd wants to start pouring some filler into his spacious cavern, I suggest he go back and start with the tiny message that was laid out in these past two chapters.

25

Pass Line

A quick reminder and a quick repeat right here: I am merely reestablishing a tiny reference to each part of the table and have no intention of going deep into the explanation of each part of that table. The basic book is the place to find that information.

If you wanna throw the dice, you gotta have a bet on the Pass Line. If you do not wanna bet the Pass Line, merely wave the dice to the next shooter and the stickman will go past you.

This is gonna be a hard pill for you long-term craps shooters to swallow, but I don't think betting the Pass Line is the greatest thing since falsies—even though both give the illusion of being something they're not. Let's elaborate on that theory.

Go to the Vigorish that the Pass Line has. If you bet just the Pass Line, the house has only a 1.41 vig, which is a good move for the Right bettor. By taking single odds, you reduce that vig to eight tenths of one percent. Imagine: less than 1 percent edge for the house.

A double odds bet is six tenths of one percent. So you can see that the player is not fighting insurmountable odds. Staying with the single odds bet and a house vig of eight tenths of one percent means that the player is not in a deep hole.

But just ask a typical Right bettor what number he would like to see come as the point, and before you can blink, he'll blurt out: "6 or 8, of course."

What he is saying is that since they are the two numbers that can be made the most number of ways for the Right bettor, he'd like them going for him and he's right. A lot of Right bettors don't like the 4 or 10 to show as the point and some even detest the 5 and 9.

But betting the Pass Line puts you in a position of having a "contract" bet. That means whatever number comes as the point, you're stuck with it. You can't take it down.

If you are place betting, you can increase your bets, decrease them or remove them anytime you want. But the house vig on placing the 6 and/or 8 is 1.51, about seven tenths of one percent higher than a Pass Line bet with single odds.

Assuming you've devoured all the information I've given you in this chapter and assuming you are a Right bettor who likes the 6 and 8, let me pose a question: Would you like to bet the Pass Line, take the single odds, fight a vig of six tenths of one percent and take the chance of getting locked into the 4,5, 9 or 10 as your point, or would you rather bypass the Pass Line and then just place the 6 or 8?

If you end up opting for the placing of the 6 and 8, your vig is 1.51, about seven tenths of one percent higher. But the plus side is you're always getting the 6 and 8 and in my opinion, the difference in the vig is not that bad.

You don't have to make your decision now, but I want you to be aware of these possibilities.

In a nutshell: The Pass Line is where you get the opportunity to bet Right along with the shooter.

We'll go deeper into the plus and minus aspects of this bet and you'll have a clearer view of what you will then decide to do.

26

Don't Pass

On the other side of the ledger we have the Don't Pass Line, where the Wrong bettors place their bets and are going against the shooter.

The Don't Pass bet is not a contract bet, as you can remove it any time you want. But never remove your Don't Pass or Don't Come bet. After you go through all the trouble of beating the 7 and 11 on the Come-Out, why remove the bet? If you don't like the number that was established, just hedge off. That'll nullify the bet, but still leave you in a positive position to grab a profit.

Let's elaborate:

I. Madork has a consistent approach to every game. The consistency party comes from the fact that he always makes the wrong assumption. When he bets Don't in craps, he hates to see the 6 or 8 become the point, because they can each be made five ways. He's right. A lot of Don't bettors hate to see the 6 or 8 show as the point.

But common arithmetic still has you with a 6:5 edge over these numbers, because the 7 can be made six ways and I'll take six ways over five ways any day of the week.

But I. Madork makes a stupid decision when either the 6 or 8 shows. He immediately tells the dealer, "No action." That means he is taking down his Don't Pass or Don't Come bet. In essence, he is giving 20 percent back to the house, which is the percentage he has going for him.

The dealer nullifies the bet and this dork starts looking around to see if anyone has watched his vigorous move. What he should have done was hedge his bet. Then he would have put himself in a position of booking the house.

Let's say you are a Don't Pass or Don't Come player betting $10 on the Don't. Six shows as the point and you don't like that number. This is what you should do:

1. Place $6 on the 6.
2. You now are betting both ways.
3. You have $10 No Six and $6 on the 6.

Here are the possible things that could happen:

a. If the 6 shows, you lose $10 Don't Pass and win seven bucks for your Place bet, for a loss of $3.

b. If the 7 shows, you lose $6 Place bet, but win $10 for your No Six for a profit of $4.

c. You are risking $3 to win $4. (Did you grasp that?)

d. Since the profit of $4 would come with a 7, you have six ways of winning, as opposed to five ways of losing by having the 6 show.

e. You are booking the house by having the edge of 6:5 on the possibility of the number showing and risking $3 to win $4. A *fabulous* position.

Read that example over and maybe you can explain it to I. Madork and get him to stop removing his bets when he is in such a good position.

I favor neither the Don't Pass or the Pass Line. The house vig is 1.41 on both, so there is actually no difference either way.

27

Chart of Combinations

This is merely a chart to show you the number of ways that each number can be made. Should you memorize this chart? Yes!

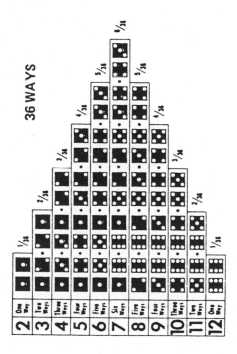

28

Come Line

When my daughters Lori and Colleen were growing up, we wanted to be sure that they had a good hot breakfast with a nourishing juice to start their day.

On the days that Cream of Wheat or Pablum was on the menu and prune juice was the drink of the day, they'd turn up their noses and refuse to eat.

So I'd go into a long tirade about how good it was by explaining all its good points, knowing in the back of my mind that I wouldn't eat it myself.

Same goes for the Come bet. I hate it, yet I have to explain it to you cause it's on the layout.

Understanding the Come line is snap city. It is exactly the same as the Pass Line, except that it can only be played after a point is established. When you put a chip in the Come box the next roll of the dice activates that bet, just as it does on the Come-Out roll with your bet on the Pass Line. If 7 or 11 shows, you win. If 2-3 or 12 shows, you lose. Any other number (4,5,6,8,9,10) shows the chip is moved by the dealer to the same corresponding box and place around that number to coincide with where you're standing at the table.

In reality, it is another Pass Line bet, cause the rules are exactly the same. You can take odds with the number that shows by simply tossing a chip to the dealer and stating: "Odds, please!"

He'll take your chip and place it on top of the basic Come bet—but off center, to indicate that it is an odds bet.

Naturally your odds can be removed any time you desire— just like on the Pass Line. But the basic bet is still a contract.

Old time craps shooters swear by the Come bet and use it all the time. I hate it and never use it.

Their contention is that if the 7 shows while your chip is in the Come box, you win that bet and that acts as a type of insurance against your other Pass Line or place bets.

My dislike is based on what happens after a number is established and a separate chapter will detail the pros and cons of this wager, as opposed to the straight place betting method.

Some of you players like the Come and will continue to play it. That's your choice. Maybe you guys also like pablum and Cream of Wheat, washed down with a tall glass of prune juice.

Well, I explained about the Come and before you make a decision as to its good and bad points, wait until it is put to a comparison.

My opinion is that you'll see a lot of holes in the Come betting technique.

29

Don't Come

Just as the Pass Line and Don't Pass are direct opposites of each other, the Come and Don't Come are also completely different from each other, except in the time that you can bet it.

You cannot bet the Don't Come until a Don't Pass number has been established. Naturally you can bet the Come or Don't Come on any roll and as often as you like after a number is established, even if you don't have a bet on either the Pass or Don't Pass line.

That's because the Come and Don't Come are separate bets unto themselves and not related to any other wager.

The Don't Come bet is also made to establish another number, but it is a good bet for the Don't bettor because it allows him to bet smaller in order to establish extra Don't numbers.

It's gonna take a little explaining, so put your thinking caps on.

I.M. Short is a little short on cash but likes the theory of having three Don't numbers working for him. His session money is $100 and he wants two additional Don't Comes after his $5 Don't Pass bet is marked.

A reminder about the rules of bank craps, which is upheld in most casinos in this country, and I said most, as in majority.

1. You can place a $5 chip on the 4-5-9-10 anytime you want

and $6 on the 6 and 8 just as often. In other words, I.M. Short could place a $5 chip on the table and tell the dealer: "Place the 4, please." And he has action.

2. You cannot bet against any number with a $5 chip. I.M. Short can't drop a $5 chip on the table and say: "No 4, please." He does not get action.

The rules state that if you want to bet against a number, you must lay enough money—plus 5 percent of the potential profit—to win four units or $20.

Inlayman's terms, it comes out like this:

"Hey Mac, if you want no four or no ten, you gotta lay $41 to win $20 (minus the 5 percent charge even if you win)."

Since the odds against the 4 or 10 coming is 2:1, you gotta lay $40 to win $20, plus $1 for the 5 percent vig.

If you wanna lay against the 5 or 9, you lay $31 to win $19. In the case of the 6 or 8, you'd lay $25 to win $19.

Since I.M. Short don't got the bread to lay $41 a pop, the only way he can't establish $5 Don't bets is by coming through the Don't Come for $5 increments. So while I abhor the Come, I strongly advise you "wrong" bettors to utilize the Don't Come and you'll get a bellyful of moves in the next section.

In a nutshell, the Don't Come:

1. Is bet made after the point is established
2. Minimum bet allowed
3. You lose if 7 or 11 shows while bet is in Don't Come box
4. You win if 2 or 3 shows
5. 12 is a push
6. You can remove any Don't Come bet after it is established
    a. Don't you dare, I. Madork, don't you dare.

Don't Come bets work on the Come-out. You can ask that there is "no action" any time that they are up there. Then you can put them back in action.

But I can't see why you would *ever* negate a Don't number from working!

30

The Field

Lotta people are swinging over to this bet and it ain't a rotten move. It's a one roll action wager and snap city to understand.

The winning numbers are listed on the layout and usually they are: 2, 3, 4, 9, 10, 11, 12. That means there are sixteen ways of winning and with the 2 and 12 getting a two to one payoff, you have a plus factor of 18.

The losing numbers are 5, 6, 7, 8, which can be made twenty ways, leaving a 20 to 18 edge for the house. Not really too shabby a play.

In fact the vigorish against the play with the field bet is lower than it is when you buy the 4 or 10, which calls for a 5 percent charge.

Plenty of times you'll hear some loud mouthed, pot-bellied, cigar chomping, super obnoxious wind-bag pick on some poor unsuspecting lady who is bothering no one and just making consistent bets on the field.

He ridicules her for making what he calls a stupid bet, yet compared to his $10 place bets on the 4 and 10, dollar bets on the Any Craps and three dollar Hard Way wagers, she is fighting less of a house edge.

There are some layouts that pay on the 5 instead of the 4 and

78

others pay triple for the 12. Naturally both of these moves aid the player and make the field bet an even more enticing wager.

So don't downplay the Field and don't worry about the Larry Loudmouth of the craps world coming down on you. It ain't as bad as its detractors would have you believe.

31

Hard Way Bets

You should already know that Hard Way bets are simply wagers made hoping that the number you choose shows as a double or hard. For instance, 4 and 4 is a Hard Eight and 5 and 3 and 6 and 2 are called Easy Eight.

Suppose you place a dollar on the Hard Eight, looking for the 9 to 1 return. That chip stays alive until either the Hard Eight shows and you win $9, or the Easy Eight or 7 shows and swallows the bet.

There is no action on Come-Out rolls as all Hard Way bets are automatically off. Naturally you can tell the dealer that your bets are "working" and you then have action.

The Vigorish against you is 11 percent and that is because the payoff of 9 to 1 should really be 10 to 1.

Here's how you figure it: There is one way for the Hard Eight to be thrown (4 and 4) and ten ways that you can lose (2 and 6, 6 and 2, 5 and 3, 3 and 5, and the six ways to make the seven).

Since they pay you 9 to 1 and you should get 10 to 1, that is why the vig is so high. To figure out the computations for the Hard Six the same figures apply.

Go to the payoff of 7 to 1 for the Hard Four and Hard Ten. Lee Tildense is a little dense on his arithmetic and can't quite grasp why you get less money for these prop bets when the chances of losing a Hard Four or Hard Ten are exactly the same as the Hard Six or Hard Eight.

What the dense one hasn't worked out is the number of ways to lose on the Hard Four or Ten. Since the four or ten can only be made two easy ways (1 and 3, 3 and 1, or 6 and 4, 4 and 6), this coupled with the six ways to make the 7 leaves you only eight ways to lose your Hard Four or Ten, so they only pay you 7 to 1.

It all reverts back to everything about the game having a logical explanation. There's absolutely nothing mystical about the table or it's payoff.

The only mystery to me is why people would play it without understanding all of these things.

I'll give you some hedges on the Hard Way bets later on and will even bow to the aggressive players and go over a disciplined progression type of approach.

32

Any Seven

I ain't gonna beat around the bush. This is the worst bet in the casino. It ranks right up there—or down there, depending on your analogy of good or bad—with the Big 6 Wheel.

Both of them tote a hefty 16.67 vigorish, but at least the bet on the Big Wheel takes about two minutes to lose. The Any Seven—which is a one roll action bet—usually goes down the drain in two seconds.

The 7 can be made six ways, as opposed to the thirty ways of losing, resulting in a 5 to 1 edge for the house. They pay 4 to 1.

That's highway robbery and even Jesse James would be embarrassed with that crime, and he used a gun.

I don't wanna go into a long discussion about this rotten wager, but I do remember an instance at a table when someone did reap a profit from this bet.

There was this wild player named Buck D. House, making all sorts of crazy wagers, trying to break the house with all of the high payoff exotic props.

There was this gorgeous redhead standing at the far end of the table. Her attributes consisted of a bust line that would make Jayne Mansfield look like a boy and a dress that was bucking the laws of gravity as it strained to perform its worldly duty to stay up.

The stickman's name was Ed, but it could have been

Cleopatra for all the attention he was getting. Even our hero, Buck D. House, had trouble keeping his mind and eyes on the table.

One particular roll he wanted to bet on the Any Seven but his mind was on anything but ("gimme the any Big Red, Ed") as he tossed a chip on the table.

The dice flew across the table. One of them took a crazy bounce, flew in the air and found a landing space in the cavern that is usually described as cleavage.

All eyes were riveted to the spot, naturally, and the offers to retrieve the lost die outnumbered the grains of sand in the movie "On the Beach."

The pit boss came over to see what was happening as Buck D. House screamed for his payoff. They tried to explain to him that the Big Seven didn't show.

He explained that he made a mistake and asked for the "any Big Red." Ed the stickman concurred that he heard the bet.

They paid Buck D. House off in four gigantic balloons.

And that's how the any Seven got it's name: The Big Red.

Don't *ever* and I mean *never* make this bet!

33

Any Craps

Another one roll action bet and this time it covers the multi rolls of 1 and 1, 6 and 6, 1 and 2, and 2 and 1.

There are four ways to make a craps and thirty-two ways to lose. The odds are 8 to 1, but you are paid 7 to 1, another high vig.

You hear the usual cries of "any craps" or "any" as the players follow their so-called hunches.

Sometimes you'll hear the old refrain; "C and E please." That merely means a bet on the Craps and a bet on the Eleven.

The layout shows a bevy of "C's" laid out next to the "E" and the reasons were already explained to you, as to this being the way the dealers know where to place the bet and who it belongs to.

The any craps bet is a good hedge for the Pass Line bettor but, just like the yo, it should also not be a hunch wager. That advice apparently falls on deaf ears.

Walk past any craps table and you'll hear the dreamers yelling out their prop bets as they toss chip after chip down the drain.

I believe the thing that attracts players to these bets is the payoff prices of 7 to 1, 15 to 1, 8 to 1 and so on.

Alas and alack, some guys never realize that everything isn't all it appears to be on the surface. You gotta strip away up-front foliage and understand that these prop bets aren't as overpowering as they appear.

They have a use as a hedge—or have I said that before?

34

The Horn

I'd be willing to bet that of the next one-hundred people to drop a chip on the table and ask for the Horn, only 50 percent of them know exactly what it is. If you ask these same one hundred people what the payoffs are, you'll get 80 percent blank stares.

It's the case of another exotic bet drawing the sheep to slaughter. Let's see if I can explain the different points of this move:

1. Proposition bets like the Aces, Any Craps, Big Red Seven, Twelve, Eleven, etc., are sucker bets.
2. Many people bet the above a dollar at a time and still get whacked.
3. The Horn bet includes each of the above. Suppose you throw $4 on the tale and say, "Horn, please!" You get:
   a. $1 on the two Aces
   b. $1 on the Aces/Deuce
   c. $1 on the two sixes
   d. $1 on the eleven

Now instead of blowing a buck on one bad bet, you get to drop $4 and have four bad moves going.

You get the opportunity of getting what is called, "Horn High." That's where you can pick any of the moves and put an extra dollar on your preference.

For instance, you toss a $5 chip to the stickman and ask for the Horn. He has to give you a dollar change and what's a lousy buck to a classy guy like you?

But by saying "Gimme the Horn-high Yo", you still get a dollar each bet plus $2 on the Yo (or whichever poison you choose) and now you don't have to worry about getting that dollar chip back.

To figure the payoff on the Horn, you gotta use a little logic, which I find prevailing in many Horn players—very little logic.

Suppose you flip a $5 chip to the stick and say Horn high aces. You get $2 on the aces and a dollar each on the ace/deuce, 12 and 11.

Let's assume the 12 shows. You lose $4 on the other prop bets and have $30 coming on the 12, for a profit of $26.

Is the Horn a good bet? Does Sophia Loren look like a boy?

Put it this way. Betting a buck with a gut feeling on the ace/deuce is like getting popped with a Mike Tyson triple jab.

Betting $5 on the Horn is like having him throw a left hook, an uppercut, a shot to the kidneys and a right cross.

Will that hurt? Yeah!!!

Will you stop betting the Horn? No way!

Are you a dork?.... (One answer, please.)

35

The World

All the world loves a lover, or is it loser? Whatever, if it's a loser they love, the casinos are a potential passion pit. 'Cause there are more losers than winners and I'm trying to show you why.

It's because so many people have a penchant for self destruction. It's like they enjoy getting their heads handed to them.

The previous chapter covered the Horn bet, which is a four times proposition suicide mission, in comparison to the guy who just flips dollar chips to the dealer and dies a slower death.

I compare the latter player with a guy who wants to commit suicide by jumping off a bridge, but wears water wings so he dies slowly.

The Horn player just dives off the roof of a building and wants to get it over quickly. But now we have a guy who wants to die even quicker than quick.

He plays the World bet. This is a step more suicidal than the Horn. When this guy jumps off a building, he brings along a gun and shoots himself in the head to make sure.

The World bet includes all of the Horn niceties, but they throw in the Any Seven. Isn't that a dandy?

But sure enough, there is I. Madork standing at the table grinning ear to ear as he pops a $5 chip on the layout and screams, "Gimme the World, Mac." Then he looks around as the other players glance over at this cat that is playing something they never heard of.

Just picture the World bet as taking the five worst things that ever happened to you during your lifetime, bringing them all together for revival night and then paying to have them happen again.

Do you get the idea that this is not the wager that makes casinos shudder when they see people make it?

If you still persist in making this nonsensical illogical bet then start looking for the highest building in your town, and don't forget the loaded gun—just to make sure.

36

Three Way Craps

Might as well explain this move now, as it'll save time later on:
1. Any Craps bet is not a good move if it is based on hunch alone.
2. It is not a bad move if there is reason for making it.
3. The Hedge bet is that reason.

Any Craps bet pays 7 to 1 and is a one roll action move. Tossing a coin onto the layout in the middle of a roll makes no sense, cause you are only making it to try and grab a quick 7 to 1 payoff.

Using it on the Come-Out roll, as a hedge against a craps, is acceptable. Let's set an amount of Pass Line bets that call for this hedge.
1. $5 Pass Line... No hedge.
2. $10 Pass Line... Optional.
   a. Could throw a buck, but you're not wrong by just letting the $10 lay naked.
3. $15 Pass Line... $1 Any Craps.
4. $20 Pass Line... $2 Any Craps.
5. $25 Pass Line... Three way craps.

Notice when we reach the level of a $25 bet, we get off the Any Craps and make it "three way craps." This is how that works when you make that play:
   a. You bet dollar on 1 and 1

b. You bet dollar on 6 and 6

c. You bet dollar on 1 and 2

Since the deuces and twelves pay 30 to 1, you've improved that payoff over the $14 for $2 you'd receive with an Any Craps bet.

The ace/deuce pays 15 to 1, so you end up a shade short of covering the $25 Pass Line bet. This could be covered by adding a dollar, asking for 3 way craps high ace/deuce. This gives you $2 on the ace/deuce, fully protecting your Pass Line bet along with a dollar on both aces and 12.

If you use the three way craps bet, you can also apply it to number four above, wherein the $20 Pass Line bet gets a three way play, rather than $2 any craps. That's your choice.

Let's just lay out a few more hedges, utilizing this play for the higher increments on the Pass Line.

1. $30 Pass Line = ($4).. three way craps, high ace/deuce

2. $40 Pass Line = ($5).. three way craps, $3 high ace/deuce

3. $50 Pass Line = ($7).. three way craps, $3 high ace/deuce

Go over the previous table and apply the use of this hedge with a spread that makes you feel comfortable.

There are many of you who will never want to hedge the Pass Line bet. That's your choice.

Some of you will want a partial hedge. This wager can be adjusted any way you like. But I do advise taking some type of hedge, at least when you get to a wager of $25 and higher.

Now you high-rollers are gonna pooh-pooh this move, but don't waste your breath. If you feel you don't have to worry about the craps on the Come-Out, don't worry about it.

But if you stand there betting $50 a shot on the line and some cat tosses three straight craps, you need quite a few hits to make that back.

You decide, but you know my feelings—at least take a partial hedge, where you cover a bet of $25 and higher.

37

Odds

I can't leave this chapter out, yet I don't wanna spend a lotta time explaining the odds, as you should know them by heart. If you don't, go back to my basic book on craps and pick up all the intangibles.

I'll briefly touch on odds to give you additional theory as to their use, but this is strickly brush-up.

If you bet the Pass Line you should always take odds. You know by now that the thirty-six rolls of the dice give the Do bettor an 8 to 4 edge on the Come-Out. It ain't like having Loni Anderson's home number, but it's better than being in the drive-in alone.

But this is the end of the edge for you Do bettors. Once the point is established, that 7 is staring you right in the eye. For instance, a $5 bet (or any amount) on the line pays even money. Yet a four or ten as the point has you sitting with 2 to 1 odds against hitting your point and for a rotten even money payoff.

By taking $5 odds, at least you'll get $15 for your $10 risk. The odds soften the blow that the Pass Line (without odds) will suffer.

Same is true of the 5 and 9 becoming the point. The 6 to 4 edge against you is too much to swallow. By taking the $6 odds, your payoff becomes $14 for an $11 risk. The odds protect your bet and increase its value.

Even the 6 and 8 becoming the point has a 6 to 5 edge against you, for an even money payoff. The $5 odds bring the total potential profit up to $11 for $10, instead of $5 for $5.

I know what runs through your mind, so let's lay it on the table. When the point becomes 4 or 10 and for some of you, also the 5 or 9, you say: "Let's forget the odds. I don't wanna lay out extra money on rough numbers."

That's because you're playing short, along with playing scared. You see guys every day making bets on the Pass Line and neglecting to take odds. A very, very stupid play.

Shorty Shortchange never takes odds when the point is 4,5,9,10, trying to save the few dollars he has for the odds on the 6 and 8. If you won't take odds, don't play the Pass Line—as you're making the basic bet a worthless move, despite the 8 to 4 edge on the 7 and 11 over any craps.

Following is the amount of single odds you should take for the various bets and the amount of their correct payout:

POINT	WAGER	$ ODDS	ODDS PAYOFF
4 or 10	$5	$5	2 to 1 or $10
5 or 9	$5	$6	3 to 2 or $9
6 or 8	$5	$5	6 to 5 or $6
4 or 10	$10	$10	$20
5 or 9	$10	$10	$15
6 or 8	$10	$10	$12

Odds never change of course, but different casinos allow you to take various amounts of odds.

Just remember this: Taking odds behind the Pass Line is a must. There ar instances where I have suggested to right bettors that the 4 and 10 can be a difficult number and for those with short bankrolls to forget taking odds on those numbers and use the money to place the 6 and 8.

That still holds true. While I admit that you should always

take odds, the guy with the short bankroll has my approval to forget taking odds on the 4 or 10 and use that money to pick up the 6 and 8.

This is strictly for the Shorty Shortchanges in the casino who insist on playing the Pass Line.

Bypass the Come-Out, then you need never worry about the 4 or 10 again.

38

Double & Triple Odds

Man, do I get heat when this discussion comes up. It has a direct tie-in with people over reacting to the power of Vigorish.

I've already told you that Vigorish is the edge the house has in any game and naturally it's important to play games where that hammer is not devastating. But you can go overboard on certain aspects of gambling and I think this is one of them.

A lot of books spit out the information that odds is the cheapest bet and the best for the player and that you should always grab as much of it as you can. I agree that odds in craps reduces the house edge, but let's not go overboard with it's value of importance.

Monee S. Tite is going through a little dry run in financial matters and right now money is tight for her. She goes shopping with the idea of budgeting her money and saving a few nickels by buying smart.

She sees a sale on bed sheets for $10 a set. If you buy two sets you pay $18 for both and if you get three sets you pay $24 for all three.

Very tempting and quite a savings if you buy in multiples. But what is Monee S. Tite going to do with three sets of bed sheets, especially since that money can buy some essentials?

She buys three sets 'cause it is ingrained in her mind to go for the bargain, then she lives on milk and crackers to make up for

94

the fact that she overspent in a certain area of her funds.

Same is true in gambling when I tell you that vig is important, but there are degrees in its importance.

Let's use the example of taking odds behind the line in Craps:

1. Pass Line bet ....Vig 1.41
2. Take Single Odds ....Vig .83
3. Taking Double Odds ....Vig .6
4. Taking Triple Odds ....Vig .46

The difference between single odds and double odds is two tenths of one percent, yet you had to lay out a whole betting increment.

The vig drops a big one tenth of one percent when you take triple odds, but now you've laid out another betting increment. Big deal—you've picked up almost four tenths of one percent when taking triple odds as opposed to single odds.

A lot of craps players believe you should take as much as the casino allows. Do you know that there are a couple of casinos who advertise ten times odds? How much of a drop off of .8 can that be? Is it worth the outlay of $50 on a $5 Pass Line bet to Monee S. Tite—or anybody else who is struggling financially? Methinks the answer is no.

My humble opinion is that bankroll is more important than vig, especially in dollar value. One or two losses with a heavy odds take is devastating to your bankroll and when your money is gone, you ain't got a prayer of a chance of competing.

Let me lay out my suggestion for the amount of

1. Single odds until shooter makes two Pass Line points.
2. Double odds until he makes his 3rd and 4th point numbers.
3. Triple odds only after shooter has made 4 Pass Line points.

Naturally the 7 and 11 on the Come-Out does not count as a point.

Following is a more conservative approach and the one I lean towards:

1. Single odds for first two Pass Line points to be made
2. Double odds from then on.

Finally, the very conservative:

1. Single odds for first three Pass Line points to be made
2. Double odds from then on.

I know you big bangers are hung up on odds and will decry this approach, but just think about the value of the edge you think you're getting—weight against the money outlay.

Y.R. Kash always takes as much odds as they allow in a casino. A couple of bad rolls and he's in the telegraph office writing out a wire for cash. In fact he is such a steady customer he has his own private desk, chair and autographed pen—compliments of his favorite casino.

One final question I'd like to ask all you supporters of the Grab-All-The-Odds-You-Can club:

If odds were such a great bet for the player, why do the casinos give you the chance to take double, triple and ten times amounts? If it's such a great deal, they wouldn't want to strengthen the player's chance of winning.

Did you ever read about the matches between the Lions and the Christians back in the Roman Empire days? I never heard anything about the Lions giving the Christians a whip and a chair to improve the odds. And at last count, the score read: Lions 386—Christians 0.

Incidentally, the reason the casinos allow the taking of heavy odds, even though they give the player a 50–50 pop, is very simple.

The casinos realize that lack of money management, lack of discipline and a drain on bankroll will eventually cream the player.

Isn't that funny: three of these things are part of the Big Four, which you need to compete.

Odds! Single odds is enough, with double odds allowed only after you reach high profit positions.

39

Odds on the Don't

While we're discussing odds and the amount of the take and lay, let's swing over to the wrong side. Here is where my theories take a complete turn-around:

    a. **PASS LINE:** Should always take odds, cause they increase value of Pass Line bet.

    b. **DON'T PASS AND DON'T COME:** Should lay odds only to protect bet in Don't Come. Otherwise I do not agree with laying odds.

That last statement is gonna bring a bevy of outcries from the Don't bettor who likes to establish a number then lay as much odds as he can. I disagree.

I've used this example before. But it's so clear that it bears repeating. The Don't bettor's biggest fear is getting banged on the Come-Out roll by the 7 or 11. Once his number is established, the odds swing over in his favor, but he must get out.

Two guys walk up to a table, both wrong bettors. Mr. A believes in laying odds. Mr. B never lays odds. They each bet $5, on the Don't Pass and 4 becomes the point.

They now have the casino backed against the wall and realistically both of them are in good stead. The four can only be made three ways versus the six ways they can win with the 7. That means they are risking $5 to win $5, and the odds are 2 to 1 in their favor.

However, Mr. A lays $10 odds against the 4, but Mr. B just lets his bet stand. Mr. A is looking to pick up an extra $5, but he is laying $10 (2 to 1) to do it.

Look at his overall bet. He is now risking $15 to win $10, while Mr. B is risking $5 to win $5. Mr. A has taken a bet, where the odds are in his favor by 2 to 1, with his dollar risk at only $5 to $5 and turned it into a wager whereby he is now risking more than he can win.

It's another case of laying more than he can win, after having the casino at a distinct disadvantage. Why reduce the value of that original bet from risking $5 to win $5 to where he is risking $7.50 for each $5 increment?

The player who lays double odds is risking $25 to win $15, after being in a $5 to $5 edge situation.

I like the opinion of Mr. B, who does not lay the odds and doesn't give in to the hogwash that odds is a 50–50 proposition that doesn't cost anything. Once that Don't number is established, the Wrong bettor is in fat city. Laying odds, even with the hard to make 4 and 10, calls for outlays of cash that may not cost any vig. But they sure as heck reduce the value of the original bet.

The only time I suggest the laying of odds is when you want to establish another one or two Don't Come numbers. In that case you would lay odds against the Don't Pass bet and go through the Don't Come with another chip to pick up additional Don'ts.

The laying of odds against the Don't Pass number protects against the seven showing on the next roll. You'd lose the Don't Come wager, but pick up a double win with the Don't Pass and Odds lay.

This is explained deeper later on, but think about the laying of odds. Why give back the beauty of a 50–50 cash risk by having to lay more money than you'll receive with the odds lay?

Old time Don't bettors will vigorishly disagree with me and state that they wanna pick up more money, especially going against the difficult Don't numbers of 4, 5, 9, and 10. That's their theory and theory is never wrong.

However, the times when that shooter bangs a number on you, especially when you're loaded with odds, means you got a long way back.

Dub L. Laye has a $20 Don't Pass bet in action and the 10 shows. He lays $80 odds and feels great, especially with a $10 Hard Ten wager, which means only the 6 to 4 and 4 to 6 combination can hurt him. He feels pretty good about his wager, especially since he has only $35 left in his kick. But this is a hard number to make and will bring him a long way back. While Dub L. Laye ponders his good fortune and begins to calculate his eventual reward, the ever present fickle finger of fate flicks him in the eye.

The shooter bangs out a 6 to 4 easy 10 and old Dub is dumbfounded. Down goes his Don't Pass bet, double odds and Hard Way hedge. In fact, down goes his chance of leaving the casino with more than car fare home.

He asks himself the time worn question of every unsuccessful wrong odds bettor who ever lived: "The odds were 18 to 1 that the easy 10 would now show. How could it happen? How could that 10 show? How? How?"

Very easy! That's why they call it gambling and I don't like to see you gamble with odds that call for heavy lays, regardless of how good they may appear. Or didn't any of you guys ever see a pair of falsies? They also appear like a lock—but that's another story!

For now, think about the laying of odds—even single ones. It ain't the worst thing you can do at a craps table. But it still ain't the best move either.

40

Place Betting

Here we go again into one of the most important chapters of the book. It is the method of handling your place bets. It is the art of handling your wagers after a win and the art of handling your bets after a loss.

If you watch 90 percent of the people who play craps, you'll see that it is a lost art and this is the part of craps that wipes out most players. They leave too much money on the table for the inevitable 7 to take a shot at.

I am going to go over place betting in very deep detail in the next section, but I want you to at least realize the importance of this facet of the game.

You know, when I think of the word "art," it immediately brings to mind a person who I picture as being masterful, coordinated, smooth and talented.

In other words, I think of someone who has mastered the activity to which he or she has concentrated their talents.

An artist, a piano player, or a dancer comes quickly to mind when I picture experts at their crafts. In baseball, Phil Niekro perfected the art of throwing a knuckle ball. Basketball had Marques Haynes as probably the greatest dribbler of all time. Barbra Streisand can hold an audience spellbound with the art of singing.

These people are all perfect in what they do. But when it

comes to gambling, people think it doesn't take any smarts or talent. They're wrong!

Art N. Shoes is a dope when it comes to playing craps. His brains are in his feet and he makes a real clod of himself at the table. He makes place bets on hunches alone.

He hasn't the foggiest idea of what vig he is fighting, when his bets work, what the correct payoffs are and mostly he doesn't know how to handle his wins and losses.

Whether you win or lose in craps will depend on how you handle your place bets.

Re-read that previous sentence 174 times and repeat it 274 times before you enter a casino. Art N. Shoes just snickered. That's why he's a dope at the tables. He thinks place betting is hunches.

I'm going to itemize the outstanding facets of place betting, so you can concentrate on the ones that give you the most trouble.

1. Place bets are the 6 numbers spread across the layout (4-5-6-8-9-10).
2. Bets can be made, taken down, increased, or decreased whenever you wish.
3. Place bets are automatically off on the Come-Out roll.
4. You can have action on the Come-Out roll by merely informing the dealer that your Place Bets are "working."
5. You can tell the dealer at any time during a roll that your place bets are "off." He will place an "off" button on your outside bet to signify that you have no action.
6. You can get back in action after one roll or as many as you like, by merely stating "back in action."
7. Place bets stay until you pull them down or the 7 does it for you.
8. Place bets do not pay true odds, but house vig on 6 and/or 8 is only 1.51 percent, one of the best bets in the house.
9. Vig on 5 and/or 9 is 4 percent.
10. Vig on 4 and/or 10 is 6.67 percent.
11. Increments in place betting is based on the payoffs.

a. 6 and 8 is $7 to $6
b. 5 and 9 is $7 to $5
c. 4 and 10 is $9 to $5

Based on the payoffs listed in number 11, the house makes the following dollar amount on each wager.

a. 6 and 8: Twenty cents on each five dollar bet
b. 5 and 9: Fifty cents on each five dollar bet
c. 4 and 10: One dollar on each five dollar bet

For instance, if you place the 4 for $5, the true odds are 2 to 1, so you should be paid $10 for the winning bet. They pay you $9. That's a buck you lose on that swing.

Obviously the 6 and 8 is the best bet. But try to tell that to Art N. Shoes. He likes to place the 4 and 10 cause the money amount is higher. Placing the 4 and 10 is one of the worst bets in the casino.

Try and tell that to your run-of-the-mill bettor. He'll give you that blank stare or tell you to shut up.

In the next chapter I will compare place betting with come betting. You can make your own decisions as to which way interests you.

But before you flip the page, make sure you understand place betting to the point that you make it an art in the handling of your bets.

If you would only realize that this part of your game will actually be 75 percent of your whole game.

41

Examining the Come

I think the best way to show the comparison between these two moves is to list the good points of each, then the bad ones. Then you can pull it apart and decide which way you'll go.

Good points of Come Bet:

1. The vig you're fighting is always only 1.41 percent, no matter what point shows.
2. By taking single odds, you reduce that vig to .8
3. By taking double odds, you reduce that vig to .6
4. While you are establishing that Come bet, a 7 or 11 will give you an instant even money payoff.

I've already explained that I think too much emphasis is placed on vigorish, especially when the difference between 1.41 percent and .8 percent is a mere .7 percent and that opinion will never change.

However, it is true that whichever number shows, you do get the house edge down to .8 just by taking single odds. But read this next statement and let it sink in: Even though the vig on making the point of 4 or 10 is only .8 percent, there are only three ways to make each of these numbers and therein lies the curse of the Come—false hope.

That statement is taken from the book of reality, chapter one, verse one. It deals with the blood and guts of gambling and the stark reality of the play: You can only make the 5 or 9 four ways each, so there you have four numbers that could become your play and all four of them are dwarfed by the all-powerful 7.

The idea of picking up a win when the 7 shows while you are making a Come bet is just defensive thinking. That same 7 will wipe out any other Come bet, plus your Pass Line bet and all odds.

Let's list the bad points of Come:

1. You gotta take the number that shows, even though it may be a hard number to make (4, 5, 9, 10).
2. You have four rolls on the Come bet which give you instant losses (any craps).
3. Come bets work on the Come-Out roll, but odds don't.
4. You gotta make the number twice—once to establish it and once to collect.
5. Come bets come down after a hit and you gotta reestablish them again to get back in action.

Start with number one. Ask any craps shooter what number he'd like to have as his Pass or Come bet and the overwhelming majority would immediately scream: 6 or 8. But with the Come bet you gotta take what shows. Even though you might not like to get stuck with the 4, 5, 9, or 10, they're gonna show and you now have a contract bet—unable to remove.

Number two is technically comparing the chances of a craps showing as to the 7 or 11, which provide an instant win. The edge is 8 to 4 in favor of the Come bettor, but adding in the 4 and 10 which many craps players don't like to see become their point, you have ten bad numbers versus eight strong ones. Think about that.

Number three is a crusher for the Right bettor. Once your Come number is established, it is working on every roll— including the subsequent Come-Out rolls after a point is made.

Man, I've been standing at craps tables since a loaf of bread cost eleven cents and I've never seen a hot roll develop at a table without at least one seven showing on the Come-Out roll.

Think about it. Here you are sitting with a $25 bet on the 9 with odds and $25 on the 8 with odds. The shooter just made his point of 6 and he's coming out. Up pops the 7.

The Pass Line wager wins, but down go both of your Come bets. Sure, you get your odds back, but now you gotta go through the Come to get back in action.

The Come purists will shout that since the Come bets work on the Come-Out, you pick up a profit. Big deal, you win the Come number that shows, but the odds are off and any craps bettor worth his salt knows that the odds bets are what increase the value of that even money payoff bet. But the casinos nullify that edge on the Come-Out. Also, the 7 brings down *all* Come bets, while you can only score on one of them at a time.

To repeat: Every hot shooter in craps has his share of sevens on the Come-Out roll. Those bets working are devastating; pure murder to the right bettor.

Read number four 162 times to make sure you get it. With the come, you gotta make that number twice—once to establish it and once to get paid. Do you know how hard it is to make the number once, just to get up there? Now you gotta bang it again to get paid.

I'm not gonna go into percentages and all that jazz, mostly because I don't know the true percentage of making the number twice before the 7, but I know the odds are stacked against it. Suppose your point is 5. We know the odds are 6 to 4 against making it once—now you gotta do it again.

Why do you think kissing on the first date is now an accepted standard? When I was in my prime, you got a thumbs-up from your buddies if you got to hold hands on the first date.

But it was so hard to get that second date that you might go two years without tasting lipstick. Now you "place" your best kiss on her lips the first time and rack it up as a score.

The stupid players working a Come system figure they'll get lucky the second date. But some cat from Seventh Avenue moves in and those guys waiting for the second date never come to bat. They get wiped out and have to start all over again.

The place bettor starts getting paid on that first hit. This is a big, big point. Please take a second look at this analogy.

Finally we get to number five. As soon as a Come bet hits, they take both the bet and the payoff and shove it over to you. There is no way to increase or decrease your bet, no chance to practice money management.

Now you gotta start all over. Just look at a quick example of what could, and does happen every day at the tables:

A Place bettor and a Come bettor are at the same table. They both have the 6 going for them and the Place bettor already collected a profit while the Come bettor was just getting established.

The shooter bangs out five more sixes. The place bettor collects on all six hits. The Come bettor collected three times. The other three times were used to just re-establish that 6.

Now come on. Would you rather be paid six times or three times? 'Nuff said.

To rehash the point of choosing your number, I want the numbers I want and not leave it to the rolls of chance. The numbers I want are the 6 and 8.

There you have an idea of the pros and cons of the Come. Next we'll do the same with the Place bet.

42

Examining the Place

Let's do the same thing as before, by listing the good and bad points of the place bet. Then you decide.

Bad points of Place Bets:

1. Have higher vigs, especially on 4, 5, 9, and 10.

That's it. The only disadvantage is in the 4 percent vig on the five and nine and 6.67 on the 4 and 10. Naturally, you could bypass those numbers, especially the 4 and 10, by never placing them.

Good points of Place Bets:

1. You have your choice of which numbers to play.
2. Place numbers automatically off on the Come-Out roll, unless you stipulate that they are working.
3. You can take Place bets down whenever you choose.
4. You can adjust bets up or down as you choose.

Number one is especially powerful for the player who doesn't like the hard numbers or 4, 5, 9, and 10 to become your bet. Place betting allows you to end up with the 6 and 8 for every single shooter.

Number two nullifies those place bets working on subsequent Come-Outs. Naturally, you might choose to have them working. But that's your choice.

Number three gives you the power to remove your bets after any roll. We'll be going over methods that call for you to take one hit as a place bet and then come down. The Come has you locked into your bet until a decision is reached.

Number four is the main one, because of the flexibility it gives you. The whole key to playing craps is the ability to manage your money. Just look at any game. Well, the ability to manipulate your place bets gives you a wide open door of multiple betting methods. What are you waiting for?

I don't wanna go into a lengthy explanation as to which bet offers the players the biggest edge. You know darn well that I lean heavily towards Place betting, even though you have a little bigger vig on a couple of the numbers.

The plus factors of money mangement and flexibility in handling your bets make the Place the place to be.

Some of you veteran players will disagree with me and that's your choice. But my intent is to show you the smartest overall way to play and in my opinion this use of the Place bets will overwhelmingly bury any Come theory.

It's only fair that I explain something now about the systems that are coming up in the next chapter. They will concentrate on Place betting moves, not Come methods.

Why should I denounce a method of play and then give you some system on playing it? You wanna play the Come, do it on your own.

43

Buying the Number

This bet seems to confuse more people than any other move at the table and that's saying a mouthful. It's my opinion that only one percent of the people who play craps knows every single part of the game, including vigorish and payoff, not to mention the sidelights that are explained in this book.

The only time you buy a number is when the 4 or 10 is your choice. The reason you are buying it is to lower the house vig. You pay 5 percent for the right to buy a number, and that means you will be paid the correct odds.

Watt S. Figg plays craps thirty times a year and can't even spell Vigorish let alone know what it means.

He'll drop $100 on the table and tell the dealer to place the 4. He likes the fact that he gets a 9 to 5 payoff, which would mean a return of $180 if that 4 shows.

However, if he had bought the 4 and paid the 5 percent charge of $5 for his wager, they would have given him true odds or $200 if the 4 showed. The 5 percent vig is attached whether you win or lose, but it is still way better than getting $180.

The reason you only buy the 4 or 10 is because the house vig for those two numbers is 6.67 with a place bet. Naturally the 5 percent charge to get a true payoff is better by 1.67 percent.

Since the 5 and 9 carry 4 percent edges and the 6 and 8 is 1.51, it's plain stupid to buy them for 5 percent when you get a better deal with the place. But there are times throughout a session when Watt S. Figg has asked the dealer if he can buy these inside numbers. A patient sharp dealer will explain that it's better to place these numbers.

Watt S. Figg can lose a lot of money by not knowing simple little things that'll save him a few dollars per bet or allow a smart hedge play.

Since I don't like the idea of paying 5 percent to have a number (4 or 10) that can only be made three ways, I steer away from this play.

Got a simple question for you. Why pay 5 percent to have these numbers that can be made three ways, when you can fight only a 1.51 vig and end up with the 6 and 8, that can be made five ways each?

Think about it—I wish Watt S. Figg would. He'd soon learn that the vig may not be the most important part of the game, but it does have some good money savings plays.

This is one of them. From a $25 wager and up, buy the 4 or 10—don't place it.

That is, if you still persist in playing those two numbers.

44

Laying Against the Number

I've explained this briefly before, but wanna elaborate just a tick cause it's gonna come up in the next section and I want you to understand what I'm saying.

When you wanna place a number from the right side, you can do it by simply dropping a $5 chip (or whatever the minimum is) on the table and say, "Place the 9 (or whatever number you choose)." The 6 and 8 require a $6 bet but the fact is that you can place the smallest amount allowed.

Not so on the Don't side. If you wanna lay against the number, say the 4, you can't lay $10 to win $5. Most casinos operate with a minimum lay of four units. If you're at a $5 table, that means you gotta lay enough money to win four units, or $20. You also must pay a vig of 5 percent to the house for making that bet, cause you don't have to come through the Don't Pass and risk getting whacked on the 7 or 11.

Since you must lay true odds, plus the 5 percent or $1 vig, following are the correct amounts you will be charged and just remember that 5 percent is taken whether you win or lose. A $20 win ends up as a profit of $19.

    a. Against the 4 or 10 ....$41 to win $19
    b. Against the 5 or 9 ....$31 to win $19
    c. Against the 6 or 8 ....$25 to win $19
    d. Against the 4 or 10 ....$51 to win $24

    e. Against the 5 or 9 ....$62 to win $38

    f. Against the 6 or 8 ....$125 to win $100

I've added the vig on both sides and to figure out the lay you desire, always compute it against the $20 minimum, then tack on the true odds lay, plus 5 percent of the potential profit.

Now why do you think the casinos set this high a minimun lay? Very simple. If they allowed anyone to stand at a table and bet $6 to win $3 against the four or ten, Don't bettors from all over the world would lay against the "hard to make" numbers all day long.

By putting a high minimum and charging a 5 percent vig, they scare away all the Don't bettors who are playing short.

Shorty Shortchange loves to bet Don't, but with his Bankroll of $63.50, a few numbers banged on him with these minimum lays and he's looking for a 10¢ bingo game.

The high minimum lays against the number keep away all the Shorty Shortchanges who are looking to stay at a table with short improper bankrolls.

Laying against the numbers is an excellent play for the Don't bettor, but they hate the fact that they must lay out true odds, so they shy away from it.

These same players who hate to lay true odds, 'cause they think it's unfair, are all smiles when they bet Right and take the odds cause the money received is always higher than the amount at risk.

What these guys don't figure is that the "risk" is always true, based on the odds of making or not making a number.

I want you serious craps players to reread these last few paragraphs again. The message will do wonders for your theory on playing this game.

Money Management

45

Just because you've heard this term and know its meaning, or know how to spell it, doesn't mean you got it.

This whole section is designed to give you methods of play and how to bet. Some of these things you have heard me speak of before and some will be advanced techniques off of the basic moves I showed you in previous books and videos.

Some of the moves border on super-conservative theories, but give them a good look, as I believe that is the smartest way to gamble.

Then there'll be an aggressive approach attached to most of these theories and you can choose the style that best suits your personality.

I honestly hope you adopt the conservative approach, 'cause once you get in the habit of leaving the casino a winner, regardless of the amount, you'll get hooked on the thrill of victory. And I believe 'tis better to win a little on a consistent basis than the constant chasing of that dream of going for big kills.

I don't give a pig's ear which way you choose to play, as long as you end up a winner.

Finally I want to capsule exactly what money management is: What you bet when you win and what you bet when you lose.

That is the entire theory of money management. The discipline theories will cover the chore of getting you to quit when you reach certain levels of your session money, but the real test is knowing how much to bet.

Don't think you decide on your bet after the dice come to a screeching halt. Those decisions are made ahead of time and every single bet is a predetermined wager that should be programmed to take advantage of trends.

Money management is an art and a necessity. It's also a chore to keep yourself regimented to a controlled way of playing. Furthermore, it's boring, restrictive and tedious.

Do you get the idea that money management is not the most joyous part of your day? Well you're right. The joy comes from the results of your strict money management, not the ongoing rigors of the game.

Go back over all the things I told you that money management was. One of those things should have popped right into your eye ball. It is a nutshell explanation of what money management is and what it means to your game.

Money management is a necessity. If you didn't know that, then you also don't know that grass is green, sky is high, water is wet, ice is cold, rocks are hard, ants are small, Dolly's are big, oops!

Anyhow, zero in on what I'm trying to say. To win consistently, you simply must perfect your money management moves.

The answers are all laid out for you.

46

The Series

The series is a run of winning rolls by a specific shooter. I call each shooter's streak a specific series.

Suppose Mae B. Hott picks up the dice and begins the game. That Come-Out roll does not begin the series, but once she establishes her point, then the Series is in action.

Let's suppose we're betting "Right" at this table and Mae B. Hott has the five dice pushed to her. We don't know if Mae will be hot or cold, so I wanna get into her series before raising my bets.

We're at a $5 table and she establishes the five as her point. Our $5 Pass Line bet is backed with $6 odds and we place the 6 and 8 for $6 each.

The series begins on that next roll and continues until Mae B. Hott either makes her point or sevens out. I didn't say craps out. Nobody ever craps out at a craps game. They seven out. I'm tired of correcting people on that term.

Suppose Mae bangs out a 9, 6, 6, 3, 10, 8, 6, 4, 5 point. That was a nice series and a strong betting pattern would have kicked off a decent return. I'm not going into that just yet, but understand that the series began as soon as the point was established and continues until a decision is reached for that particular point.

Naturally you don't want a series of point 5, 6, seven out.

That's a rotten series and a couple of these each session will have you inventing new curse words.

The series also applies to the Don't bettor and to the Place bettor. Let's say you bypass the Pass Line but place the 6 and 8 after a number is established.

The series applies to her whole roll, and your job is to keep track of how many winning series there are at a table and how many losing ones.

Once I had a guy ask me: "How do I know if I'm winning at a certain table?"

I said: "If you start with $100 and after three shooters you only got $40 left, it means you're losing. If you got $140, it means you're winning."

He just looked at me blank-faced and his question was the smartest one I got that night.

Let's get back to Mae B. Hott and pick up where she made her point of 5. She'll come out to establish another point and then another series will begin. How you handle these series will determine your success. How you bet them is the key—coming up soon.

47

Regression System

In 1983 I wrote a book on blackjack that explained this method of betting. I believe it is hands-down the most powerful approach to money management ever put out.

It is primarily aimed at even bets, such as blackjack, baccarat, outside bets of roulette, sports betting, 6 and 8 in craps and the Don't Pass line, excluding laying odds.

If you don't know the theory by now, you oughta hang your head, but just for smiles I'll go over it again, cause it's gonna get a lot of play in my systems.

The basic idea is to bet higher than the minimum, and after a win, regress back down to the minimum, thereby wrapping up a profit.

That means you can win as many hands as the house, yet be guaranteed a profit. The key to the system is the second bet, whereby you regress the next wager.

You must always bet higher than the table minimum, in order to give you room to go down, and the amount of that first bet is based on your own personal bankroll. I'll start by giving you the method as it pertains to $5 increments.

You're at a $5 blackjack table, so your first bet is $10. If you win, the dealer slides $10 profit to you and you've got $20 in front of you. Here's the key move.

Take back the $10 you started with, plus $5 of the winning

payoff and bet $5. At this point you're in fat city. You've got your original $10 back, plus a profit of $5 and even if you lose the next bet, your series shows a $5 profit.

Most people, after a win, bet the same amount or go up one unit or even two. If a loss occurs on that second bet, they're in a position where they won a bet, lost a bet and are either even, or—heavens to Betsy—out a unit or two.

Four guys walk up to a table and each bets $10 at a $5 table. Each wins their bet, yet each has a different theory as to what the next bet should be:

a) Player A pulls back $10 profit and bets $10.
b) Player B pulls back $5 and bets $15.
c) Player C pulls back nothing and bets $20.
d) Player D pulls back $15 and bets $5.

Let's say they all lose the next hand. Look at the results:

a) Player A won a hand, lost a hand and he's even.
b) Player B won a hand, lost a hand and he's out $5, even though he held the house even.
c) Player C won a hand, lost a hand and is out $10, even though he won as many hands as the house.
d) Player D ends up with a $5 profit, although he ended up 1 to 1 with the house.

Once the profit is locked into that series, you can become aggressive with your wagers. For instance, you win that second bet of $5. The dealer slides a $5 chip over to you and you let the whole $10 ride, rully cognizant of the fact that the series is in a profit lock.

Suppose you win that third bet of $10. At this point you revert to Up-and-Pull, a powerful method of money management that has a couple of chapters dedicated to its use a little later in this section.

Anyhow, you win the bet at $10 and incorporate the Up-and-Pull theory. Raise your bet *Up* to $15 and *Pull* back a profit of $5, which further increases the previous profit for the Series, which was gleaned by regressing after the first win.

If that $15 bet also wins, you now go *Up* to $20 and *Pull* back $10. You could have gone *Up* to $25 and *Pulled* back $5, and that is strictly up to you. Naturally I would have you up only $5, but I like the conservative approach.

BUT EVERY WINNING BET MUST GIVE YOU A PROFIT, SO DON'T THINK YOU CAN RAISE THE SUBSEQUENT BET BY THE FULL AMOUNT OF THE WIN. EVERY WINNING BET MUST RESULT IN A PROFIT BEING PULLED BACK!

Stop right here, my friend, and go back over the last paragraph. It was meant for every single solitary one of you and it should be memorized backwards and forwards.

When you get into your series, be absolutely sure you take back a profit after every winning score. I cannot stress enough the power of this move, nor the necessity of it. Guys like Imus Pressit and Y.R. Kash, Frank Lee Board, Low N. Shirt and P. Weebrane will scoff at this theory and claim you can't win serious money by being conservative.

But all I'm asking you to do is give up that second winning bet in a series, lock up a profit and then go into your aggressive increase in bets.

Besides, what's so hard about taking back a profit after each winning hand or roll. I'm still letting you increase your bets. All I'm asking is that you take back a profit. You'll get more of this in the Up-and-Pull chapter, so let's finish the theory on regression.

As you continue to win, you can raise your bets, as long as each win results in a profit being stashed. Naturally you can also insert another regression into your series and the smarter players will want to do that. It just means you lock up a bigger profit at a specific time in your series and then start back up.

Let's finish that winning series you were in. You won at $15 and had the option of going to either $20 or $25. We'll say you went to $20. Suppose you win again and the dealer slides $20 over to you, this time you get a little more aggressive and raise the bet to $35, while pulling back $5.

Again you get a winning hand and $35 is slid over to you. At this point you slap another regression bet into your series. Take back the $35 and regress your bet:

a) All the way down to $10
b) Partial Regress to $20
c) Partial Regress to $25
d) One Unit drop to $30

Choose any of the above and you're not wrong. Then you can start back up. For instance, Connie Conservative drops her next bet all the way to $10 and each subsequent winning hand is increased by $5. I love her!!

Aggie Aggressive likes the regression but drops her next bet to $30 and every succeeding win is pulled back and another $5 lopped off her bet. For instance, she wins at $30 and then bets $25. Then, wins at $25 and drops to $20, or even a spin-off of that method.

The variations go on and on and on. The next chapter gives you tables to follow, and of course, you could come up with your own.

Just remember that after a loss, you revert back to the beginning bet of the series and start over.

I might just warn you, or maybe you know already: You ain't gonna win forever, so you better think about incorporating second regressions into your series. It'll soften the blow when that inevitable loss does occur.

I've talked a lot about the regression and this was a long chapter but a necessary one. There is also a method of betting called Off-Amounts that comes into play at the blackjack and roulette tables—not in craps, so I won't explain it here.

A few months ago I released a book entitled, *So You Wanna Be A Gambler: Advanced Roulette*. It covers Off-Amounts and four chapters on the regression and a bellyful of theories of betting this method.

It wouldn't hurt you to spring for the book and it would give you a firm grip on this tremendous betting method. The game may be roulette, but the theory of betting is the same.

I don't give a rat's tail if you think I'm trying to hawk a book.

I'm trying to get you to fully understand this whole concept of betting, even as it applies to other games which have no bearing on craps.

Since you should be keyed in on this regression system right now, swing right into the next chapter and take a look at some series.

48

Regression Series

Since you're going to be getting a lot of series for the handling of the 6 and 8, I won't go into that in this chapter. But I wanna give you an idea of running series in blackjack or roulette in order to acquaint you fully with the method.

$5 TABLE

	A	B	C	D	E
First Bet	$15	$15	$20	$20	$20
Second Bet	$10	$10	$10	$10	$10
Third Bet	$15	$10	$15	$15	$15
Fourth Bet	$25	$20	$20	$25	$20
Fifth Bet	$35	$25	$30	$45	$10
Sixth Bet	$45	$20	$40	$25	$20
Seventh Bet	$50	$15	$50	$45	$40

$10 TABLE

	A	B	C	D	E
First Bet	$15	$15	$20	$20	$20
Second Bet	$10	$10	$10	$10	$10
Third Bet	$15	$10	$15	$15	$15
Fourth Bet	$25	$20	$20	$25	$20
Fifth Bet	$35	$25	$30	$45	$10
Sixth Bet	$45	$20	$40	$25	$20
Seventh Bet	$50	$15	$50	$45	$40

You have more room for various series as the betting increments increase, but the $10 table should also have five times your table minimum as your maximum bet ($50) until you reach the plateau part of your win goal. It'll be explained later.

$25 TABLE

	A	B	C	D	E
First Bet	$35	$40	$50	$50	$40
Second Bet	$25	$25	$25	$25	$25
Third Bet	$35	$30	$35	$30	$30
Fourth Bet	$50	$60	$60	$50	$50
Fifth Bet	$75	$60	$90	$75	$70
Sixth Bet	$100	$100	$90	$100	$50
Seventh Bet	$125	$100	$60	$75	$75

You know, you could go to a $5 table and make first bet $30 and second $5, to have spread of $25 in your profit regress. It'll also hold down the amount of your risk factor from $50 to $30, in the event you lose that first bet.

So don't think you must go to a $25 table to get a $25 spread. It can be done at the lower tables.

$100 TABLE

	A	B	C	D	E
First Bet	$150	$150	$200	$200	$150
Second Bet	$100	$100	$100	$100	$100
Third Bet	$125	$150	$150	$150	$150
Fourth Bet	$150	$200	$200	$250	$200
Fifth Bet	$200	$300	$350	$150	$300
Sixth Bet	$250	$400	$500	$250	$200
Seventh Bet	$300	$500	$400	$150	$300

Naturally you'll come up with your own offshoots, but just remember to regress after the first win and it ain't a bad idea to incorporate another regression move in your series.

Maybe you'll feel somebody will think you're a cheapskate for using a double regression. But I got a scoop for you. More people will think you're a sharp cat—and I'll be the first one to pat you on the back.

You should now have a complete grasp of the regression method. If you don't, go back and read the last two chapters before going on.

49

Regression in Craps

Like I said, the best way to handle the regression system on the table is in the place betting for the 6 and 8. Since the vig is only 1.51 percent and the payoff is $7 to $6, you have the perfect opportunity to put this in play.

Let's base it on a minimum bet to get you started. The least you can bet is $6 on the 6 and 8, but in this case you place them for $12 each.

As soon as you get a score on one of those numbers, the dealer pays you $14. You're in fat city. You simply say: "Break my 6 and 8 down to $6 each." At this point you have $12 at risk and $14 profit, meaning even a seven out will give you a profit of $2, and there is no risk factor.

Suppose the 8 shows. You get another $7 payoff and here is where a multiple amount of betting variations spring up. Following are some examples as to what you would do:

a) Same bet—take the $7
b) Press the 6
c) Press the 8
d) Take down both the 6 and 8
e) Place the 5 and 9

All of this will be covered in great detail in later chapters, plus what you'll do on each succeeding hit.

The intent at this time is to make sure you grasp the theory of the regression. By the time you reach the off-shoots of betting series, you'll have different ideas as to conservative series, or aggressive series.

Go back over these three chapters and re-read them slowly. This is an approach that 90 percent of you will use one way or another.

Mark my words, it's effective.

50

Betting Right

You already know the object of craps and you know how the "correct" theory of play has been handed down through the years:

1) Bet the Pass Line
2) Take as much odds as you can
3) Make two Come bets
4) Again, take full odds

First of all, you know how I feel about the Come bet. I hate it! Don't play the Come.

The Theory remains the same, and that is that you have three numbers working for you but you can place them. I'm agreeable to this approach as long as you have the proper bankroll.

We've already gone over this, but a quick reminder is in order, 'cause this is a solid rule that will apply to every system.

The amount you bet on the first shooter is the amount you should bet for every shooter at that session.

You should have enough money for ten shooters around the table, at an amount equal to what you bet on the first shooter. Finally, you should have enough for at least three sessions, so that reverts back to your bankroll.

If your bankroll does not allow three sessions, with each session having the proper money, don't play this system and I mean don't!

When you utilize the place numbers, the 6 and 8 should automatically be the key. There are many people who like to place the 5 and 9 or the 4 and 10 and I vehemently disagree with this thinking.

The 6 and 8 has the lowest vig of all the numbers and can be made the most number of ways (five). They should always be your key place numbers.

To go back to the basic approach of Pass Line bet, odds and two Place bets, let's first hit the odds theory.

I strongly suggest single odds and then working up to double odds as your profits increase. But don't start with double odds even if your bankroll allows it. See if the table you're at is running your way.

Bett N. Small has a decent $600 bankroll that he breaks into three sessions of $200 each.

He starts with $5 on the Pass Line and takes single odds. As soon as the point is established, he swings into picking up two place numbers, with the 6 and 8 always included.

Here's the formula for the proper place betting moves:

1) If 4 is the point, place 6 and 8.
2) If 5 is the point, place 6 and 8.
3) If 9 is the point, place 6 and 8.
4) If 10 is the point, place 6 and 8.
5) If 6 is the point, place 5 and 8.
6) If 8 is the point, place 6 and 9.

In a nutshell, whatever number (4-5-9 or 10) becomes the point, always place the 6 and 8. If either the 6 or 8 becomes the point, surround the number.

For instance, if 6 is the point, place the 5 and 8. This does not mean the 5 has a better chance of showing when 6 is the point, but it does keep you disciplined.

This way you can't go home at night and lament that you shoulda played the 5 or you shoulda played the 9.

With this predetermined setup, you play the same way all the time and can never second-guess yourself.

F. Ida is the champion second guesser of all time. As soon as something happens he screams: "Man if I'da bet that way I'da won." He's always bemoaning what he mighta done.

I want you to eliminate that weak willy-nilly type of second guessing. With this approach, you know exactly what numbers you will have.

F. Ida can never say "if I'da" again! But he'll find something else to moan about.

The final thing in this area I want you to remember has to do with basic amounts. If you bet $5 on the Pass Line and take single odds, then your place bets should be of like value. You can place bet for lower amounts, but I don't want you place betting for higher amounts.

If you are a $5 bettor, then your place bets should be $6 6 and $6 8.

A $10 Pass Line bet allows you to have two unit bets on the 6 and 8, which means $12 6 and $12 8, or you could have $6 on each.

Suppose your Pass Line bet is $25. Take single odds and abide by one of the following:

1) Place 6 and 8 for $6 each
2) Or place 6 and 8 for $12 each
3) Or place 6 and 8 for $18 each
4) Or place 6 and 8 for $24 each

In the beginning of a session, I suggested $18 each with a $25 Pass Line bet. If you are a $50 bettor, use the same formula approach.

My opinion, with a $50 line bet, would be $30 6, $30 8. That gives you plenty of room for making adjustable bets when you start getting into some hot rolls.

This shows you which numbers to play. Next we go into how much you play.

51

How Much Do I Bet?

We're zeroing in on the correct way to play "Right," as has been handed down to us through the years. The theory of having three numbers going for you is a powerful tool.

Just remember it is not the only system available, but it does give you a start.

Starting with a $5 table and a session amount of $230, you begin by charting the tables.

Three shooters in a row make at least one point and also pop out anywhere between 4 to 5 inside numbers, so you buy in.

Your session money calls for a $5 Pass Line bet. Seven shows and you win $5. Under no circumstances whatsoever should you increase that bet to $10. Just make another $5 wager, by pulling the $5 profit into your pile.

Frank Lee Board just had a fit. He's bored with this conservative style, but increasing that Pass Line bet after a 7 or 11 kicks off a point is a stupid move.

Suppose you let $10 ride on the roll after the 7 showed. If craps then popped out, you'd lose the $10 bet, which would result in an overall $5 loss, even though you won just as many rolls as you lost.

Furthermore, let's assume 7 hit and you let $10 ride. Eight became the point and you take $10 odds. If the 7 then showed, you would have a $15 loss, even though you had a win and a loss.

130

Maybe Frank Lee Board is bored, but that's his problem. After a 7 or 11 shows on the Come-Out, take your profit and make the same bet, regardless of the amount and this includes no soft increases for you $25 bettors.

Back to the Pass Line. After the point is established, you take single odds and make your two place bets.

If the shooter makes the point, you again come out with a $5 Pass Line bet and take single odds. Do not increase your Pass Line wager until that shooter makes at least two points.

It does not matter how many inside numbers he bangs out. Your Pass Line betting is based on that phase only. If he makes two point numbers, then you can increase your Pass Line bet. Take a look:

1) Bet $5 on first roll.
2) If point is made, against bet $5 and take single odds.
3) If the second point is made, you have two options:
   a) Again bet $5, or,
   b) Go up to $10 Pass Line with single odds.
4) If that third number is made and you were betting $10, again make $10 wager.
5) If shooter makes that second point at $10, which would be his fourth score, you can go up to $15 pass line with option to take double odds.
6) You'd want two hits at this $15 level before going up to a $20 Pass Line wager.

Let's put it into as simple terms as possible. With a $5 bettor, the maximum Pass Line bet should be $25, or five times the amount of your initial wager.

You wanna make two hits at each level Pass Line bet and only raise that wager after you've made two hits on the Pass Line.

For instance, you'd bet $5 Pass, $5 Pass, $10 Pass, $10 Pass, $15 Pass, $15 Pass, etc. Taking single odds keeps a nice profit coming in and keeps potential losses down.

When you reach the $15 Pass Line bet, you can stay at single odds, but you also have option of going to double odds.

Naturally the rule calls for two hits at the $15 bet before

moving onto the $20 bet and now I'd like to add a little logic to your approach.

Nothing goes on forever, so if you've banged out wins at the $5, $10 and $15 increments, that's six winning scores and a nice profit in your kick.

At this time you have several options:

a) Go up to $20 Pass Line.

b) Stay at $15 Pass Line.

c) Regress to $10 Pass Line.

d) Go down to $5 Pass Line.

Think about it. There's nothing written in stone that says you gotta keep going up, 'cause that 7 is lurking in the wood somewhere.

Staying the same, or even going down to a $10 bet with double odds will still give you a nice profit and if that hit, you could again start up the ladder till you reached the $25 bet.

Make these plans ahead of time, but don't be like I. Madork and have a super-heavy Pass Line bet at risk with triple odds and then have a nice profitable roll eaten up with one 7.

Personally I'd use (c) regression bet to $10 after a hit on that second score of $15.

The smart player accepts these consistent returns, holds potential losses down and never leaves himself open to give back decent profits.

Maybe that one big roll will come early and be your profit for that day.

This is the rule for the $5 bettor and the next chapter goes over higher increments. Just remember:

1) Two hits at each increment ($5, $10, $15).

2) No increasing bets after seven or eleven scores on Come-Out.

3) Double odds after the fourth hit—and then only as an option.

52

Betting Higher

The theory doesn't change as you bet higher, but the money outlay has variations. The previous chapter restricted the $5 bettor to a set conservative increase in betting units.

As you move into wagers of $10 or $25 or $50 or $100 Pass Line bets, that same approach should be used. For example:

a) $25 Pass Line (9 becomes point).

b) Place 6 and 8 for $24 each.

c) Shooter must make two point numbers at $25 bet with single odds.

d) After two points made, third and fourth bets could be $50 each, with single odds.

e) If third and fourth points are made, fifth bet could be raised to $75, with option of double odds.

That's the same pattern that is used as a basic approach, but the higher chip outlay opens variations and these offshoots might appeal to each of you in a different vein.

Most players have no predetermined plan of betting, which is a stupid approach. These offshoots have both conservative and aggressive overtures, so you pick the one you want.

The first bet of Pass Line, single odds and two place numbers should be one tenth of that Session money, or have I already said that? But it's important.

$10 BETTOR

PASS LINE	PLACE BETS	POINT DECISION
1st Bet—$10	Two Units each	Win
2nd Bet—$10	One Unit each	Win
3rd Bet—$15	Two Units each	Win
4th Bet—$20	Two Units each	Win
5th Bet—$25	Three Units each	Win
6th Bet—$15	Two Units each	Lose

Start over at $10 Pass Line.

Just glance at that table and see how it differs from the basic approach.

Notice that there are several things that changed, including partial increases, regressions and differences in the units bet as place numbers.

1) Third bet only went to $15, yet it could have been $20.
2) Second bet had place bets reduced to one unit each.
3) Fourth bet again only went up five dollar increase, while it could have gone up two units.
4) Fifth bet showed place numbers at three units each, while they could have been four each.
5) Sixth bet showed Pass Line regressed to $15.
   a) It could have gone to $35
   b) It could have gone to $30
   c) It could have stayed at $25
   d) It could have regressed to $10 or $20.

Do you see all the variations available to you? They are innumerable and the possibilities increase after every single decision. The only constants are these and they are non-negotiable.

a) First Pass Line bet, with place numbers, should be within amount of ten shooters around that table (man I'm tired of saying that).
b) You *cannot* increase your Pass Line wagers until you win the first two points at the basic bet.
c) After that, you can increase for maximum increment

amount of first bet or in partial increments.
1) If first bet is $10, you can never increase Pass Line by
   more than two increments at a time:
   $10-$10-$20-$20-$30-$30-$40-$40 etc.
2) You cannot do this:
   $10-$10-$20-$40-$60.
   d) Place bets can never start or be higher than the
      amount of your Pass Line bet.
1) Place bets will be deeply covered later and will have
   their own set of moves.

This chapter covered the $10 initial wager and gave you
offshoots of soft increases as you continued to win.

But get this straight: These examples are based on hot rolls
and you must always revert back to the basic minimum bet after
a loss, whether that shooter makes one point or three or eight,
or whatever.

There are very few red-hot rolls per session, so don't think
these examples are the rule. I'm just giving you ways to handle
the hot runs.

As you can see, this was a very trying chapter, one of the
roughest so far; yet one of the most important. It is zeroing in on
the way the Right bettor must control his pass line bets and
keep him from betting crazy amounts.

The worst thing the Right bettor does is get a hot roll and find
that when the 7 shows he has all the profit on the table.

I'm trying to get you to avoid that. Will you listen? Would a
dog eat a ten-pound steak and then walk away from another one?
No way!

And neither will the craps player abide by these rules, but
that's another story.

53

Quarter Pass Line

I hope you go back and read the last few chapters again before you start this one. The message is exactly the same, only the increments are being raised.

We're at a $25 bet level and the same rules of session money prevail (10 times the amount of initial bet—pretty soon I won't have to say it).

The variations now begin to multiply, and this is to the benefit of that particular type player.

Your Pass Line bet is $25, single odds, with placing the 6 and 8 for either $18 each or $24 each. If the point is made, your second line bet is exactly the same. Let's say the point is made.

Here's where we run into a little bet of egotism. Most players who bet the green $25 chips look upon themselves as sort of dashing, daring, devil-may-care swingers and the temptation is to bang up those green chips to the black $100 level.

And here's where I come along to throw a bucket of ice water on their aggressive dreams. It's not that I'm trying to be a party pooper, it's just that this is the moment of truth for all crap shooters.

The hitting of that first point with odds has kicked off a decent profit to that player and I cringe as I see Lett R. Wride let the whole bundle ride on the next come-out.

Why-o-why do crap players fall prey to that greedy approach?

Why sacrifice two scores with the 50–50 chance of giving it all back? Yet that is the curse of all the Lette R. Wrides who long to bang out those chips in an uncontrolled fashion.

Look at the options that are hanging out for you for that third bet.

a) Normal increase to $50 Pass Line.

b) Go up to $30 Pass Line, or $35 or $40 or $45.

c) Regress to $20 Pass Line, or $15 or $10.

d) Stay at same $25 bet.

If you've got the last few chapters still fresh in your mind, you know all of these options by heart. But let me touch your unwilling subconscious for just a moment.

Would it really be like blowing a date with Loni Anderson if you were to swallow your inflated pride and give the regression a shot?

I know you think this is a blow to your pride and other players at the table will probably throw rocks at you and question your manhood, but I'm asking for a regression bet. Come out with a $15 Pass Line, single odds and place the 6 and 8 for $12 each.

If you lose, the losses will be only a small dent in your series win, that now includes two point scores.

If you win, now you start the Up-and-Pull process, and it can be aggressive, all based on wins on the Pass Line (You've won that third Pass Line wager).

Fourth Bet: $30 Pass Line, $24 6 and 8.

Fifth Bet: $50 Pass Line, $30 6 and 8.

Sixth Bet: $75 Pass Line, $30 6 and 8.

Seventh Bet: option

1) $100 Pass Line, $60 6 and 8.

2) $50 Pass Line, $30 6 and 8.

Notice you can always add another regression in the middle of your run. The aggressive player can continue to increase by multiples of $25 per Come-Out.

Another note worth mentioning: The amounts I place on the 6 and 8 are only to stay in line with Pass Line amount, but you're gonna see chapters that put strict restrictive controls on these bets that will only regress as the 6 and 8 shows, not based on the fact that the Pass Line wagers are increasing.

That previous paragraph says a mouthful, so if you didn't grasp it, go back until you digest it, and this means you Lett R. Wride.

I know there are gonna be many of you who'll agree with my method of handling the Pass Line bets and many of you will vehemently disagree. That is your choice.

But all I'm asking you to do is slap a regression bet in there every once in awhile and lock up some profits in the event of a loss.

Even if you won't regress, you absolutely must abide by the super strict basic betting mode:

a) You cannot increase your Pass Line bet until at least two point numbers are made.

b) Sevens and elevens don't count.

c) Your increase cannot exceed the increment value of your first bet: such as $25-$25-$50-$50-$75-$75 etc.

d) A loss reverts you back to your original bet.

e) Before increasing your Pass Line bet, you must have two scores each at that betting increment, although you can regress any time you want (Lett R. Wride just fainted).

I ain't gonna give you betting increments for $100 tables and all the others in between, 'cause you can easily adjust the theory to these higher levels.

The trick is to set these bets ahead of time, even if it entails your taking the time to write these plays out beforehand, and adhere to them religiously.

My apologies for a bevy of long winded chapters, but once this groundwork is laid, you'll grasp the theory.

For you advocates of the Pass Line, the key to successful wagering in that area was covered in detail over these past pages—devour the information.

54

Following the Trend

Take a good look at this approach. It's gonna take a lot of discipline and a lot of adjusting to the swing in trends at a table, but it has a lot of merit, and is a strong approach to craps play.

It's called Follow the Trend and that's easy to grasp. The theory is simply to follow whichever previous decision emerged. With this system you are neither a Right bettor or a Wrong bettor. You are looking to catch a trend, whether it be on the Right or Wrong side.

Buck D. Trenn is a typical hard-headed, stubborn, persistent player who feels that if you buck a certain trend long enough, it'll eventually turn and go your way.

Hey baby, I've seen players hold the dice for over an hour and clean out every wrong bettor who persisted in hanging in there waiting for that 7.

Same is true for the Right player who stays glued to games where a point hasn't been made in three swings around that table.

Blackjack players lose eleven hands in a row and spit out the crap that "things are due to change." I've seen black show eighteen times in a row at roulette and Less Hope will stand there betting red, with the hope that red will show. He has less brains than he has money and both will wipe him out.

139

There is always the chance that you can play Follow the Trend and end up with a pattern of win, lose, win, lose, etc. That's a chopping table and a killer to any player but you have your loss limit to protect you, plus four losses at the start of a session signal the end of that session, so you're well protected. Stop worrying.

Let's get to Follow the Trend. First of all you chart the tables till you find one that is running either hot or cold—it doesn't matter.

At least a trend is showing at that table. But don't settle in at a game where one shooter makes a point then sevens out. Next shooter makes four points and sevens out. Next shooter doesn't make any points, next one makes one Pass.

That's a chopping pattern and too dangerous. Get one with a definite edge.

After the buy-in, wait for a decision from the present player.

1) If he makes his point, the next Come-Out bet Right.
2) If he sevened out on that prior roll, bet Wrong.
3) Continue to bet on the line decision that shows on the previous roll.

This way you catch a hot roll when one develops on the Right side and are still in tune at a cold table, 'cause you're following along with that dry spell.

The big key is recognizing the chop and being able to avoid being ground out. If you begin your play following a Don't and a point is made and you swing over and bet Right and the shooter sevens out, you've lost two quick plays.

If you lose four in a row to start a session, wrap it up immediately; you're in a chopping pattern. If this chopping situation pops up during the course of your play, you have the 50 percent loss limit to protect you and you darn well better remember your loss limits at every session.

If you drew a blank when I mentioned loss limits, you better zip right back to that chapter.

This is a strong method of play and you diehard Right bettors who refuse to ever bet wrong can either follow this method or use the variation move in the next chapter.

If Buck D. Trenn scoffs at this switching technique, let's see how long he'll last at a table, continually trying to buck a trend running against him.

55

Varieties of Patrick Hedge

Staying with the $25 Pass Line bet and $4 three way craps, you could also place $22 inside, working. This way you pick up the possibility of having the 5 or 9 show as the point and immediately getting a $7 profit, minus the craps loss for a $3 win.

Now you skeptics can claim that it ain't worth the trouble for $3, but you're missing the fact that you are also looking to cover the $4 three way craps hedge, which is used to protect the $25 Pass Line bet.

Hedging is another word for protection and falls under the category of minimizing losses. There are thousands of craps shooters who put $25 on the Pass Line, with no protection in the event a craps shows.

The reason they don't protect it is because they feel the grind of $3 or $4 per Come-Out is too great. There's nothing wrong with that thinking, as you'll find sessions that never have a craps show on the Come-Out, and that constant small drop begins to add up.

An another table some guy will Come-Out with 12-12-2-3 in an attempt to establish a number and all the players with no craps hedge will get whacked. It's a matter of choice. Mine happens to be hedge.

Here's what happens if you bet $25 Pass Line, $4 three way craps and $22 inside:

a) 2 or 12 shows: plus $2

b) 3 shows: plus $3

c) 4 or 10 shows: minus $4

d) 5 or 9 shows: plus $3

e) 6 or 8 shows: plus $3

f) 7 shows: minus $1

g) 11 shows: plus $21

I don't wanna go into a lengthy breakdown, but the previous chart comes out to twelve losing rolls for a minus $30 as compared to twenty-four winning rolls and a plus of $106.

The 11 stays constant whether you make the inside numbers work or not, but the difference is whether you want the six ways of the 7 giving you a $21 profit or the profit spread over the hits on the 5-6-8 and 9. Without the inside bets, the three ways craps hedge keeps chopping away at you.

The next chapter gives more plays off of different unit amounts, but before you look at these moves, be sure you've got the theory completely understood.

56

Wrapping up Patrick Hedge

OK, you've got the idea of this play and probably have already decided whether you wanna use it or not.

This chapter will simply give you plays at the $10 level and $50 level, for the group like Kan I. Kount, who can't.

If you have $10 on the Pass Line, you don't need three way craps and a buck on the Any Craps is strictly optional. I'd say let it slide and ride with the $10 being naked.

But you could also place the 6 and 8 for $6 each, giving you ten ways of picking up a score there, plus the two ways for the 11, increasing the profit potential per roll from four ways to twelve ways.

You might ask what happens after a point is established. That's easy and you should know it by now.

Simply revert to your basic style of Right betting. This play is strictly to increase the number of ways to win on the Come-Out.

If your session money allows for a $50 bet or higher and you want to use the hedge, you have to decide if you'll go for the full hedge or just partial. The options are innumerable and remember that each of these examples will include $8 three ways craps, but you can adjust it to $6 or even down to $4, even though your Pass Line bet is $50:

    a) Thirty-two across, which leaves the 7 also eligible for a payoff if it shows.

1) This partial place bet hedge is the one I like, 'cause it
   opens up all place numbers for a score, plus the 7.
   b) Forty-four inside, which uses up the payoff on the 7,
   but increases payoff on numbers.
   c) Eighteen each on the 6 and 8, which also leaves room
   for the 7 to kick off a profit.

I could list spinoffs that encompass every type of full or
partial hedge, but you got the idea.

I like (a) because it gives me a score on thirty-two numbers,
all while offsetting the chances of the craps hurting you. If you
decide to use the Patrick Hedge, and have the bankroll to break
into high sessions, you just might wanna give this approach a
second look. Every number from 4 through 11 will kick off a
profit.

For you old-time street shooting crap players who get a
headache reading my conservative approaches, I ask you to bear
with my theories until you can prove they're useless, which they
are not.

My intent is to teach you how to win and the first step is to
minimize losses.

I've said it before, but for the benefit of a couple of friends of
mine, Monee S. Tite and Lou N. Shirt and D.C. Plinn and Y.R.
Kash, these hedges will come in quite handy.

In fact, it may start them on the road to picking up a few
winning sessions and that's the name of the game!

Isn't it?

57

Come System

In case you skipped over the chapters where I blasted the Come line, I just wanna be sure you're clear on how I feel about this move.

No, I ain't gonna give you a system on the Come—I just wanted you stubborn Come players to get suckered into reading this chapter, so I can take another shot at you.

Jean E. Yuss is a math wizard. She can actually get a row of numbers to talk to you. I listen to her give seminars on how to use a mathematical equation in order to shovel your driveway in quicker time.

I listened in one night when she was talking with her friend, Sir Count D. Waze III. He even had a numerical title, and listening to their conversation had me bent fourteen ways north and south. They didn't talk with words, they used numbers.

They saw me listening in, so I came up with a quick question: "By the way, could you direct me to the Parkway?" "Sure," replied Sir Count, "You'll be there in five minutes. Take your shirt size, minus the number of dents in your car, divide it by your lucky number, add twenty-eight, the number of days in February, subtract your telephone number, multiplied by the number of times you got stood up on a date the last four weeks, add the number of times your second cousin was caught cheating on his wife and you get the number of numbered

146

streets there are to the Parkway."

I thought the guy was nuts but I did what he told me and sure enough I got to the Parkway in three minutes.

The reason I was early was because I lied about the number of times I was stood up in the last four weeks. I put down twice while actually it was eleven times, but that's another story.

The point is that these geniouses like Jean E. Yuss can make figures say anything.

So when you read that the Come bet is a good mathematical move, just nod your head in agreement, but don't play the Come.

I can only make it as simple as it actually is. Betting the Come means you gotta make the number twice. Betting the Place means you only gotta make it once to get paid. Man, if you don't understand that, then you're a bigger dope than I had you figured for.

Let me count the ways.

58

Reality

Don't skip over this chapter, 'cause it's a big, big part of your approach to gambling, regardless of which game you play.

Actually this message belongs in the Discipline section, but since it is so important, I decided to make you aware of it now and then bang it out to you again later on.

It is something that most players lose when they enter a casino and it happens long before they reach into their pockets for money.

They lose touch with reality!

The beauty and splendor of the casino takes them right into a never-never land. The soft lights, beautiful music, gorgeous cocktail waitresses, the multitude of people betting thousands and thousands of dollars make the outside world seem dull and boring.

All of a sudden that $300 bankroll that you struggled to save for four months has lost its true value. The $100 you were hoping to win becomes a memory. You wanna become a part of this whirlwind-type existence and you feel that the way to do it is to bet big and bet freely.

You want the Big Score. You feel cheap betting $5 when the guy standing next to you is betting black hundred chips. You now envision gambling as the vehicle that will make you rich.

The goal you now set with that paltry $300 is up to $3,000.

You have lost all touch with reality.

The environment has eaten into your normal common sense approach to handling money, and you end up making stupid illogical bets, trying for the big kill.

Betting big amounts does not increase your chances of winning. It is imperative that you understand that you never have better than a 50–50 chance of winning at gambling... never!

Your predetermined conservative approach is swept away as you continue to play and even if you get ahead $300, it seems paltry by comparison to the thousands of dollars you see sitting in front of the dealer.

You won't quit when you double your starting bankroll but keep right on banging away, looking for your Utopia.

Eventually the inevitable losing streak takes over and your winnings are swallowed up faster than a donkey can swallow a piece of sugar.

Only this time it's the jackass that gets swallowed.

You crawl away from the table, dead broke. Every dime of that $300 is pushed into action trying to recoup just what you started with.

As you reach the street, away from the glitter of "that world" you are brought back to reality. Now you find out what a dork you really are.

A few hours ago you ran your $300 bankroll up to a profit of $500 but refused to quit, hoping for more, more, more.

Now you're broke and you realize you didn't lose $300, you lost $800. Admittedly you find it hard to accept, but it all goes back to your approach to gambling, which in most cases is illogical.

Remember the Little Three? Of course you don't—you skipped over that chapter cause you didn't think it applied to you.

The Little Three are Theory, Logic, and Trends. Logic! Anything to do with gambling has a logical explanation.

Setting a win goal of 10 percent or 20 percent is a logical

approach to a game whereby you have only a 50–50 chance of winning.

Going for the gigantic score is illogical, stupid and beyond the realm of reality.

You gotta use common sense in setting your win goals and loss limits and forget about your dream killing.

The reality of it all comes down to you yourself understanding the limitations of beating the house for thousands of dollars.

Reality! I think too many people lose touch with it when they enter the world of gambling.

59

Final Word on Pass Line

This is gonna be short although it may not be sweet to your ears. It has to do with my approach to playing craps from the Right side.

It is not written in stone that you *must* bet the Pass Line when you are not shooting. Bypassing the Come-Out and placing the numbers is the way I play, and the reason is that I get to pick the numbers I want going for me.

This theory of play gives away a Vigorish of eight tenths of a percent that you have going for you with a Pass Line bet with single odds versus the 1.51 percent you fight by placing the 6 and 8.

But as I've said before, the seven tenths of a percent that I give up is worth it, cause I always have the 'easy' numbers of 6 and 8 going for me.

Think about it. You might like to give this theory a shot.

Next we're going into place betting, the real blood and guts of craps.

60

Place Betting

I don't wanna belabor the art of Place betting, but this is where the sharp craps player really shines.

These are the things to remember about Place betting:

1) You get your choice of numbers.

2) You have to hit the numbers only *once* to get paid.

3) You can adjust your bets any way you choose.
   a) Press
   b) Regress
   c) Stay the same
   d) Take down

4) Bets are off on the Come-Out, unless you stipulate differently.

Go back over those explanations one by one and see if you can finally grasp the difference in Placing as to playing the Come.

When you bet the Come:

1) You don't get your choice of number—you gotta take the number that comes.

2) The Come bettor has to pop the number to get established and again to get paid.

3) After a score with a Come bet, you gotta come down and re-establish that number all over again.
   a) The place bettor can go right into money management.

4) If you're betting the Pass Line and a 7 shows, you'll win

152

the bet, but all bets that you had established through the Come get beat and you gotta re-establish them again.

Finally we come to the vig. The experts tell us that the Come has only six tenths of one percent vig for the house on the Come, when you take double odds, as opposed to the higher amounts on the Place bets (6 and 8 are only 1.51 percent).

But those figures were acquired through millions of computerized runs. Reality dictates you're only gonna be at a table an average of two hours per session.

Give yourself the best chance of winning by making the moves that are in your best interests for these short time periods of play.

As we swing into the Place betting moves, you're gonna find that the whole key is in how you bet:

1) What you bet after a Win.

2) What you bet after a Loss.

61

Key Numbers

Since the 6 and 8 are the numbers that can be made the most number of ways, they are always gonna be my starting plays and they always are played together.

In other words, just because the 6 hit five times in a row doesn't mean that I'll stop playing the 6. It only means I'll be betting more on the 6, to take advantage of that streak and less on the sister number 8 until it starts to pop.

You're gonna find that I like the use of the regression system as the main key to most of the series, but since I am also aware of the thousands of players that have short bankrolls, you're gonna find moves that are geared to other approaches.

That's because some people do not have the bread to bet higher on the first roll, which of course is the key to the regression. So if you are playing with smaller funds don't feel embarrassed, just heed the moves that are laid out for you.

Penny Pore loves the game of craps, but has run into a series of bad luck in her personal life and hasn't got the money to comfortably bet $12 each on the 6 and 8.

Since $150 is the total amount of her stake, I don't want a $24 risk on the two numbers that key the regression. She must start with $6 on each and the first chapter is pointed to Penny Pore and many of you that are playing tight.

But first a message to Penny and her cousin Nick L. Tite.

Nick L. Tite wouldn't spend a dime to learn how to play any casino game, but he'll take a handful of quarters, a roll of singles and a stray five dollar bill up to a craps table and make all types of silly bets, trying to quadruple his money.

Most times this nickel-plated lame-brain will bemoan his rotten luck, but he has neither the proper bankroll or knowledge of the best bets on the table to properly compete.

Nick L. Tite usually bets the 4 and 10, 'cause he likes the higher pay-offs of 9 to 5. He likes to bet the Yo and the Horn and the Snake Eyes and the Box Cars all tempt him with higher pay-offs of 15 to 1 and 30 to 1.

The bottom line is that these bets are harder to make, hence the inflated payoffs. My opening suggestions are geared to people like Penny Pore and Nick L. Tite. They can act as cool or calm as they like at a table, trying to hide their scared and stupid play.

A few minutes of watching their illogical moves will have them standing out for all the world to see—bad players.

There is absolutely no crime in having a limited bankroll, in comparison to the guys betting green and black chips.

The crime is how you handle that bankroll.

62

Hit and Down

Let's start at square one for the easiest place betting method of all. You will leave yourself vulnerable for a loss, for only as long as it takes you to get one score.

And just to save myself the necessity of having to repeat the instructions over and over, take a good long hard look at what you must do before you play.

1) Break bankroll into sessions.
2) Chart the tables.
3) Set win goals
4) Set loss limit

As we pop through these chapters, it'll save a lot of time if you understand that these four things must be done at every single table.

The amount of your bankroll is the sole determining factor as to the amount of your bets. (Should be ten times the amount of first bet.)

The following table describes the Hit and Run method, whereby placing the 6 and 8 is the total amount of your play:

Session Amount	Bet
$120	$6 on 6 & 8
$240	$12 on 6 & 8

156

$360 $18 on 6 & 8
$480 $24 on 6 & 8

OK, that explains the amount of money needed, and naturally the Session amount dictates what your bets will be. This is all you do:

1) Bypass the Come-Out roll.
2) Place the 6 and 8 for $6 each. (**Note:** If your Session amount is $240, you'd place $12 each. If it was $480, you'd place them for $24 each, etc.)
3) Take one hit on either the 6 or 8 and come right down on both.

With this play, you are looking for one hit on either the 6 or 8 and then immediately coming down on both bets. It calls for one hit and coming down on that shooter.

You do not make another bet until the shooter either makes his point or sevens out. You then wait for another point to be established, either by the same shooter or the next roller.

You're looking for a quick score and then coming down. Right away I can hear the cries of protest from guys like Frank Lee Board, who feels he will be bored to death with this play.

Hold your britches, my friend, as there is an offshoot to this play.

Based on the size of your session money, you will set a goal whereby you'll increase the number of hits before you come down.

Suppose you started with $120 and placed the 6 and 8 for $6 each. After a score, you'd come down and wait for another point to be established.

With the grinding type of method that this system calls for, your win goal is changed from 20 percent to 50 percent, due strictly to the fact that your risk factor is so low.

Continue taking one hit per established point, until you reach the win goal of 50 percent. At that point you do the following:

1) Break 50% Win Goal in half ($60).

2) Put starting session amount in your pocket ($120).
3) Put one half of win goal in your pocket ($30). This is your guarantee. You're guaranteed to leave that table with a profit.
4) The other $30 is your excess and you continue with that session, using the $30.

However, now you increase the number of hits on the 6 and 8 to two. This is how you will play:

1) Bypass the Come-Out.
2) Place the 6 and 8 for same amount you started with, based on your session amount.
3) Take two hits on any combination of 6 or 8 and come down.
4) Do not make another bet until another point number is established.

This isn't hard to understand, and even Frank Lee Board should be able to accept the so-called challenge of going for that second score.

There are two things that call for explanations, so let me get to them before I am deluged by letters.

1) You place the six and eight all the time—even if the 6 or 8 becomes the point.
2) You only stay at that table until your loss limit is hit, or you lose three consecutive shooters in a row.

The first statement is self-explanatory, the second calls for a comment. If you chart the table and find the 6 and 8 coming for several shooters in a row and then have it change when you get to a table, don't start crying and pouting. It's gonna happen.

But also don't stand there getting whacked. If you lose on the first three shooters, leave. In fact, at any time during the course of that session whereby three consecutive shooters beat you, close out that session, even if you haven't reached your loss limit.

This is a snap system to play and while it may seem boring and super-conservative, it works. Upcoming chapters dress up the moves you'll make as you continue to win and also addresses the matter that has crossed the minds of all you crap shooters that have been rolling those bones since the beginning of time:

"Yeah, this system is okay, but I'm gonna lose all those red-hot rolls that'll come along!"

I'll let you think of your own answer before I give you reality.

63

$12 Six and Eight

As we move into the stronger Place betting methods, I'd like you to start concentrating with both of your heads, cause this is the method I highly endorse.

Naturally it'll include my regression system but in the long run this is the theory of play that I believe will become the focal point of all Right bettors.

The method is snap city to learn and the variations off of the play will allow you a tremendous amount of offshoots that you will come up with yourself.

As usual you'll bypass the Come-Out roll and then place $12 6 and 8, based on the fact that you're at a $5 table. You're giving yourself room to regress to $6 each after a score, but if there are some who cannot handle this size layout, then you must go back to the basic play of 6 and 8.

This Session calls for $240, due to the initial $24 risk and of course you have a 50 percent loss limit and 20 percent win goal. Series will progress as follows:

a) 1st hit—regress both bets to $6 each.

That's the key move in the whole play. At this point you have $14 in your kick and $12 at risk. This shooter cannot hurt you. Even if he sevens out on the next roll, you have a $2 profit.

By regressing your bets to $6 each, you have your money back and two free bets on the table.

Imus Pressit ain't gonna like this method. He wants to go right on pressing his bets to the full amount of his score. He's wrong and so are all you cats that have the singular thought of constantly attacking the house.

All I'm asking you to do is give up the second score of a series, by regressing down after a win. After that you'll see that the play allows you to go up.

Let's start all over:

a) 1st hit—regress both bets to $6 each

b) 2nd hit—place the 5 and 9

Stop again and look at the great position you're in. When that second 6 or 8 showed, the dealer slid $7 to you. Take $3 from your rack and tell him to place the 5 and 9. Since you were already plus $2 after the first score, the total amount you have to risk for this shooter is $1, and you have $22 on the table.

You're looking for one more hit on either the 5, 6, 8 or 9 and then come down on everything. You're risking $1 to win $28.

Now before you start bellowing all over again about coming down after that third hit, I'll remind you again—the chapters on Plateaus will give you options.

Go back over this play and grasp the full impact.

a) After the first hit you have a profit of $2

b) After the second hit you are out only $1

c) After the third hit you have a profit of $28

Naturally after the first and second hits you have the opportunity of coming down on your bets and ending up with a profit of either $14 or $21 respectively.

Bottom line is that all you're looking for is one rotten lousy hit and you're home free.

This is a great approach.

64

Another Variation

You're still starting with $12 6 and 8 but now the move after the first score will vary.

a) First hit—place $22 inside

b) Second hit—whether it is on the 5, 6, 8 or 9, come down on everything.

Okay, let's pick this theory apart and see if you catch the approach.

After the first score, you have $14 in your rack and $22 spread over the inside numbers. At this point, a 7 will give you a minus $8 for that shooter, but a score on either the 5, 6, 8 or 9 will result in a $21 profit.

You are risking $8 to win $21 and the beauty of this play is that you need only two hits per shooter, whereas the initial system called for three.

The plus factor in the initial play was that after the first score you are up a deuce, while this variation has you going right to four place bets working, while opening up a possible $8 deficit.

Take a moment right now to seriously review the theory behind both these plays. Both are geared for the initial score on the 6 or 8, but then comes the key move of setting up that second bet. Right there is where the sharp player protects that particular series.

Stand at a crap table and watch the moves that the various players make in their series. Most of them change each shooter and most of them are geared to super aggressive plays.

They never come down! When than inevitable 7 finally does show, there stands Ding Dong Dotty with $188 spread all over the table, a loss of $9 for that shooter and a stupid grin on her face, as she gives the high-five to the shooter for having such a great roll.

Sure he had a hot roll. But Ding Dong didn't make a dang nickel out of it.

The next shooter picks up the dice and Dotty starts all over again. In all honesty it doesn't matter if that shooter is ice-cold or red-hot, Ding Dong Dotty doesn't know how to grab a profit.

Go over these past two chapters which start with $12 on both the 6 and 8. Get a solid read on the theory 'cause next we go into higher starting amounts which lead to more variations.

65

$18 Six and Eight

Now we start at $18 six, $18 eight with a $360 session amount.

Again we're looking for one hit, which will make that series either a full profit, a wash, or minimizing the loss for that shooter. In other words, the amount of the regression after the first score will determine how little we lose for that series.

I'll give you basic drops, like all the way back to $6 six and $6 eight after a score and you decide if that is your play or if you just go to $12 and $12.

The thing to realize is that you drop both the 6 and 8 after one hit and not just the one that scores or the opposite. Both work together.

Let's go to a move:

a) **First Hit**—Regress both bets to $6 each.

b) **Second Hit**—Go to $22 inside.

c) **Third Hit**—(on either the 5, 6, 8 or 9) Press the 6 and 8

d) **Fourth Hit**—all down.

Okay, for the benefit of Watt E. Cey, who hasn't the foggiest idea of what I said, let me explain it one more time.

But Watt E. Cey better start paying attention, cause this theory is not tough to digest.

After the first hit on either the 6 or 8, you have $21 in your rack and $12 at risk, which means you're a plus $9 even if the shooter bangs a 7.

The second hit gives you another $7 and you take $3 from your rack and place the 5 and 9.

Right now you have $22 inside and $6 profit, which means this shooter can't hurt you. Now maybe you'll scoff at the $6 profit but that $22 inside is a free bet.

Naturally if the 7 shows, you end up with a profit of $6 and start all over again with $18 and $18. Again I repeat for the benefit of both Rhee Repeet and Watt E. Cey—if you lose on the first four shooters at a session, whereby no score at all comes, you absolutely must leave that table.

Okay, back to the series. If you catch a hit on any of these inside bets as your third score, you have many options.

The one I laid out was pressing the 6 and 8 for $6 each. That means you now have $12 on both the 6 and 8 and $5 on both the 5 and 9, and a buck profit. All of the bets on the table are free—in the event of a 7.

The option on this play is that after the third hit, you would take everything down. You'd have a $35 profit for that shooter.

Naturally my move is down but I'm giving you a choice.

Go back over this play, keeping in mind the two main themes.

a) First hit, you regress both bets.

b) Second hit, exercise options of both conservative and aggressive.

Please re-read this approach until you grasp the full impact of its potential.

66

Option Off $18 Each

Let's shift your thinking into second gear as we give you an option off the first hit:

a) **First Hit**—$22 inside

b) **Second Hit**—all down

In this case you immediately go to $22 inside after the first score. You've got $21 win, minus $22 at risk for a situation whereby you are risking $1 to win $28.

It ain't hard to grasp this option. The hardest part is when you have to say, "Take me down!"

Let's go to another move, still starting with $18 and $18.

a) **First Hit**—regress to $12 on both the 6 and 8.

b) **Second Hit**—place the 5 and 9 for $5 each.

c) **Third Hit**—go to $44 inside.

d) **Fourth Hit**—Regress to $22 inside.

e) **Fifth Hit**—all down.

On this play you're taking a shot after the second hit by using this shooter as an aggressive move but the return is always far greater than the risk.

a) After the first hit you have $24 at risk with potential loss of $3.

b) After second hit you have $34 on board with potential profit of $1.
c) On the third hit, regardless of whether it is on $12 6 or 8, or $5 5 or 9, you go $44 inside. The worst you could be is to have $44 on the board with potential loss of $2.
d) Fourth hit will give you a payoff of $14 on all four numbers and immediately regress to $22 inside, leaving you with a guaranteed profit of at least $34 and a free $22 bet on board.
   1) You could come down after the fourth hit.
   2) Last hit must come down on everything.

This is a powerful play for the medium-hot table, and offers you several spinoffs along the way.

67

$24 Six and Eight

The required session amount is $480 with a total bankroll of at least $1,440. The first move is strictly on the 6 and 8 and this will be the final starting amount that regresses all the way back to $6 6 and 8.

The more options off of the regression, the wider base of plays after that first hit and that ties in with your starting bankroll. If you have a short bankroll, you're gonna have to stay with basic moves. If you have a larger stack of chips, you'll increase the chances of winning, because you need a lesser number of hits.

Les N. Lessor is a craps shooter who has less knowledge of the game of craps than a new father who has never been in a casino and his only idea of craps is when it's his turn to change the diapers.

Les N. Lessor has been reading this book but doesn't take the time to grasp the theory of what I'm trying to get across.

The statement I made about a large bankroll giving you a better chance of picking up a profit with less hits is a snap to understand.

A guy with a $100 session amount needs two or three scores on the place numbers to show a profit for a shooter, because of all the same bet moves he must make.

A guy with a $480 session amount needs only one hit, 'cause after the first score he can immediately drop to $6 6 and 8 and

have a guaranteed $16 profit salted away. Remember this, Less
N. Lessor! The less you have, the more you need, and the more
you have, the less you need.

So while Les N. Lessor digests the information that will help
him more and more with his approach to craps, let's stop the
crap and get onto the game of craps—if you get my drift.

Again, begin with $24 on both the 6 and 8, after thoroughly
charting the tables:

    a) **First Hit**—Regress to $22 inside.
    b) **Second Hit**—Press the 6 and 8 one unit each.
    c) **Third Hit**—Press the 5 and 9 one unit each.
    d) **Fourth Hit**—Again, regress to $22 inside.
    e) **Fifth Hit**—All down.

With this play you have a strong use of double regression in
the series and as we increase the amount of the bets, I'd like you
to increase the amount of times you'll use the regression.

Another offshoot:

    a) **First Hit**—Go to $34 inside (That's $12 6 and 8, $5 5 and 9).
    b) **Second Hit**—Regardless of number, go to $44 inside.
    c) **Third Hit**—Regress to $22 inside.
    d) **Fourth Hit**—All down.

This play calls for only four scores to complete a series and
lets you use second regression after third hit. The drawback
comes after the first hit, where a score leaves you with a hit of
$28 and an investment of $34 on board.

You are not setting aside a profit after that first hit, although
your risk is only $6 versus a potential profit of at least $35 (if the
5 or 9 shows) if you were to come right down after the second
hit.

If the 6 or 8 shows on that second score, naturally you'd have
a $42 profit if you came right down.

Since I called for a move of $44 inside after the second hit,
you are now risking $2 to show a profit of at least $49 (with
possible plus $56) and it only took three hits, the average

number of hits per shooter, after the point is established.

Sure, you would then take everything down after that third score, but I give you an option of going down to $22 inside.

After awhile you'll settle in on the number of hits you'll be satisfied with.

Methinks you'll swing over to my conservative style.

For the thousandth time, let me again say: You can come *down* any time you like after that first or second hit. I am carrying out the series for the benefit of the aggressive player.

But you will notice I *never* go for more than five hits and that's stretching it!

68

Options Off $24 Inside

I get the feeling that my old friend Buck D. House is dying to find an aggressive system whereby he takes a good pop against the house, but he doesn't realize he's bucking tremendous odds.

When he starts with $24 on both the 6 and 8, his dreams are for stupendous returns. As the dealer slides the $28 win towards him, he'll drop another $20 on the table and say, "Go up to $48 each." Then as an afterthought he'll drop another handful of chips on the table and blurt,"Oh, and give me $10 5 and 9, all the hardways, Horn high Yo, $5 on the field for that good looking blonde in the corner. If there's anything left, give me $30 across the board on Big Shot Bucky in the fourth at Aqueduct."

I mean, what does this dork take in his water? He didn't just win the New York Lottery, he won a lousy $28 when the 6 showed and right away he starts giving the money away.

If you think you're gonna find moves like that in this book, you'll also believe I can have the Penthouse Pet of the month kicking down your door in fifteen minutes.

There's no way to win with super-colossal stupid moves.

If you get a score with $24 6 and 8, here's another play:

a) **First Hit**—drop to $12 6 and 8.

b) **Second Hit**—$22 inside.

c) **Third Hit**—press the 6 and 8 one unit each

d) **Fourth Hit**—press 5 and 9 $5 each.

e) **Fifth Hit**—regress to $22 inside.

f) **Sixth Hit**—all down

There you have an intelligent series that utilizes a double regression but also allows for double unit bets on all the inside numbers after the fourth hit.

I don't wanna belabor going over your profit and loss after each hit, cause by now you can figure that out yourself, but you'll find you were never in trouble after that first hit.

The last example called for a drop to $12 and $12 after first hit, but now we'll give another offshoot:

a) **First Hit**—go to $18 6 and 8

b) **Second Hit**—place 5 and 9 for $10 each

c) **Third Hit**—same bet

d) **Fourth Hit**—go to $44 inside

e) **Fifth Hit**—drop to $22 inside

f) **Sixth Hit**—take me down

This example kept you in double and triple units for a good spell and then worked down.

Get something straight right now: It is very, very, very hard to catch 4, 5, 6 hits per shooter. When you do find a succession of hot shooters, you'll curse the day you ever heard of my conservative style.

But most of the time you'll be getting one or two scores per shooter and this conservative regression style attack will keep putting small gains in your pocket and holding losses down.

You'll praise the fact that you discovered the regression system and think I walk on water.

I do—but that's another story.

69

$22 Inside

Before going on with the place betting that starts with 6 and 8, let's touch on the guys who would like to have four numbers working for them instead of two.

There are plenty of guys who go up to a table and bet $22 inside and get whacked by the 7. It's gonna happen, just like the 7 can whack you when you just place the 6 and 8.

Charting the table is a snap but this is what you're looking for:

a) Two shooters in a row to make at least two inside numbers.

b) Or, three shooters in a row making at least one inside number.

You still bypass the Come-Out and then drop your chips on the table and say "22 inside."

The dealer will give you $5 on both the 5 and 9 and $6 on both the 6 and 8.

You're now risking $22 as your first bet so you should have at least $220 session money and 20 percent win goal and 50 percent loss limit set.

I'd like you to go for two hits on any combination of inside numbers and then all down.

Do that until you get ahead $50, then go for three hits until a profit of $100 and so on.

I know a lot of you won't do that and the prime reason is universal:

INTIMIDATION

You're so afraid to look cheap at the table or conservative or that the dealer will see you pulling back after a couple of hits while everyone else is banging away.

Too many of you are just too darn concerned with what other people think. Deep down in your hearts you know I do not speak with forked tongue and still you ain't got the guts to follow this advice.

Anyhow, back to the tables and pick up with this $22 inside move. You got eighteen numbers working for you but the key is in staying up only for short runs.

I've already told you to take two hits on any combination until you reach plus $50, so let's pick up the moves from there.

Once you get ahead $50 this will be a series:

a) **First Hit**—same bet regardless of what number hit
b) **Second Hit**—take down your 5 and 9
c) **Third Hit**—press the 6 and 8
d) **Fourth Hit**—all down

If at any time you drop below a plus $50, you must go back to the basic two hits and down, until you reestablish you $50 profit.

Let's shoot off a variation:

a) **First Hit**—same bet
b) **Second Hit**—take down 5 and 9
c) **Third Hit**—go back to $22 inside
d) **Fourth Hit**—all down

I'm giving you ample chance to get four hits in a series and that's plenty.

When we reach the $100 profit mark we'll allow for more fluctuation but for right now, just hold your britches.

70

$44 Inside

This move can be made with higher bankrolls:
a) You have at least $440 session money when you come to the
   table.
b) You have reached a profit of $100, starting with $22 inside
   and want to increase starting bets.

Here's where you can get into some deep regression spinoffs,
'cause you have more numbers working for you. As usual, the
key to making the series work is right after the first hit, as you
lay out the bets for the next roll. It all happens right there:
a) **First Hit**—regress all bets to $22 inside
b) **Second Hit**—same bet
c) **Third Hit**—press 6 and 8
d) **Fourth Hit**—press 5 and 9
e) **Fifth Hit**—all down

Go back to where you stood after the first hit. You pick up a
$14 payoff and leave $22 at risk. One more hit gives you a profit
of $21 with a potential loss of only $8.

You've protected that series after the first hit, making sure it
wouldn't be a wipe out, yet it took only one hit to make sure.

The second hit gives you another $7 score, leaving you $21 in
payoffs and $22 on the table with four numbers working.

175

The third hit allows for a press on the 6 and 8 and if you'd like to come down after the fourth hit, be my guest. But for the more aggressive player, I gave you a press on the 5 and 9 and then down after the fifth hit.

In this series you have your risk factor down pretty low after one hit and then you can stay out there for several more shots.

Phil O. Krapps thinks I'm full of crap for telling you to come down after four or five scores 'cause he feels that maybe this could be the roll of the day.

Sometimes he'll be right, but most times it will be Phil O. who is full of. Sure it's nice to catch that hot roll and sure you'd like to be a part of a potential Bonanza, but the down side is the reality of what happens to all right bettors. That 7 is always lurking.

Another allusion to this rebuttal on Phil O. Krapps theory. If he stays up there with $44 across after picking up a profit, he has to get three more scores on any combination of these numbers just to break even.

In other words, he has $44 inside and he needs to pop three straight $14 payoffs to offset the chance of that 7 showing the next three rolls. Four hits and he'll have himself only an extra $12 profit. Four hits!

Do you realize how hard it is to get these scores? Well, you'd better.

Phil O. Krapps would be better off filling the air with the sound of "Take me down, please."

But he won't—he won't.

71

Option Off $44 Inside

If you started with $22 inside and worked your way up to where your profits allowed for starting with $44 inside, you can follow right along with us.

The series that you will use will be the exact same ones that I'll be giving to people who are buying in for $440 or more and will begin with $44 inside.

The one difference is that there will be times when you might hit a little snag in your play and the table will become a little choppy.

Please, and I'm begging on this one: don't be afraid to either leave that table, or at least go back and start your series off at $22 inside. You can work your way right back to the $44 level.

Let's have a little spin off in the initial $44 series as show in the past chapter:

a) **First Hit**—Regress all bets to $22 inside
b) **Second Hit**—Down on 5 and 9
c) **Third Hit**—Press 6 and 8
d) **Fourth Hit**—Place 5 and 9
e) **Fifth Hit**—Go to $22 inside
f) **Sixth Hit**—All down

In that series you're coming down quickly on the 5 and 9 but going back up after you pick up a few hits.

a) **First Hit**—Regress all bets to $22 inside
b) **Second Hit**—Same bet
c) **Third Hit**—Press up to $44 inside
c) **Fourth Hit**—Press 6 and 8
e) **Fifth Hit**—Regress to $22 inside
f) **Sixth Hit**—Press 6 and 8
g) **Seventh Hit**—Again press 6 and 8 to $18 each
h) **Eighth Hit**—Again down to $22 inside. You stay up, but revert back to Sixth Hit and follow along as long as hits come. The absolute maximum amount you will have on any number will never exceed five units.

I want you to review that series and note that I left you up on the four inside numbers but kept sticking in regression moves, while limiting the total amount on any number of five units.

A lot of you big boppers will scoff at that, but that's the way the ding dongs when you start a series.

I'm gonna give you one more series starting with $44 inside and this one will get you a little more aggressive after you've got a few bucks packed away.

a) **First Hit**—Regress to $22 inside
b) **Second Hit**—Same bet
c) **Third Hit**—Press 6 and 8 up to $12 each
d) **Fourth Hit**—Press 6 and 8 up to $18 each
e) **Fifth Hit**—Press 5 and 9 up to $10 each
f) **Sixth Hit**—Same bet
g) **Seventh Hit**—Press 6 and 8 up to $24 each
h) **Eighth Hit**—Press 5 and 9 up to $15 each
i) **Ninth Hit**—Regress all bets to $44 inside
j) **Tenth Hit**—Press 6 and 8 to $18 each
k) **Eleventh Hit**—Press 6 and 8 to $24 each
l) **Twelfth Hit**—Press 5 and 9 to $15 each
m) **Thirteenth Hit**—Regress all to $44 inside
n) Continue going for two increases and then regressing back to $44 inside.

First off, you're gonna find very few long runs but when you do, use this table I just gave you, or come up with your own offshoots.

But be sure you incorporate enough regressions in your series. It'll take guts on your part but do it or even blurt out the three power words: "Take me down!"

Don't get upset because of the restriction of five units per number. The key words for the craps shooter are "Take me down." I'm going against the grain by allowing this aggressive five unit play.

You wanna win more—bring more!! Starting with a $44 inside bet should never exceed $110 inside. You don't realize it yet, but this is excellent advice.

72

Big Six and Eight

For the benefit of you who play in Vegas and points west and use the Big Six and Big Eight, let me give you some powerful advice. Don't play them. Period!!!

You'll find this bet on most western lay-outs and it should be entitled "Suckers Welcome."

The Big Six and Big Eight are large enough to cover the oversized jaws of the biggest mouth at a craps table and it's for a purpose.

Unsuspecting bettors can drop their chips on the lay-out without having to deal with the dealer and this is inviting to the intimidated players. But they fail to see the drawbacks of that bet.

It only pays even money. If you place the 6 and 8 you get paid $7 to $6. If you play the Big Six or Big Eight you get only even money. That's a big whack out of your packet and has you fighting a vig of 9.09 percent as opposed to the small 1.52 you fight by placing these same two numbers.

In Atlantic City they used to have the Big Six and Big Eight on the lay-out but were required by the Casino Control Commission to pay off at the proper $7 to $6 amount.

The lay-outs have since been changed to eliminate that Big 6 and Big 8 bet, but all you gotta do is place it with the dealer and get $7 to $6.

For you people who play in Vegas and see this bet on the lay-out—don't go near it.

I don't care how intimidated you may feel about having the dealer handle your bets, don't play the Big Six or Big Eight under any circumstances. Never!

73

Aggressive $44 Inside

This chapter is for the player like Igott Bred who has a heavy bankroll and breaks it down to where his session amount is at least double the amount of his initial bet.

In straight talk I'm telling a guy who brings at least $880 to the table that his initial bet, which could call for $88 inside, will be restricted to $44 inside but will incorporate a little more aggressive move.

The reason, naturally, is that the loss limit will take longer to reach and the heavier bread that Igott Bred has will give him extra shooters in which to catch a streak.

The drawback for guys like Igott Bred is that just because they have a heavier bankroll than Lil Tilchot, they think they have to bet green and black chips. They're dead wrongsky.

I want them to use the bankroll to give them longer stays at the table by starting with smaller place amounts.

So even though your buy in is $880 or higher, try this series beginning with $44 inside:

a) **First Hit**—Same bet
b) **Second Hit**—Regress to $22 inside
c) **Third Hit**—Go back up to $44 inside
d) **Fourth Hit**—Same bet
e) **Fifth Hit**—Go up to $66 inside
f) **Sixth Hit**—Same bet

g) **Seventh Hit**—Regress 5 and 9 to ten dollars each
h) **Eighth Hit**—Press 6 and 8 to $24 each
i) **Ninth Hit**—Press 5 and 9 to $15 each
j) **Tenth Hit**—Go to $88 inside
k) **Eleventh Hit**—Same bet
l) **Twelfth Hit**—Go up to $110 inside
m) **Thirteenth Hit**—Same bet

Keep alternating subsequent scores with "same bet" and upping each inside number by one unit.

However, with a starting amount of $44 inside, your absolute maximum bet will be not one penny more than $176 inside. (That's $48 each on the 6 and 8 and $40 each on the 5 and 9.)

At that point you take one more "same bet" and then all the way back to $44 inside, before starting back up.

I am not going to give any offshoots or variations of this type of series but you'll be able to easily set up your own increases. Just be sure you incorporate a couple of regressions and hold to the maximum of $176 inside.

As an aside to all you players who have decent bankrolls as stated in the beginning of this chapter, I'd love to see you incorporate lower starting amounts as your place bets and the gradually work up the ladder.

You'll find all of the following start to happen:
a) Losses will be minimized.
b) There'll be more winning series.
c) Less money will be on table when 7 does come.
d) You'll get in the habit of accepting consistent smaller returns.
e) You won't be such a grouch when you get home from the casino.

All of the above will tend to make you a stronger player. Igott Bred will have a very tough time playing small amounts in the beginning of sessions, but he'd have to give me a couple of solid reasons as to why this theory of mine isn't worth a good shot.

And handing me the garbage that he's got the bread to get bigger doesn't hold water with me.

Betting "smarter" is always better than betting "bigger."

Please, please, please re-read (c) where it states you'll have less money on the table when that 7 does show.

The crusher for the craps shooter is always the fact that when he goes down, he has a mint of money on the board.

I'm trying to get you to change this pattern!

74

Jargon

Before going on with some series bets, I'd like to break the tension of concentrating on series offshoots and just touch on the use of craps terms that the dealers like you to use.

Craps is a fast moving game and they like to see the payoffs handled as swiftly as possible so as to keep the action flowing.

That's why it's important that you have a handle on the way the requests should be made.

Several weeks ago, two budding craps players were standing at a table trying to understand the lingo. Each time they heard a new word they would look at each other and discuss what they thought it meant.

They didn't have a clue as to what the players were saying, and it all sounded like a foreign language to them.

Yet both of these guys admitted to having played the game and still couldn't understand what they were supposed to say.

My original book on craps goes over this in greater detail. But I just wanna repeat a few of them for people like Noah Little, who cause the action to slow down at a table due to his inability to say the right things concerning his intended bets.

a) **Press:** Increase the amount of your place bet.

b) **Press up one unit:** If you're betting $12 6 and get paid $14, you increase to $18 and take back $8.

c)**Press it all:** You've got $15 on the 5 and get a hit, giving you

$21. You'd be asking dealer to increase it all the way up to $35 and get $1 back.

d) **Move it to the nine:** You've got $12 6 and 8 placed from previous shooter with $10 on Pass Line. Eight becomes the point. They move $10 from the 8 to the 9 and return $2 to you.

e) **Off on this roll:** For some reason you want to call off your place bets for a roll or series of rolls. Instead of taking your bets down, they just place an "off" button on one of them and you have no action until you again inform the dealer that your bets work.

f) **Working:** Place bets and hard way bets are off on the come-out roll. By saying "Working," you now have action.

g) **Partial Odds:** You have $5 on Don't Pass and 5 becomes the point. You can lay $15 to $10 or $9 to $6. Partial odds would be $6 to win $4.

h) **Big Red:** Bet on any seven (never make this bet).

i) **Horn High Yo:** Throw $5 on table and you get dollar each on the deuces, 12, 3, and $2 on the 11.

j) **Natural:** 7 or 11 on the Come out.

k) **Make It Look Like:** Suppose you have $24 on the 8 and it shows. "Make it look like $12" means they'll drop the 8 to $12 and give you $28 plus $12 back.

l) **Lay Bet:** You're betting against the number: for instance you lay $41 against the 4 to win $19.

m) **Buy the Number:** Only two numbers you'd buy is 4 or 10 for minimum of $25. You'd pay 5 percent charge, reducing house vig from 6.67 percent to 5 percent and being paid true odds of 2 to 1 ($50 for $25), instead of 9 to 5 ($45 for $25).

n) **One Roll Action Bets:** They work only on the next roll, such as Field bets, any craps, Yo, Big Red, Horn bets.

o) **World Bet:** Two aces, two sixes, ace-deuces, yo, and any seven. To say it is a sucker bet is to say grass is green, sky is high, rain is wet and Dolly is big.

p) **Tow Way "Hard Way":** By dropping $4 on the table and

saying "Two Way Hard Six and Eight" means you have a dollar Hard Six and Hard Eight for yourself and a buck on each for the dealers.

Noah Little, who knows very little about the proper way to conduct himself at a table, took a look at this list and stared back in amazement.

"Gee, I thought the World Bet was every number on the board and action meant all the female dealers were available."

I asked him about the Field and buying the numbers and he winked and said: "I figured playing the Field meant you got your choice of any chick at the table and buying a number meant you got the unlisted number of Miss Casino 1990."

I can't believe there are guys at the table who really don't understand all the jargon of the game. Yet there are.

75

Placing the 4 and 10

This chapter shouldn't be too long cause I don't have any variations to spin off to. The reason I don't have any variations to spin to is because I don't have any system to give you on placing the 4 and/or 10.

Perhaps the best way to explain why I don't place the 4 and 10 is by giving you some questions and letting you give me some intelligent answers:

1) Why place the 4 or 10 that can be made three ways each, when I can place the 5 or 9 that can be made four ways each?

2) Why place the 4 or 10 that carries a 6.67 percent house vig when 5 and 9 are only 4 percent?

3) Why place 4 and 10 that can be made three ways each when I can place 6 and 8 that can be made five ways each?

4) Why place the 4 or 10 that carries a house vig of 6.67 percent when I can place the 6 and 8 that carries only a house vig of 1.51 percent?

If you've got some intelligent answers to these questions, I'd love to hear them.

I do not place the 4 or 10, even if I'm in the middle of a

scorching run and the shooter is banging out every number except Sophia Loren's private masterpiece.

And the reasons are all locked in the four questions I just laid out. I see no reason to elaborate further.

76

Buying the 4 and 10

Way off in the distance I can hear Don B. Leve telling one and all that he didn't believe word I was saying. The only thing he believes is that:

1) You should bet as high and as often as you can.
2) That if you're going to lose, you might as well lose quick and painlessly.
   a) How he can say losing is painless I don't grasp.
3) That making the 4 or 10 is just as easy as making the 6 or 8 cause the dice have no memory.
   a) I don't wanna go trying to explain to him that something that will occur 5 times is easier to make than something that'll occur 3 times.
4) The payoff on the 4 and 10 is $9 to $5, which is better than $7 to $6 or $7 to $5.

Comparing the payoffs of 4 and 10 versus 6 and 8 over a projected roll of thirty-six numbers on the dice, the 4 and 10 will be made six times at a payoff of $9 each for a total of $54.

Based on the same projected number of thirty-six rolls, the 6 and 8 can be made ten ways. At $7 per payoff, that comes to $70. Even if you minus the probable loss of $10 for each roll of the 7 versus the 4 and 10 and $12 per loss versus the 6 and 8, the result will always favor the inner numbers.

190

Let's go to buying the 4 and 10. This is a move that the house allows you to make when you wager at least $25 on the 4 or 10.

Instead of placing your bet and getting $45 for your $25, you can pay a charge of 5 percent and get paid true odds of 2 to 1. That means you have reduced the house vig from 6.67 percent down to 5 percent. But it's still higher than 4 percent or 1.51 percent.

To elaborate, suppose a guy walked to a table and made a $100 place wager on the 4. If the house paid him 9 to 5, he'd get $180 for his score.

By paying a 5 percent charge, he'd get true odds of $200 for his $100 by buying the number. But that still doesn't change my advice to you about playing the 4 and 10.

I want the numbers that can be made the most number of times and if Don B. Leve doesn't believe in my theory, let him bank away at those tough numbers.

No wonder they build casinos all over the world.

77

$30 Six and Eight

Let's swing back to the method of bypassing the Come-Out and placing the 6 and 8. The offshoot play of betting all the inside numbers, after a point is established, is just as effective as the ones featuring just the 6 and 8. So it is up to you to decide which one is the path you'll follow.

Then again you'll also come up with your own set of plays based on suggestions from all or any of these predetermined series.

Placing 6 and 8 for $30 each calls for session amount of $600 and bankroll of at least $1,800.

Following are series:

a) **First Hit**—Go to $44 inside
b) **Second Hit**—Press the 6 and 8 $6 each
c) **Third Hit**—Press the 5 and 9 $5 each (regardless of number that showed)
d) **Fourth Hit**—Same bet
e) **Fifth Hit**—Regress to $44 inside
f) **Sixth Hit**—All down except $12 6 and 8, and now use regular spin-off for these amounts.

That was double regression play but kept you in action after the sixth hit.

This one is more conservative:

a) **First Hit**—Regress to $44 inside
b) **Second Hit**—Same bet
c) **Third Hit**—Same bet
d) **Fourth Hit**—All down except $12 six and eight and revert to basic increases.

This one is more aggressive:
a) **First Hit**—Regress to $44 inside
b) **Second Hit**—Press the six and eight $12 each
c) **Third Hit**—Same bet
d) **Fourth Hit**—Go to $88 inside
e) **Fifth Hit**—Same bet
f) **Sixth Hit**—Go to $110 inside
g) **Seventh Hit**—Regress to $44 inside

On these plays I did not go off but you know dog-gone well that after the fourth hit, you are not wrong to start thinking along these lines.

As my old pappy used to say: "He who retreats on a given day, has money to bet for another day."

Go over these examples and pick the ones that interest you, even with your adding some revisions. But never start making those changes in the middle of a series. You must stay with your pre-determined series.

Will E. Swaye sways in the wind like a little whore, jumping from one system to another, never settling in with one brand of play.

He ends up out-guessing himself with no firm disciplined play to follow. Now I ain't telling you to be like Rock O. Ages, who is stubbornly rock-hard in his persistence to play the same system all the time, whether it is winning or losing.

I want you to be able to adjust your play, to adapt to a table that is semi-hot, or chopping, or scorching. But those variations should have been set hours and hours before you made your first bet.

Will E. Swaye will swear to change his roving style but just like the times when a "lady of the night" will sway his thinking, a change of direction at the table will sway his playing and he's in big trouble in both cases.

Take one or two or all of the series I laid out for you, master the ones you will use and stay with that series.

Watch how you'll begin to minimize losses.

78

$60 Six and Eight

We'll jump past some other numbers and go right to $60 for the 6 and 8, and this session calls for $1,200 table amount and bankroll of at least $3,600.

Remember that your initial bet can be $60 each or spread out over the inside numbers. The choice is yours.

But the theory never changes. I want a regression after the first hit:

a) **First Hit**—Regress to $44 inside
b) **Second Hit**—Press the 6 and 8 by one unit each
c) **Third Hit**—Press all bets one unit each
d) **Fourth Hit**—Same bet
e) **Fifth Hit**—Regress all to $44 inside
f) **Sixth Hit**—Press all numbers one unit each
g) **Seventh Hit**—Same bet
h) **Eighth Hit**—Go to $66 inside
i) **Ninth Hit**—Regress all numbers one unit each
j) Continue regressing one unit each and leveling off at "Same Bet" when you reach $44 inside.

I liked that series and was anxious to give it to you, cause it has triple regression and my Up-and-Pull theory all lumped together.

You'll notice that there are more options available and that's because you had a higher bankroll to start with. It always goes back to the Big Four and what you need to win consistently.

Bankroll is right there at number oneski!

Let's go to a variation:

a) **First Hit**—Regress to $30 6 and 8
b) **Second Hit**—Go to $44 inside
c) **Third Hit**—Go to $56 inside
d) **Fourth Hit**—Same bet
e) **Fifth Hit**—Regress to $44 inside
f) **Sixth Hit**—Go to $66 inside
g) **Seventh Hit**—Regress all numbers one unit each
h) Continue regressing one unit each until you reach $44 inside. Then start back up, increasing 6 and 8 one unit each.

I could write 846 pages of variations and each one would be tempting. I don't give a rat's tail which series you use. But make sure you have a regression or two and revert to the Up-and-Pull method.

79

$120 Six and Eight

These'll be the last starting amounts I'll give you and this time you should have at least $2,400 buy-in and $7,200 bankroll.

I'm well aware that very few of you have this much bread, but in a way I'm trying to reach out and get a message across to all the cats who start off with $120 on both the 6 and 8, with a buy-in that rarely exceeds a lousy $500 start.

How anyone can risk approximately 50 percent of their session money on the first roll is foreign to me. It has something to do with them being bored by betting lesser amounts.

Well if you need real excitement in your life, try walking through Central Park in New York at 2:00 A.M. some hot Friday night, wearing a pair of purple shorts with a twenty-dollar bill hanging from each ear and a red nose pinned to your britches.

If you get out alive, you'll never need excitement again; that is the ultimate test. But in a casino, a move whereby you risk more that 10 percent of your starting money is considered insane, not exciting.

Let's look at a series:
a) **First Hit**—Regress to $30 6 and 8
b) **Second Hit**—Go to $66 inside
c) **Third Hit**—Increase each number by one unit
d) **Fourth Hit**—Same bet
e) **Fifth Hit**—Increase each number by two units

f) **Sixth Hit**—Regress to $66 inside
g) **Seventh Hit**—Increase each number by one unit each
h) **Eighth Hit**—Increase each number by two units each
i) **Ninth Hit**—Same bet
k) **Tenth Hit**—Regress to $66 inside
k) Continue alternating between same bets and one unit increases

You're aware that these examples are geared to the long runs you'll occasionally get, with all of the protection in the first couple of hits.

I am all in favor of you betting low and getting off by the fifth or sixth hit, but these examples are geared to the aggressive player, even though they may "seem" conservative.

One more series:

a) **First Hit**—Regress to $44 inside
b) **Second Hit**—Increase each number one unit each
c) **Third Hit**—Same bet
d) **Fourth Hit**—Increase each number one unit each
e) **Fifth Hit**—Same bet
f) **Sixth Hit**—Go to $110 inside
g) **Seventh Hit**—Same bet
h) **Eighth Hit**—Go to $66 inside
i) **Ninth Hit**—Continue alternating "Same bet" and one unit increases

Again I ask you to take the time to examine these series and either follow one of them or set up your own pattern.

How powerful a player you will become! And watch how the regression move that is incorporated early will minimize losses.

80

Art of Place Betting

Let's lay something on the table right now. The previous batch of chapters on Place betting is too deep to pick up the first time through.

It's gonna take you many repeat readings to grasp the theory, understand the importance, and then set up your own predetermined series.

A lot of you will balk at the conservative and monotonus repetition factor, but therein lies the power of money management.

The whole key to winning in gambling is being able to take advantage of streaks. The rotten part of life is that we never know when we're gonna run into the good trends.

Heck, if I knew on Sunday that the following Saturday I'd hold the dice for two hours and twenty minutes, throwing number after number, then I'd sleep Monday through Friday, not even going near a table.

Then on Saturday I'd bring every dime I could beg, borrow, or find and go for the jugular.

The killer is that we don't know when that streak will come, so I give you series that wrap up small sure-pop gains after the first score, to keep you alive.

After you have a few bucks salted away as your guarantee, then you make your aggressive moves.

Go back and look at these series. Notice that they all have one thing in common: they sacrifice the bet after the first score in order to give you a little breathing room.

Buck D. Trend will say that the only way to score big is to buck the trend by banging away with big bets, shooter after shooter. He will never realize the fallacy of his play. You have two choices:

2) Buck that trend and get swallowed on days when things are going against you.

2) Follow my method of holding losses down and increasing your bets *only* after you lock up a profit.

The choice is yours.

Way way back in one of the chapters I stated that place betting was the key to playing craps. Naturally I meant that only if you were a Right bettor.

The past several chapters zeroes in on how to set up series, always keying on the inside numbers. Personally I only bet the Pass Line when I shoot, and concentrate on placing the numbers after a Come-Out number is established.

You are free to bet from the right side any way you wish and there were even moves that included the Pass Line. So make up your own mind.

If you decide to stay strictly with Place Bets, just absorb these tips:

1) Chart the tables—that is important.
2) Set Win Goals and Loss Limits.
3) Have predetermined series set up.
4) Bypass the Come-Out roll.
5) You then can pick any numbers you choose.
6) Make sure the amount of your first bet is not higher than one tenth of your session money.
7) Pre-determine if you will use all inside numbers or just the 6 and 8.
8) Please incorporate the regression method at least once in a series.

9) Nothing wrong with two and three regression moves in a series.
10) Utilize Up-and-Pull theory every time you get deep into a successful run.
11) Don't be afraid of saying, "take me down."
12) Re-read number eleven again and again and again.
13) Always try to win a certain amount per shooter.
14) Take another look at the method of regressing your bet one unit at a time as explained in next chapter.
15) Have the guts to quit when you lose four straight shooters.

I guess that about wraps up place betting and now it comes down to each of you individually as to how you accept the play. If you think it's gonna be easy, you got a couple more thinks coming.

In ain't easy at all. In fact, there will be days you'll curse the controlled play—especially after somebody has a particularly great run.

But look at the whole picture and not isolated instances that tend to back up your antiquated approach to this game.

Place betting is an art. You can become the master—if you'd only give it the proper shot.

81

Regressing One Unit

This book is taking me two years to write, much longer than the other six. The reason is that I wanna get across as many variations as possible.

Every now and then I remember something that should go in and sometimes I forget if it was already covered. Guess I'm getting a little senile, but that's okay cause I had no other place to go this weekend.

Anyhow, I think I forgot to explain the theory of regressing one unit at a time, as you continue to win. So we'll take a chapter to go over its motive in case there are any of you that are missing the drift.

With this play, you are grabbing a profit, staying in action, yet regressing your bets a unit at a time.

I will probably say this a few times but I should say it four thousand times so that you'll catch it.

This move can be made when you start your series or when you have reached a high point in the excess part of your win goal!

My friend Watt E. Cey is right on cue with his standard question: "What did you say!"

Well I ain't gonna repeat it, but I'll try to explain it.

Suppose you were at a $5 table and your first bet was $30 6 and 8. The first score would give you $35. You take your bet and tell the dealer:

"Make my bets $24 and $24." He gives you back $12 and regresses both bets from $40 to $24.

Then you hit one of them again. Dealer pays you $28 and again you tell him:

"Make my bets $18 and $18." He gives you another $12 back and drops both bets from $24 each to $18 each.

Watt E. Cey is smiling and nodding so I think we've reached him.

The point I want to make is that you can do this anytime. Even when you reach a level where a hot roll has run your bets up to $60 and $60 after a $12 and $12 start.

You don't want to go all the way back to $12 and $12 so you start reducing your bets either one unit or two units each, after each score.

You're still picking up decent profits while keeping adequate money at risk. You're also reducing total wipe-outs, by regressing your risk after each winning score.

It's a strong way to play and very effective. Just for smiles let me throw out the two series theories that I always harp on. Both have strong merit and one will appeal to the aggressive player while the other will tickle the fancy of the conservative player:

1) Up-and-Pull.
2) Regress one unit per score.

Both have the same underlying approach whereby after each score, you grab a profit and move your basic bet.

We may be losing Watt E. Cey again, but just hang tight my friend and it'll fall into place.

Suppose player number one and player number two each had $60 placed on both the 6 and 8.

A 6 showed and this is what happened:
a) Player number one took his $70 and regressed both bets to $24 each.
b) Player number two took his $70 and regressed both bets to $54 each.

Again a 6 or 8 showed:

a) Player number one took his $28 and upped both bets to $30 each.

b) Player number two took his $63 and regressed both bets to $48 each.

Notice that player number one is using the Up-and-Pull method which I love. Player number two is using the consistent regression method which I love.

In all honesty I love both approaches, so whichever one you choose is hunky-dory with me. But pick one of them.

Watt E. Cey is still sitting there trying to figure out what hunky-dory means and I thought I was going senile.

The use of this one unit regression method is fantastically effective. Notice that allows you to grab a profit, while still staying up on your numbers, while at the same time reducing your risk.

Give this regression off shoot a big big second look.

82

Up-and-Pull

I know—I know I've covered this before, but while I'm in a groove and have my mind into handling series, there is no reason for me not to take a few minutes and bang away at this method.

Again I'll tell you that the key to winning consistently is to grab a profit after single winning hand or roll or ball game.

Imus Pressit is addicted to stupidity. How in the name of heaven can he have $30 6 and 8, get a score of $35 and then drop another $25 on the table and tell the dealer:

"All the way up!"

Next hit will again have him having all the profits on the table. Sure he looks like Benny the Brain as the numbers continue to show but he also looks like Dippy the Dope when a seven shows and bangs down all those profits.

Of course Imus will then look for someone at the table to blame:

1) One guy hit the dice with his hand.
2) The shooter didn't set the dice right.
3) He didn't hit both dice against the back board.
4) He threw dice too high.
5) He should have only hit one die against the board.
6) Shooter used wrong hand.
7) Shooter threw too fast.

8) Shooter took too long.

9) One guy was breathing too hard.

Imus has everyone to blame but himself. Yet the answer is in the betting series—nothing else.

When he grabbed that $35 profit with the $30 6 or 8, he could have gone right to Up-and-Pull. He should:

a) Up both bets to $36 each.

b) Pull back $23 profit.

c) He has upped his bet and pulled a profit.

If the 6 or 8 shows again:

a) Up both bets to $42 each.

b) Pull back $30 profit.

c) He has upped his bets and pulled back a profit.

That's why I want you to predetermine your series, incorporating an intelligent Up-and-Pull series.

Notice that the prior example allowed you to increase your wagers, while still salting away profits. Every single hit should allow you to pull back something, regardless of the amount.

That's why it is imperative that you learn both of these systems so that you can incorporate both the Up-and-Pull and regression in the same series.

Imus is getting a half baked grin inching its way across his motley puss. Maybe, just maybe he is beginning to get smart.

Before he can ask the next question, I'll answer it for him. No, no, a thousand times no! You cannot go right into the Up-and-Pull theory after the first hit.

If you place the 6 and 8 for $30 each and an 8 shows, you cannot go up to $36 each and pull back $23. If you lost that $72, you'd be out $49 for that shooter.

First you gotta regress your bet—then you can go Up-and-Pull as long as you're in a position where a loss won't eat up all the profits.

By the way, the question that ding dong Imus Pressit was

gonna ask was: "Can I immediately go to Up-and-Pull on the first score?"

Here I thought we were finally reaching that dork, but all the time it was just his feeble mind finding a reason for him to press his bet.

The Up-and-Pull is a super powerful move after you reach the excess part of your win goal and have set up plateaus to handle and take advantage of hot rolls.

This should cover Up-and-Pull and as we head off towards another system, we leave Watt E. Cey and Imus Pressit trying to explain to each other how to play craps. There are thousands of players like these two.

83

Hard Way Plays

Don't worry, we'll get back to Place betting due to its importance to the game, but let's swing over and get into the way to handle Hard Way action.

I use Hard Way Bets to hedge Don't bets on the 4, 6, 8, or 10 when betting wrong and that'll be covered in the Hedge portion of Don't betting.

But there is a way to play them straight up, if play them you must. What I don't want to see is an uncontrolled, undisciplined way of playing, whereby you make bets just for the sake of keeping your mouth moving.

Happ Hazard had a haphazard way of playing craps. Everything is done on a whim, with no pattern, no control, and no system to his betting.

He'll make Any Craps bets at various times during a roll and not to protect his pass line bet, but because he "feels" such and such a thing will happen.

When Happ Hazard does make a score, he hasn't the faintest idea as to what his next bet will be.

a. Sometimes he takes it all down.
b. Sometimes he presses all the way up.
c. Sometimes he moves it to another prop bet.

There is no set pattern and that's where the hazard of Happ's play is.

The proper way is to milk a run if it's scoring and pull back if it ain't.

Betting the Hard Way is a game within a game and should be handled in a predetermined manner. Let's say you're betting Right on a certain day and you wanna have side action on the Hard Ways. You set aside your session money and then include an amount to be allocated for the Hard Ways.

Let's say you're gonna begin with $12 6 and $12 8. That means you need $240 for that session.

Now you wanna work the Hard Way numbers. Decide if you're gonna do all the Hard Ways—or just the 6 and 8 and how many shots per session.

We'll say Hard 6 and 8 will be your play and you'll give it ten shooters, with a dollar in both the 6 and 8. That means $2 per shooter for ten shooters or $20 per session.

So your buy-in would be $260 to cover both the Place betting and Hard Way moves. Your bankroll must be at least $780. Naturally you won't use this play at a cold table and four shooters that finish their roll without ever making one Hard Way hit means you wrap up that type of play for that session.

However, if you're banging out easy sixes and eights you wouldn't kill the Session—only that part of it that included the Hard Way bets.

Following is a guide that will lay out needed money per session, based on your mode of play. It shows the intended bet and the needed money.

	Type	Bet	Session Amount
a.	Hard 6 and 8	$1.00 each	$20.00
b.	Hard 4 and 10	$1.00 each	$20.00
c.	All the Hard Ways	$1.00 each	$40.00
d.	Hard 6 and 8	$2.00 each	$40.00

e.	Hard 4 and 10	$2.00 each	$40.00
f.	All the Hard Ways	$2.00 each	$80.00
g.	Hard 6 and 8	$5.00 each	$100.00
h.	Hard 4 and 10	$5.00 each	$100.00
i.	All the Hard Ways	$5.00 each	$200.00

Of course you set a win goal and loss limit to apply to this play and the percentages are still 20 percent and 50 percent respectively and four shooters in a row throwing blanks is a signal to stop.

Happ Hazard feels that I'm taking the fun out of tossing a few chips on the table with certain shooters just for the heck of it— and he's right!

I want this Hard Way to be controlled. You've seen how to set aside your session amount, next we go into the action.

84

Hard Way Action

If you didn't understand the previous chapter, go back over it until the theory jumps out and bangs you in the face.

First of all I am condoning your making a play on a move that carries a higher vig than the simple placing of the 6 and 8 and even the 4, 5, 9 and 10. Then I am putting up restrictions, such as setting aside certain amounts of chips, for the attack on the Hard numbers including win goals and loss limits.

Simply put—there are people gonna play the Hard Way regardless of whether I condone it or not, but let me give you ways to properly funnel your bets in the direction of a hot table.

The previous chapter outlined the amount of money you should set aside per session for the Hard Way play and naturally to attach its own goals and limits.

In essence you are looking for a table that is banging out numbers and now you wanna grind out a certain return from these plays.

Let's suppose you are using (A) from the previous chapter, whereby you've allocated $1 each for both the Hard 6 and 8. That's an extra $20 for that session.

After a point is established, you play one buck each on both the Hard 6 and 8. Now don't go looking at the shooter and try and determine if he "looks" like a guy who's gonna throw Hard numbers, just play every upcoming shooter.

211

The loss limit for the Hard Way play at a session is five shooters in a row not making any of the Hard numbers you are playing.

Since Hard 6 and 8 is your play, you better have at least one of the next five shooters throw either one Hard 6 or 8. If they don't, that's it for the Hard Way play at that session.

But you may be banging out easy numbers, so it's OK to keep playing in that vein. But don't go bellyaching if one of the upcoming shooters begins banging out Hard numbers, after you have pulled off.

That loss limit is gonna save you a bundle of money on other days.

Remember the examples we'll be going over in these chapters on Hard Way bets will apply to only that part of your betting at a particular session and has absolutely no bearing at all on other Place betting moves you may or may not be making at the same session.

OK, point is established and you take $1 Hard 6 and $1 Hard 8. If the shooter completes his roll by making his point, I personally don't let the Hard Way bets work on the Come-Out roll, since they're automatically off.

My friend Y. Knott wants to know why not let them work on the Come-Out roll, and actually there's no real answer either pro or con. If you wanna let them work, just inform the dealer that "they're working" but I just try to give them less work to do and play within the regular flow.

If you wanna make these changes, why not do it if it makes you comfortable?

As that great philosopher Y. Knott would say, "Why not?"

Anyhow, you make your own decision and either way is acceptable.

Suppose a hard 6 hits. You now have $9 coming and immediately you spring into the Up-and-Pull theory. The method of the money management will vary slightly according to your own preference, but the theory remains the same.

1. You will Up your future bets and Pull back a profit.

2. These moves should be predetermined beforehand and never deviated from.

You've got $9 pushed over to you and one of the following options should now be employed (remember: you still have Hard 6 and Hard 8 working for a buck each). Do one of the following:
1. Go to $2 Hard 6 and $2 Hard 8.
2. Go to $4 Hard 6 (the one that scores) and leave the other one at one dollar.
3. Increase Hard 6 and 8 to $2 each, plus a buck each on the Hard 4 and Hard 10.
4. Increase Hard 6 and Hard 8 to $3 each.
5. Leave hard 6 and 8 at a buck apiece and start Hard 4 and Hard 10 at a dollar each.

Those are just five options and naturally you'll come up with some others, but in each instance you increased your bets and pulled back a profit.

Each has merit, and if pressed for the one I would use, it'd be (3). With the $9 I have to work with, I've increased my money on both the 6 and 8 to $2 each and also picked up the Hard 4 and 10. A 7 would knock down $6, leaving me with a profit of $3 and I'd start all over.

If any of these four Hard numbers hit, I'd raise each of them one dollar each, pulling back the difference.

If any hit again, I'd raise each of them $2 each.

As they continue to hit, regardless of which one it is, the bets all stay on each Hard Way number and the increases would be in increments of $2 each, then $3 each, then $4 each and so on.

This next paragraph is of the utmost importance, so read it over and over until you grasp it in its entirety.

There will be times when easy numbers will knock down one of the Hard Way bets, so you start that series over again with a dollar chip. All subsequent winnings will be brought along in the usual increments. In other words, in the absence of a 7 but in situations where easy numbers are popping up, you could have 6 off with the following amounts working: four dollars Hard 8, $2 Hard 4 and $7 Hard 10.

The worst thing a Hard Way player can do is keep bringing his bets even with each other. The previous paragraph explains that losses on a Hard number could have various amounts working. That merely means the higher amounts are on the Hard numbers that are hitting and the lower amounts signal cold numbers.

Another "don't miss," message: naturally, there will be times during a hot roll whereby the Hard 6 and Hard 10 may be up around $9 or $10 each, while the Hard 8 and Hard 4 might only be a buck each. It could be that the Hard 4 keeps getting banged back to a buck because the Easy 4 is showing. If a Hard 4 shows and kicks off a $7 payoff, all the other hard numbers are increased a buck each, not the multiple amount that may be called for if a higher heeled Hard 6 were to come.

You *must must must* Pull back a profit after a hit, so you adjust the Up part of the next bet to insure that you take a profit.

Watt E. Cey is having a heck of a time by now, but if any of you are in the dark over the past two messages, you better flip back and grab the theory before moving on.

Next we have variations in play, but don't move on until you're with me one-hundred percent and in full grasp of what I am saying.

85

Variations of Hard Ways

Since you've reached this stage of the play, I'll assume you understand the fact that each winning Hard Way bet must allow you the comfort of setting aside a profit before you up any of the bets.

You don't have to be a mathematical whiz to see that there are hundreds of offshoots of various increases and decreases you can make with the Hard Way bets.

I surely don't intend to bore you with all of these offshoots because the respective payoffs of 7 to 1 and 9 to 1 give you a lot of chances to make attractive increases as you get into a roll.

But if you clearly understand the basic theory of Up-and-Pull you'll have all the variables set up ahead of time.

Go all the way back to chapter 82 and pick up another mode of play. This time we'll go to (F) all the Hard Ways at $2 each.

You've got $80 set aside for Hard Way play at that session and start with a deuce on each number. Here are some initial plays:
1) Increase each number $1 each.
2) Increase each number $2 each.
3) Increase Six and Eight $2 each and 4 and 10 $1 each.
4) Increase just the Hard Way that hit by $2 and leave each of the others as same bet.

As usual, each of these moves allow you to pull back a profit while upping your bet.

As you continue to win, you will incorporate a method to follow whereby each succeeding score on one of the hard Way bets will call for an increase and a pull-back. Go back to the previous chapter to pick up the idea and then incorporate your own.

My preference is to keep increasing all Hard Way bets by equal amounts and after three such scores, incorporate the regression.

You knew I was gonna get to it and here it is. There's nothing wrong with starting each Hard Way bet at a deuce apiece and after a combination of these scores on any of the Hard Ways, slipping a regression bet all the way back to $2 each.

Let's try one more pop from chapter 82 and this time we'll go to (i), where we start at $5 each on all the Hard Ways. This calls for $200 set aside for that session on these plays. You're gonna find a fantastic amount of variables on both the first score and all subsequent hits, so be sure you have zeroed in on the moves that you like best. All right, you've popped $5 on each Hard Way and we'll say Hard Way 10 shows. You have $35 coming and bets still working.

A quick word to those of you who play in Casinos whereby they give you back the initial bet along with the payoff. This done in many Vegas Casinos. Immediately re-establish the bet that was hit and now you have $35 to work with.

a) Increase all the Hard Ways by $3 each.

b) Increase all the Hard Ways by $5 each.

c) Increase the 4 and 10 by $5 each and 6 and 8 by $3 each.

d) Regress all the Hard Ways to $3 each.

e) Increase the Hard 6 and 8 to $10 each and leave the 4 and 10 at $5 each.

You get the idea, and if pushed I'd lean towards (B) where you go up $5 each Hard Way.

If you hit again, Regress all to $3 each and every subsequent increase would be in increments of $2 each, then $3 each, then $5 each, then $8 each and so on.

Naturally an "easy" hit would reduce that particular number to the starting point and would then leave it eligible to have a new series started for that particular number.

You can see the fantastic amount of variables. I want you to look over these suggestions and come up with your own series.

The next chapter will give you my thoughts, but work out your own beforehand.

86

Prop Systems

Of all the tempting parts of the craps table, the biggest seems to be the center of the table called the "PITs" or Prop bets.

All the dreamers with illusions of big payoffs keep tossing chips to the dealers, screaming "Gimme the World," "Gimme the Horn," "Any Craps," "Five Dollar Yo," "Horn High Twelve," "Three Way Craps," "Gimme the Big Red."

Where they get the idea that this is the road to riches is beyond me. All of these bets are one-roll action jobs. You're gonna get clobbered with these stupid plays, yet the casinos vibrate from the shrills of people who get lousy $7 return for a buck bet on the "any Craps", while that same player bypasses the smarter moves on the Line and Place bets.

The Prop bets get their popularity from the high pay-off possibilities. Getting a 15 to 1 pay off with an eleven sends shivers up the spine of Yellow Jack Korner.

This yellow-bellied, chicken-hearted, penny pinching loud mouth wouldn't place $6 on the 6 and 8, yet he'll make $1 plays on the high-paying Snake Eyes and Box Cars.

He mocks the other players who get zapped with a 7 and screeches in delight when the dealer slides a $15 payoff over to him on one of the rare times that he makes a score.

Let's just look at a few of the bets that Yellow Jack makes. He'll drop a couple of chips on the table and yell: "Gimme $2

218

Yo, $5 Horn High Yo and $2 each on Box Cars and Snake Eyes."

That's $11 he has riding on the next roll.

The dice are coming out and as any craps shooter should know, there are six numbers on each die that could show. That's twelve separate numbers in all. Let's say a 4 shows on just one of these monsters. There's absolutely no way that any of his bets can be won.

Suppose a 3 shows on one of the dice. This guy's nowhere, with not a prayer of a chance of getting a return. In simple mathematics, these four numbers will swallow his whole batch of chips. Suppose a deuce shows on one of the dice. His Yo bet and Box Car bet is history, along with Snake Eyes. His only hope is a one in six chance of popping an ace on the other die and picking up a partial return on his Horn bet.

Same is true if a 5 shows on one dice. He's alive for the Yo and partial Horn, but his Craps, Aces, and Twelve bets are now part of the casino's bankroll.

Take a look at these Prop bet possibilities and see if you can write three or even two good things about them.

Sure you can use them as hedges against Don't betting, which I'll get into later, but you sure won't get writers cramp listing positive things to say about these sucker bets.

Yellow Jack Korner would be better off standing in the corner making some 6 and 8 plays.

I ain't gonna give you any system on Prop bets because I don't believe any of them will kick off any consistent returns.

You want my opinion on these Prop bets, even if it is only for an occasional dollar or two fling? (Not counting hedges!)

Don't do it. Never, never, never, ever never ever do it. Period!

Before you split a gut thinking I've just contradicted myself, back up a second. I am knocking the one roll Prop bets—not the use of a money management system on the Hard Way plays.

87

Field Place System

In my basic book on Craps I went over this system and called it the "Umbrella." That's because it covers so many numbers.

I also indicated that it wasn't one of my favorites but felt that it warranted an explanation, due to the large number of players who were employing it.

Well, I still don't like it. In fact my feelings of disdain for it have reached the point of advising you not to play it.

My friend Thomas Doutin is a doubting Thomas who doubts my opinion on this play because he feels it is a powerful move that covers the majority of numbers and gives the Right bettor a lot of chances for a score.

First let's explain what the play is, then we'll analyze it.

The move is bet the Field and place the 5, 6 and 8 at the same time. Purists can see right away that you now have coverted the 2, 3, 4, 9, 10, 11 and 12 in the Field and the 5, 6, and 8 on the side. The only thing that can hurt you is the 7.

Using the word "only" when describing the 7 is like saying war ain't so bad, except for the bombs, bullets, dying, misery, and disaster.

When that 7 shows, it's gonna whack you for all four bets. But that ain't the bad part. The rotten part is in the payoffs.

It's my opinion that the six ways to make a 7 coupled with the fourteen ways of making the 5, 6 and 8 make a total of twenty fairly unproductive rolls.

Look, if the 5, 6 or 8 shows, you get a $7 payoff, but lose the $5 wager on the Field. So you lose all of those power numbers in the middle of the board, where you end up with a lousy net $2 every time one of them shows.

Take a gander at this chart:

NUMBER	WAYS TO MAKE	NET RESULT
5	Four	Plus $2
6	Five	Plus $2
7	Six	Minus $22
8	Five	Plus $2

A close look at the above chart points out that based on the laws of probability, you're really getting a wash with the use of this whole play.

In effect it seems just as easy to just play the Field. It all comes down to my feelings on minimizing losses. A couple of sevens in a row puts you in the position of needing a good long run of Field numbers to make up that deficit.

It's sure gonna be hard to grind back from two losses with the 7, when you're ending up with only a $2 pop for the 5, 6 or 8.

Go over the idea of the Field-Place method and then look over my opposing theories. See which way you are swaying.

Then take a look at the next chapter, whereby I talk about strictly Field betting.

Incidentally, if you decide that this method will be your play, I'm not gonna put a contract out on you.

But my opinion is that you shouldn't weaken the sock of the payoff on the 6 and 8 when you are a Right bettor. This method takes away too much money when that 5, 6 or 8 shows.

I just don't advise this to be your play.

88

Betting the Field

I've already mentioned this but let's put that nonsense about the Field being a bad bet to bed right now.

It doesn't rank up there with being marooned on an island with Loni Anderson but it's better than having a date with Bobbi Cexpott and finding out that she's a he. Now that's what I call rotten.

Yet purists who claim to know the game of craps have been calling the Field bet a rotten move for years and years.

The house vig is less than buying or placing the 4 and 10 and beats all the Prop bet plays, yet it gets frowned on by most players.

I'm gonna go over this play again, even though you've heard it before—but I believe it is worth a pop at a table when Field numbers are showing.

Naturally it involves following the trend and using the regression but what else is new? That's the key to any gambling foray.

If you've noticed during your charting duties that a lot of Field numbers are popping, use one of the following plays:

a) Follow the Field
b) Straight Field play

Of course (b) is simple to understand, 'cause it merely means you'll play the Field every roll, using the regression system.

I add a touch of trends to my play by waiting for a Field number to appear, and then using the regression. In other words, if a 5, 6, 7 or 8 shows, I don't play.

I'm looking for a streak. You've also been told about the 1-2-2, the 1-2-3 and the 1-2-4 mini Martingale approach. There's nothing wrong with employing one of these approaches with the Field, but three losses in a row is the absolute wrap on that session.

For those of you who are still unaware of these three aforementioned moves, they are explained in detail in my baccarat book. These methods of play are very strong on any of the following "flat" bets!

1) Baccarat
2) Outside bets of roulette
3) Don't Pass line in craps
4) Blackjack
5) Placing the 6 and 8
6) Playing the Field

For my friend Ivor Gett, who forgot, the next couple of chapters will touch on this play, because it is controlled from a standpoint of allowing an aggressive approach.

To finally wrap up my opinion of the Field, let me make something clear.

The bet has a 20 to 18 edge for the Casino and this is reduced to 20 to 19 when a house pays triple on the 12. Look at this chart one more time:

Number	Ways to Make
2	1 (Pays double)
3	2
4	3
9	4
10	3
11	2
12	1 (Pays double)

Adding the pay-off of 2 to 1 on the two and twelve, you have a possible payoff of eighteen units (nineteen if the 12 pays triple).

The numbers that can break you are:

Number	Ways to Make
5	4
6	5
7	6
8	5

That's 20 versus 18 and while it ain't steak, it also ain't dog food you're asked to swallow.

One final note as a suggestion for playing the Field, using either the regression or 1 - 2 - 2 etc. methods.

You could use it in conjunction with the Hard Way betting systems I went over a few chapters back. They could be used at the same time, as sort of a hedge against each other, and allows for those people with short bankrolls to hold down their bets.

I know that Ivor Gett forgot what the Hard Way system entails, so it you're in the same category—go back and look it over.

As for the regression play, I'll lay out a few examples, you pick out your own series. You know the theory.

	(A)	(B)	(C)	(D)	(E)	(F)
1st Bet	$ 8	7	10	10	20	25
2nd Bet	$ 5	5	5	5	10	10
3rd Bet	$10	6	10	10	15	15
4th Bet	$10	8	15	15	25	20
5th Bet	$15	10	20	15	20	30
6th Bet	$20	15	25	10	30	40
7th Bet	$15	20	15	5	20	50

Don't discount the Field as a way to play. It is not that bad and you've got a couple of money management methods to use if you so desire to give it a pop.

89

Smart Place System

We've just spent a ton of time going over the various moves on Right Side betting and perhaps you're confused as to exactly which system you want to zero in on.

That's gonna be your choice and through the years you'll come up with different spinoffs of my theories but there is one thing that will remain constant.

That's the three key words at the craps table: "take me down." The day you realize this is the day you become a player.

I ain't no high roller in a craps game and rarely ever get a big score. But they don't hang me out to dry because of these magic three words.

Sure I miss out on a lot of red-hot rolls and sure I feel the eyes of the other players glance at the chicken who just pulled back. But I know in my heart that it is the way to play. One more time I give you this example and you can apply it to any level bet.

Suppose you bet $22 Inside, take two hits for a profit of $14 and call your bets off. You got a profit for that roll.

The guy who stays up must hit three more numbers to collect $21 and still he's a buck short of being even. The bottom line is he has to bang out four extra hits after I took my profit of $14, to show an additional profit of $6. That's a lot of times to buck the 7.

The times you miss out on a hot roll is more than made up for the times you'll save those bets. Yes, you'll feel intimidated but in the long run, it's the smart move.

Here is how I suggest you play, assuming you had a $440 session amount. Read on and absorb it:

1) Chart the tables to find one kicking off numbers.
2) Bypass the Come-Out.
3) After point is established, take $44 Inside.
4) After first hit, take $14 and regress to $22 Inside.
5) One more hit and OFF.
6) When reach profit of $150, change starting amount.
7) Bypass Come-Out.
8) Start with $66 Inside.
9) After first hit, regress to $22 Inside.
10) After second hit come OFF.
11) When reach profit of $300, change starting amount.
12) Bypass Come-Out.
13) After point established, place $88 Inside.
14) After first hit, go to $44 Inside.
15) After second hit, come OFF.
16) When reach profit of $450, change starting Series.
17) Bypass Come-Out.
18) Place $120 Inside.
19) After first hit, regress to $66 Inside.
20) After second hit, regress to $44 Inside, or $22 Inside.
21) After third hit, Come OFF.

Keep increasing your starting series as you reach $150 profit plateaus.

The amount you start with is based on your bankroll, but I've used $44 Inside as a perfect start for 70 percent of the players in a casino.

You'll notice I gave you three hits when you get deep into a Winning Series. That is your option—you can stay with two hits if you like.

I don't know what you paid for this book, but I believe it is worth one-hundred times more than the cost, if you follow everything I tell you to do.

And this chapter is one of the granddaddies of importance. Read and re-read it over and over again. It contains the answer for you doubting Thomases that never believed that discipline is a big part of gambling.

Will you pay attention to this advice and follow the suggestions in this chapter?

No way will you do it. What a pity!

90

Don't Betting

I think I've pretty much hammered out a lot of Right bettor betting methods for you, so perhaps we should look at the Don't side.

I'll be coming back to you Do boys, so don't think you've had your finish of instruction, but a look at the Don't bettors is on the schedule now.

I don't give a rat's tail which way you play—Right or Wrong, 'cause both have a plus potential, but I do care that you play intelligently. That means money management to you people who still don't grasp what gambling is all about.

Don't betting is more of a grind and requires a lot of patience. In fact it is rare that a colossal score is a normal thing for the Don't bettor. He is more apt to be looking for a day's pay as he grinds out small consistent returns.

I covered Don't betting very heavily in my basic book on craps and again I suggest you spring for a couple of bucks and read those pages.

If Don't betting is your bag, there will be certain things that I am dead set against and one of them is laying odds for substantial amounts and leaving them up for long periods of time.

I know that statement is gonna irritate many Wrong bettors but the next chapter explains why I dislike laying odds.

Again I repeat that if Wrong betting is your thing, the same amount of charting should be put into play, also the strict discipline of backing off.

Incidentally, it ain't gonna hurt you Right bettors to look at this approach; you might pick up some discipline.

91

Vig on Don't

Again, I gotta make quick mention of the vig on the Don't, even though you should know it by now.

1) Don't Pass ....1.41 percent
2) Don't Come ....1.41 percent
3) Single Odds ....0.83 percent
4) Double Odds ....0.59 percent

Sure it's a small vig when you start laying odds, but just remember that you're laying out a lot of bread with the laying of odds and a loss puts a big dent in your bankroll.

You'll see how I'd like you to lay odds, strictly as a protection through the Don't Come, but other than that I hate laying out that extra money.

Let's go to a little example that I've used many many times, so if you've heard it before, just close your eyes, skip over the next few paragraphs and don't even listen to the words jumping off the page.

Suppose Pat and Mike were at a table, each betting $5 on the Don't Pass. Ten became the point and Pat laid $10 odds against the point. Mike stayed with his flat $5 Don't Pass.

Look at the situation from a standpoint of where they were as soon as the point of 10 was set.

They had the house against the wall, cause they had six ways of winning and only three ways of losing, while risking $5 to win $5. That's fat city. As soon as you beat that 7 or 11 on the Come Out, you are booking the house.

But Pat lays $10 odds because he read in a book somewhere that laying odds was a great move and that there was no vig attached.

There's that word vig again. The book also states that by laying double odds, you reduce the house edge from eight tenths of one percent to six tenths of one percent. Big deal! You save two tenths of a percent.

Personally I can hardly tell the difference. I just don't think there is that much difference either way.

But look at the real tangible Pat is risking. He's laying an extra $10 to win $5, making his total risk $15 to win $10, while Mike is only putting up $5 to win $5.

It is my humble opinion that Pat took away a lot of edge that he had against the Casino by weakening the profit versus risk position he was in.

A lot of you will disagree with my theory on this, but before you start another "hate mail" campaign, look over this example. I prefer holding my risk to profit potential down and don't like laying odds for a lousy two tenths of a percent.

The difference in Vigorish is minimal and winning a few extra bucks is not worth the possible loss through true odds.

92

Simple Don't Pass

You don't have to be a genius to understand the simplest form of Don't betting, so we'll breeze through the basic moves.
1) Place $5 on the Don't Pass.
2) When point is established, just sit and wait for 7 to show before your number.

That is the easiest and most basic approach to Don't betting. Naturally odds are optional, but the idea is that you are looking for just one number to be set and you sit and wait for a 7.

The important thing to remember is that you only buck a shooter for a certain amount of points. You can set either two or three as your limit.

If he bangs three straight losses on you and that includes both making his point or popping a 7 or 11 on the Come-Out, you must pull back from fighting that shooter and wait till he's done.

You gotta realize that the biggest thing going against the Don't bettor is that rotten 7 or 11 on the Come-Out. Naturally you win on a 2 or 3, which offsets the 11, but it sure is discouraging watching your bets get banged on that Come-Out.

However, after the point is established we now have the odds working in our favor with an edge of either 6 to 3 or 6 to 4 or 6 to 5 over the house.

So sitting with a single bet on the Don't Pass is a grind, but not a bad way to start off.

93

Two Number Don't

We go a step further by looking for two numbers to be established and again it's snap city to grasp.

A) Place $5 Don't Pass.

B) After point is established, lay single odds against the point and place $5 in the Don't Come.

C) As soon as Don't Come number is established, remove your odds and sit with your two Don't numbers.

Nothing hard about that, and while I am using $5 examples, you can adjust the theory to whatever increment chip you use.

The amount of your bets must be in line with your total bankroll. They should be no more than 10 percent of your session amount. In other words, you should have ten times the amount of your series bet as your session amount.

If you go for two numbers at $10 each, that's $20 for that particular shooter. You must have ten times the $20, or $200 to play at that session.

Since I want at least three sessions per day, your total bankroll must be at least $600. This was all explained previously but if you forgot, go back to the Bankroll section and re-read it.

I can just picture Thomas Doubting, doubting the validity of my suggestion. But doubting Thomases like Thomas Doubting bring a rotten $50 to a $10 table and play like a scared jackrabbit, failing to make the proper moves because of their short bankrolls. Heed what I say about bankrolls.

OK, so you've adopted the two number Don't method but just remember that the same rules of replacing Don't Come numbers only twice still holds true.

You should also restrict your Don't Pass losses to three and that's because of the ever present danger of 7 and 11.

I don't wanna belabor this method as even a dope like Jean E. Yuss should be able to grasp it.

94

Laying Behind

Before we get to the three number Don't, I think it's only right to explain why you can't just place $5 or $10 Don't Come bets against any number you want, just like the Right bettor.

The answer is logical. When you place a $5 bet on the 10, you got three ways of winning and six ways of losing. They pay you 9 to 5 instead of 10 to 5, which is the true odds. The house makes a profit on these plays so they allow the bettors to make as small a wager as they want.

But if they allowed the Don't bettor to bet against any number he wanted, there would be 8,643 guys betting against the 4 or 10 for a lousy $5 per pop.

So the Casinos reach into their bag of rules and put a stipulation on betting against a number:

a) you gotta pay 5 percent Vig,

b) You gotta make a wager that calls for at least four units versus the number you choose.

Now the first part is not too big a factor for most players but the second one is a granddaddy of a block.

Shorty Shortkash is a bonafide Don't player but he doesn't have the bread to lay out $41 to fight a No 4 or No 10. He brings a ten-dollar bill, two fives, a handful of singles, three rolls of quarters, twenty nickels, six unused stamps and a lot of prayers to the Casino.

He ain't gonna risk a four time bet, 'cause he realizes one or two losses and he's in left field without a glove or worse still, in the casino without any money and the casinos know this. That's why they put up those barriers, to keep the smaller-heeled players from tying up the tables for hours on end.

If you wanna lay against a number, here are the amounts:

a) No 4 or No 10; you lay $41 to win $19.

b) No 5 or No 9; you lay $31 to win $19.

c) No 6 or No 8; you lay $25 to win $19.

Notice they take the dollar vig whether you win or lose. For instance on the No 10 you must lay 2 to 1 odds which means at least $40 to win $20. Then you are charged 5 percent of the possible win, which means 5 percent of $20 which equals $1.

They take this back when you win or when you lose.

I ain't knocking the play and in fact I'm gonna give you a system that utilizes these lays.

But at least I wanna make you aware of why you have to utilize the Don't Come to establish small Don't bets.

Jean E. Yuss thinks she understands what I'm saying but I think a re-read of the explanation wouldn't hurt her.

95

Variations of Bets

This is a variation that permits you to avoid having to lay odds. Your first bet is $10 on the Don't Pass.

Suppose the 4 becomes the point and you want two additional Don't Comes. Instead of laying $20 odds against that 4, just reduce the amount of your Don't Come bet.

With a $10 No 4 on the Don't Pass, you now put $5 in the Don't Come and the 7 can't hurt you. If the 7 does how, you lose the $5 Don't Come but pick up $10 on your No 4 for $5 profit.

Suppose the 9 showed with the $5 Don't Come bet. That $5 chip moves behind the 9 and you can stop here or go for another Don't Come.

Since you have a $15 edge with the 7, you can now increase the amount of the next Don't Come bet to $10, or you can stay at $5.

My suggestion would be to go for $10, since the total No bets on the 4 and 9 are $15 and you have the protection to go for the higher play.

This is the way I would like you to play the basic Don't. It eliminates your ever having to lay odds. Realize that the key is in a higher bet on the Come-Out to establish that first number.

Once that is down, you have the option of coming through the

Don't Come with reduced amounts and reduced risks on the original Don't Pass wager.

The next chapter goes into higher plays, so swing right into it while your mind is clicking. But this is the proper and cheapest way to get three Don't bets in action without a high risk factor.

96

Higher Variations

As you increase the amount of your Don't Pass bet, the number of variations increase. You have more opportunities to stagger subsequent wagers.

But again I caution you that your Session amount *must* be sufficient to withstand possible losses, cause you're gonna be getting more aggressive.

Suppose $20 is your Don't Pass play. Now you decide if you want a partial hedge on the 11.

Personally, when I reach this amount I'll throw a buck on the 11 to keep from leaving that $20 wager naked. You still have the aces and ace deuce going for you as a profit potential, so it's worth the buck to cover part of the numbers that could whack you.

Let's say 9 becomes the point. You're in fat city with an option to just sit, to take a partial or full hedge or to use the bet to protect a romp into the world of the Don't Come.

Here are options for the Don't Come:
a) $5 Don't Come.
b) $10 Don't Come.
c) $15 Don't Come, buck on the Yo.
d) $6 6 and 8, and $5 Don't Come.

Hold off on (d) right now as we'll get to that in the hedging chapters but at least you know it's available.

I would opt for (b) which calls for $10 Don't Come. You still have $10 potential profit on the 7 and a load of options if you can get that $10 Don't Come established. Suppose the 8 shows. The $10 moves behind the 8 and now you have $30 protection to manuever. Your next move will be:

a) Bet $5 Don't Come.

b) Bet $10 Don't Come.

c) Bet $15 or $20 or $25 Don't Come.

d) Use the hedges.

My choice is hedges, but since that is not available yet, I'd go for $15 Don't Come and $1 on the 11.

Let's say the 6 shows. $15 Don't moves behind the 6.

You now have $20 Don't Pass 9, $10 Don't 8 and $15 Don't 6. You can replace twice and no more, and the replacement bets should be for the amount that goes down. The buck on the Yo is used only if $15 or higher is bet in the Don't Come.

I don't have to give you variations off of each level bet, such as starting with Don't amount of $25, $30, $40, $50 etc. as you should get the idea of how to use it and come up with your own theories.

However, I will make a point here as directed to you higher rollers that think your nose will grow six feet at the table if you don't bet high amounts on every roll.

Sure it's a plus to your ego to have people stare at you as you drop those green and black chips on the lay-out, but I've spoken to enough of you in private to realize you can withstand only so many losing days before the losses start to eat at your gut.

So don't be too proud to read what I have to say about cutting back bets, in an effort to prevent complete wash-outs.

Suppose you're a green chip Don't player and want to utilize the theory. You could start with $35 on the Don't Pass and $2 Yo:

a) After point is established, don't lay odds but reduce Don't Come bet to leave 7 working for you,

b) Put $20 in Don't Come plus $1 Yo.

c) When that Don't number is established, you'll have $55 protected by the 7 and the important thing is that one number won't whack you, as you have wagers spread over two numbers and gives you a chance to withstand total wipeout.

d) If you want third Don't, go for $40 Don't Come, ($2 Yo), or any amount *lower* than $55, so that you'll at least show some profit if 7 hits.

As soon as third Don't is in place, sit and wait for 7 and you can either replace twice or even ride out the roll with one or no replacements.

There are dozens of offshoots and it is up to you to implement the ones you're most comfortable with. I can't lay out 242 different approaches, so I expect you to grasp theory and use your head—which most of you *don't* do in the casinos.

97

Hedging the 6 and 8

We're swinging into heavier Don't playing and before we go too far along, I want you to be aware that hedging will become a big part of your approach.

The 6 and 8 example will throw some light on the subject so be sure you understand this move.

When I play Right I always have the 6 and 8 working for me because they can be made the most number of ways. In that same vein, betting Wrong leaves us dreading having to go against the 6 and 8.

It's a dumb move to take your bets off when they become No 6 or No 8 cause you're giving up a 6 to 5 edge on the house, but there is another way to handle it. Hedge bets!

Suppose you have $10 on the Don't Pass and 10 shows. You lay odds against the 10 and put $10 in the Don't Come. Six comes.

The dealer moves your bet behind the 6 and you have a 6 to 5 chance of winning. I've heard guys tell the dealer "No bet" and he leaves that $10 bet in the Don't Come box. That's a stupid move.

You go to all the trouble of beating the 7 and 11 then get a Don't Come number and you tell the dealer to forget it.

I realize the 6 and 8 are the easiest numbers to make but you still have the 6 to 5 edge with the 7. That's gold!

There are three things you can do after he moves that bet behind the 6.

(1) Just sit and wait for 7.

(2) Put $1 Hard 6.

(3) Place $6 6.

Number one is self-explanatory as you wait for a decision to effect that bet. Number two is easy to understand as a bet on the Hard Way reduces the potential losing ways from 5 to 4 'cause a Hard Six will kick off $9.

There's nothing wrong with hedging it with the Hard Way bet, but let me show you a smarter way. Place $6 on the 6 or 8 , whichever was the Don't number. Look what happens.

(a) You are risking $3 to win $4.

(b) You have 6 to 5 edge on the house with less *money at risk*.

You are now "booking" the house with this move:

(a) If 6 shows, you lose $10 Don't Come and win $7 Place 6 for loss of $3.

(b) If 7 shows, you lose $6 Place 6 and win $10 No 6 for profit of $4.

You're in a better position than if Raquel Welch was kicking down your door. (Well, maybe not that good).

But look what you've done. You've taken a bet that you're a little shaky about and turned it into a position where you are the boss. Risking $3 to win $4, while having the 7 give you a 6 to 5 edge on the 6 (or 8) is a strong position.

Whenever I have $10 Don't Pass or Don't Come, I always use the $6 Hedge—always. But wait until you have reached the number of Don't bets you predetermined to set, before starting your hedging.

For instance if 6 or 8 showed on the Come Out, you have a couple of options to set your Don't Come numbers with that $10 Don't:

(1) Lay odds on 6 (or 8), take a couple bucks Hard Way, and put $10 in Don't Come, or

(2) Bet $5 Don't Come.

Let's say 4 comes. You now have two Don'ts working. You immediately place the 6 (or 8) for $6. But you waited until your series was in place.

I use the Hard Ways to help when the point is 6 or 8 but I don't hedge off until my Don't Come numbers are all set.

But I *always* hedge my sixes and eights. The next chapter will give you examples of multiple increment hedges, but be sure you understand the theory.

98

Multiple 6 and 8 Hedges

I like to think of hedge betting as I look at my hedges around the house. I trim the hedges to cut off excess.

In gambling, I trim my exposure to make the overall bet more attractive. It cuts losses while still leaving decent profit potential.

My friend Imus Pressit looks at hedges as a means of cutting chances of bigger wins. He also sees a garden of hedges, but he sees green, as in money, and doesn't want to go for the small returns. He goes for the kill and presses his Don't bet to the moon by laying quadruple odds. Sure it's great when he wins but his losses are devastating.

Imus Pressit hates hedges so much that he even takes it out on the hedges around his house. He cuts them to the root and never gets to see the beauty of his hedges. Just like he never gets to see the beauty of a 6 and 8 hedge.

Following are Don't Bets on either the Don't Pass or Don't Come and my suggestion for the hedge, and remember this is strictly for the No 6 or No 8:

Don't Bet	Hedge (Place)
$10	$6
$15	$6 and $1 Hard
$20	$12
$25	$18

$30	$18 and $1 Hard
$40	$30
$50	$36 and $2 Hard
$60	$42 and $3 Hard
$100	$72 and $3 Hard

The chart is strictly suggestions for those of you who want to hedge. I personally strongly suggest that you do, and the examples I gave were based on minimum amounts.

For example, look at your Don't Bet of $30. I gave you $18 Place and a buck Hard Way. That gives you only a possible loss of $10 if 6 or 8 showed soft, with profit of $11 if 7 pops.

But there are many many offshoots for that amount of $30 and you pick the one you like best.

(a) Hedge for $24
(b) Hedge for $30
    (1) You cannot lose a dime if 7 shows but win $5 if six shows.
(c) Hedge for $12 and $4 Hard Way.

The number and amount of variations are fantastic, especially as you increase the amount of your Don't bet. Just for smiles, let's say you bet $100 Don't Pass and 8 shows.

You could come up with a dozen different hedges of placing and/or Hard Ways to complete your approach. My job is to make you aware of the approach. Your job is to apply the hedge you're most comfortable with.

If you bet Don't and $10 is your bet, I strongly feel that you should use this method of placing the 6 and/or 8 for $6.

For you people who feel comfortable just throwing a buck on the Hard number, be my guest.

For you people who feel comfortable just sitting on the Don't, be my guest. Any of these approaches are acceptable.

For you people who say "No Action" where 6 or 8 shows, you're 100 percent wrong. Make that 200 percent wrong. No, make it 1,000,000 percent wrong.

Those people are Charter members of the "I Am A Dork" club.

99

Option Off Hedge Betting

Hey, I ain't saying hedging is for everybody. If everyone liked the same thing, it'd be a crazy world.

I don't like mushrooms, hot cereal, fatty food, stew, peanuts, almonds, oysters, showoffs, cigarettes, beer, noisy players, bad losers, milk, cold coffee, lamb chops, cooking, cutting the grass, airplanes, or loud music. Yet there are guys who like all or some of the above. It just proves that everybody is not the same.

So if you don't like hedge betting, that doesn't make you wrong. Nor does it make me right for playing that way. But I want you to know it's available.

On the other side of the coin, there are some things that I like that you may not agree with.

I like hedge betting, ice cream, cream candy, soda, cake, turkey, spaghetti, shrimp, gravy, good poker hands, fast pitch softball, Manhattans, Sophia Loren, high living, fast women, slow cars, and soft music.

There are plenty of guys who won't agree with any of these. So be it. That's what makes the ding-dong. Being different.

So when I show you a conservative approach to gambling, I hope you'll take it. But if you don't, I'm more than understanding about the fact that there are aggressive styles which many people like.

But even though I can understand you're disagreeing with the theory, at least take the time to give these hedges a long hard look.

100

The Ricochet

All Don't bettors realize that the killer in their style of play is the dreaded 7 or 11 on the Come-Out. The 2 and 3 soften the blow, but it still is a plus five in favor of the 7 and 11.

The way to combat it is to make the second number your dominant Don't and forgetting the Come-Out roll. With this method, you never have to worry about the 7 or 11 being your major obstacles.

The simplest way of handling this play is to bypass the Come-Out roll and start your moves after a point is established. Whichever number becomes the point will be the number you lay against.

This system is called the Ricochet system and is spearheaded by one of my good friends Les Scally. Les, along with all the guys mentioned on the acknowledgement page, has been teaching casino games with me for nine years. He has refined this method of play and calls it the Ricochet system.

Let's pick up the play exactly as Les plays:

(a) Bypass Come-Out roll.

(b) Whichever point is established, bet against that number:

(1) 6 or 8, lay $25.

(2) 5 or 9, lay $31.

(3) 4 or 10, lay $41.

(c) At the same time you make your lay bet, place $15 in don't

Come and a buck on the 11.

(d) As soon as point is established with the Don't Come wager, remove your lay bet.

(e) The Don't Come now becomes your dominant Don't.

(f) Sit and wait for a decision.

Les is a dyed-in-the-wool Don't bettor and plays all types of Wrong betting but seems to settle in on this one as his main move.

The method has a lot going for it, including the fact that the 7 or 11 cannot hurt you. In fact your biggest fear will come with the shooter coming right back with the point, or as the system suggests—a ricochet.

Since you are laying in the heaviest amount of bread against the point, in an effort to establish your dominant Don't Come, a repeat will take you down for $25 or $31 or $41 or whichever amount you lay against the point.

Once the Don't Come is set, the $15 moves behind that number and by removing your lay bet, you cut down your possible total loss.

Naturally there are spinoffs, but Les has been quite successful with this play and I heartily agree with the system.

101

Analyzing the Ricochet

Thomas Doubting is against this method because he ends with no bet against the point and he is a devout Don't bettor who becomes a doubting Thomas whenever he sees a system that goes against the time worn method of betting the Don't Pass and laying quintuple odds versus the point.

But he won't take the time to grasp the theory of this play. All I'm asking you to do is make the second number your point instead of the first one. That's because I wanna eliminate the 7 and 11 from crushing you. This method does that.

The object is in putting yourself into a position whereby your Don't bet is equal to your possible win amount, yet the odds will be in your favor.

Let's say the point becomes a 6 and you lay $25 No 6 and put $15 in the Don't Come. 9 shows and you kill the $25 lay and now have $15 Don't 9 with odds 6 to 4 in your favor that you'll win. The 7 or 11 could not beat you and most of all, your probable loss of $15 is equal to your probable win of $15 with the odds in your favor, and it only cost you the buck you put on the Yo when you came through the Don't Come.

It just means the second number is your dominant and not the first.

Bank—now Thomas Doubting jumps off his chair screaming and yelling—"I got it—I got the flaw in your system," he's almost delirious with joy cause this dork is more interested in restricting his knowledge than adding to it.

You've probably already figured it out, so let's hear Thomas Doubting get it off his chest.

Suppose 10 becomes the point on the Come-Out roll and you now lay $41 No 10, put a $15 bet in the Don't Come, a buck on the Yo and 8 shows!

You now have 8 as your dominant instead of 10 and since 10 is harder to make than 8, you've put yourself in a position of going against a number (8) that is easier to make than 10.

He is so happy that his face is beginning to crack, cause it's the first time he's smiled in six years.

He's right you know. In this instance he's 100 percent right and I told him so. This made his thirty-three inch chest pass his forty inch waist. In fact his chest stuck out so far his pants fell down.

But then I showed him the breakdown and his world shattered.

Based on the number of Come-Out numbers that could be established, the 6 and 8 will come up only ten times as compared to the fourteen times that the 4, 5, 9 or 10 will show. That means that you have a 14 to 10 chance of getting a better number when you come through the Don't Come and still not have to worry about the 7 or 11.

Thomas Doubting, the doubting Thomas of all time, was speechless for the first time in his life.

Sure you're gonna find times when you end up with No 6 or 8 on the Don't Come after 4, 5, 9 or 10 was the point but the odds are that it'll be the other way around.

Also, the opportunity of dropping a buck on the Hard 6 or Hard 8 brings the loss probability back down to four ways you can be hurt, instead of five.

Les Scally grinds away with this method. This is the basic approach and a good way to get started on this system.

102

$41 No 10

Veterans of my video tapes and book on craps will recognize this system so I ain't gonna elaborate on it, but since it is not a bad play, it's only right to go over it.

Instead of the process of waiting for a number to be established and laying against that point, this system offers an offshoot approach:

    (1) Whichever number becomes the point, lay $41 No 10, put a buck on the 11 and place $15 in the Don't Come.

    (2) This way you always have the hardest number to make (10 or 4) as your protection on the Don't Come wager.

    (3) Putting a $5 Hard 10 is optional, but since it is a good way to cut total ways to lose from three to two, it's not a bad idea.

I. C. Goode is a good friend of mine and a decent gambler but he has a hard time seeing the good in a lot of my systems cause they are too conservative.

Most times I. C. Goode will look at a system and say "I don't see anything good about it."

But he does like the Richochet system and when I first showed it to him, I. C. Goode said, "I see a lot of good things about it."

Anyhow, when I showed him the offset method of laying $41

No 10 (or No 4), no matter what the point was, he was even more elated. I. C. Goode said he saw a lot of good in this approach because of the fewer ways to lose.

The fact remains that you do have a possible loss factor of $41 if the ten shows and $46 if it shows easy. Just want you to be aware of this.

Even though you are betting against a strong No 10 or No 4, losses can put you in a hole, and a whole lot of holes can put a hole in the approach. Don't discount this paragraph.

I. C. Goode is holding his breath waiting for a direction to take.

Okay, let's put it in perspective and you make your decision. I like Richochet and the idea of betting against the point, 'cause the shooter has to make that point right back to cause damage and that's when you're vulnerable, but the only time.

Laying the No 10 or No 4 to protect that Don't Come wager is also strong because there's only a few ways to get beat. But that $41 possible loss does loom in my head.

A run of two or three straight $41 losses means you need nine $15 wins to come even. So even though I like the fewer ways of losing, I hate the higher possible losing dollar amount.

You decide which way you prefer but a least keep the theory intact in your mind. It's a great way to get your dominant Don't in action. That means the Don't Come bet!

I. C. Goode sees good in both ways but says he'll reserve judgement for a few chapters.

103

Hedging the 41 No 10

Before we go any further, let me give you something to store in your head so I don't have to keep repeating it. When I talk about the "No 10 System" or "Hedging the No 10" I also want you to vision it as a No 4 method also.

It doesn't have to be that you bet just No 10, cause the 4 is in the same percentage category. So when I give you these methods, they can be applied to either one of these two numbers to use as a Lay hedge.

OK, now that you understand that (Watt E. Cey hasn't the foggiest idea of what was just said), let's touch the hedges.

Whenever you use the $41 No 10, it is mostly because there are only three ways to get beat—6 and 4, 4 and 6, and 5 and 5. A couple of bucks on the Hard 10 is simply a way to reduce your ways of losing from three down to two. The choice is strictly yours.

I am very conservative and believe in holding down losses. Naturally I grab all the hedges I can, so as to reduce my chances of losing. When I play $41 No 10, there is always $4 or $5 dumped on the Hard 10.

Sure it's possible to lose an extra $5 but it's also possible to cut a $41 loss down to $6 with a $5 Hard 10. But you're not wrong either way you play: with or without the Hard Way offset.

Let's go to another aspect of using the No 10 to protect your

255

inside bets. When I bet Right, the only numbers I place are 5, 6, 8, and 9. Based on a single chip wager, that's $22 Inside.

You can leave these bets naked while they're in action or you can protect them from the 7 by getting $41 No 10. Look what happens with $22 Inside and $41 No 10.

(a) If 7 shows, you lose $22 but win $19, 'cause 7 came before a 10. You've cut your loss to $3.

(b) You still win if any inside number comes.

(c) But a 10 gives you a loss of $41.

Now you must decide if the possible loss of $41 with a number that can be made three ways is less a chance that fighting the 7 which can be made six ways, producing a $22 whack. Tough decision!

Mathematical experts will tell you it is better to lay $41 No 10 as your hedge, 'cause based on the laws of probability you'll lose $41 three times, for a total of minus $123, while the place amounts naked could result in a loss of $132.

Naturally I believe the laws of probability do not come up unless you spread them over thousands and thousands of spins.

I've stood at roulette tables for centuries (or so it seems) and in a roll of thirty-eight numbers, I've never seen all different thirty-eight numbers show. There are always doubles and triples.

I love placing the inside numbers and taking two hits and sure, I fear that 7. The No 10 does protect versus the 7, but I hate losing $41 when the 10 shows.

If $44 Inside is your play, lay $41 No 10 and $41 No 4. They can't make both numbers at once. A 7 gives you a payoff on both No bets and your worst loss will be $41 anyhow.

The thing to remember is that you are nullifying the 7. If you do not fear the 7 when you get Inside—then by no means should you lay the No 10 or No 4! But it is up to you to decide what your play will be. Think about it before making a decision.

104

No Ten and Place 6 and 8

The last part of the previous chapter points out that you've neutralized the 7, but still leave yourself open for a possible loss of $41 if either 10 or 4 shows. So you gotta put your thinking cap on.

To go a step further, let's look at No 10 versus Place bets of 6 and 8. This means we've eliminated the 5 and 9 as potential profit makers, but the 7 is now in the position of kicking off a return:

(a) If 6 or 8 shows, you win $7.

(b) If 7 shows, you lose $12 on your 6 and 8 and win $19 No Ten for a profit of $7.

The following variation cuts down that $41 total possible loss. Here's how you'd spread your bets:

(a) $41 No Ten.

(b) $6 6 and 8.

(c) Place the 10 for $10.

By placing the 10 for $10, you've cut the total possible loss on the No 10 down to $23 cause the place 10 bet will take an $18 bite from the initial loss of $41.

Of course a 7 will result in a loss of $3 with the payoff of $19 not hardly covering the loss of $22 on the place 6, 8, and 10.

Here again realize that the purpose of the No 10 is to reduce

257

the poison punch of the 7, but be sure to understand all drawbacks.

Some of you won't like the hedge, while others will utilize it. Placing $10 on the 10 to soften the $41 No 10 is not like losing your little black book and deserves another look.

105

An Example of Hedging

At this very fraction of a moment I am in my living room waiting for the 1990 Super Bowl to begin. It is 4:21 P.M., exactly fifty-nine minutes before the kickoff and I have over $9,000 in bets on the game.

Yet I can't lose more than a couple of hundred dollars. That's because everything is hedged. The bets go both ways. I'm not really gambling at all cause I realize how tough it is to win.

My risk factor was at its highest last summer when the biggest gamble had to be made: Who would win the Super Bowl?

Along with my great friend Howie Goldstein, one of the sharpest players in the country, we analyzed all the teams. Naturally you throw out the Jets, Falcons, Bucs, etc., and then go to eliminating the decent teams such as the Dolphins, Cards, Seahawks, etc., and zero in on the powerhouses.

San Francisco outlasted all the others and became the choice, based on the process of elimination. The Big Board stated that a future bet on the 49ers to win the Super Bowl was 3 to 1. They were the favorites and to win $3,000 you must lay $1,000.

So a bet of $3,000 was made, with a pot of gold worth $9,000 hanging in the balance. The fact that they cruised through the regular season was not surprising, 'cause actually the goal was for them to reach the Playoffs in order to qualify for the shot at the Super Bowl.

History will show that they also cruised through the Playoffs.

Denver was the enemy. In the true sense of odds, the 49ers should be nine, maybe ten point favorites, but the super hype attached to Joe Montana and friends throws the fear of God, or worse still the fear of losing money, into the hearts of the bookmakers of the world.

They know that a line of nine on the 49ers will bring a ton of money on San Francisco and set up a possible Black Sunday if they win. So they release a line which is obviously an "overlay." They make San Francisco a twelve point favorite. Now the betting is split, as bettors have a number that results in wagering on both teams.

Not so with yours truly, Charlie Chicken. I got S.F. with no points laid, so I'm sitting in Racquel Welch's bedroom and her husband is stranded in Tokyo.

But alas and alack, just as he is boarding a chartered flight for the trip home, I am thinking of the possible loss of $3,000 that could occur if (gulp) Denver does win.

So just as I would avert a bad night in the event that plane gets back on time, I'd make a call to Dolly Parton to see if she's free. It's called hedging.

Well I also hedged the 49ers wager. I grabbed Denver with 12 ½ for $5,000 and look where I stand.

(1) If S.F. wins by thirteen or more, I lose $5,000 but win $9,000 for a profit of $4,000.

(2) If Denver wins outright, I lose the $3,000 on S.F. but win $5,000 on the Broncos for a profit of $2,000.

(3) If S.F. wins by one through 12, I win $9,000 plus $5,000 for a profit of $14,000.

That means I win $2,000 or $4,000 or $14,000. That's hedging. Sure, a lot of wheeler-dealers will say I'm a jerk for giving up the chance to win $9,000 with the 49ers laying no points. There is still the matter of $3,000 if Denver wins outright. Maybe they won't and maybe they can't. But there is still... "what if!"

When the game is over and if S.F. wins by more than 12½, I

may twitch for four or five seconds, but reality will set in and I'll know it was the best way to go. The hurt will go away.

Whether you non-hedgers can ever grasp this theory is hard to tell but it sure is comfortable sitting here, knowing I'm in a no-lose situation with now only thirty-two seconds to kick-off.

Do I have a real rooting interest in the outcome? Sure, I'd love a middle or at least for S.F. to win. I'll root against Denver but even if they win outright, a profit of $2,000 ain't gonna cause me to go looking for a bridge to use as a spring board.

But I do have one problem. My spies tell me that the chartered plane from Tokyo took off in time and Dolly's phone is busy. I can't use my hedge system.

See, even hedge bettors run into situations where they have no control.

I'll have to get Dolly a beeper or myself a pair of running shoes in case the plane lands before her phone comes free.... The problems of a hedge bettor.

106

No 4 and No Ten

The biggest drawback in placing $44 Inside or $22 Inside or $66 Inside or $88 Inside is the fact that a 7 can be made the most number of ways.

The biggest drawback with laying $41 No 10 is the loss of $41 or $82 or $410 on one little 10 showing, even though you've cut your total amount of losing ways down to three.

So you've got drawbacks on both sides and the trick is to cut down the things that could hurt you the most.

Igott Bredd goes to the casino with a $50,000 line of credit, so obviously losing a couple of thousand dollar bets doesn't have him fingering the number for the suicide hotline.

But 90 percent of the people who enter a casino play with short bankrolls and if you still can't grasp, accept, or zero in on this theory, go back and read the entire bankroll section again and again and again. . . .

But I know you're in this category, hence the reason I implore you to try hedging.

Let's get back to a way of reducing a total loss of $41 if you employ the No 10 theory. This calls for you to bet $41 No 10 and $41 No 4 at the same time. Now you've got a profit potential of $38 if the 7 shows, protecting a wager of $44 Inside and eliminating the necessity of betting $82 No 10 to protect those numbers.

The good part is that the worst you can lose is $41 'cause the 4 and 10 cannot come up at the same time.

The bad part is that now you've stretched the number of ways to lose from 3 to 6 (same number as 7) but the 7 is still neutralized. You make your choice but my feeling is that if you apply the hedge, I don't want $82 as a loss amount staring you in the face, regardless of whether you use Hard Way plays or not.

Let's swing down to the guy who plays $22 Inside and wants to use the No 10 theory but is scared to risk $41. Here's what you do:

(1) Place $22 Inside.

(2) Play $41 No 10 and $41 No 4 at the same time.

(3) Place $10 10 and $10 4 at the same time.

    (a) the worst that happens with a 10 or 4 is minus $41 plus $18 for possible loss of $23.

These options are strong and naturally it's up to you to decide if you want them or not.

107

Full Hedge

Once you establish a Don't Number, the edge at the table swings strictly in favor of the Wrong bettor, but you already know that.

The trick is to know how to handle the edge. You can sit on your Don't or try to establish more Don't Come numbers and when the amount of the numbers you want are in place, now you make your move.

If you are a $5 bettor, then all your Don't bets should remain naked. Don't hedge them.

As you climb to the level of $10 bets, you should always hedge the No 6 or 8:

(1) $1 Hard 6 or Hard 8,
(2) Place the 6 or 8 for $6
    (a) I always place the 6 or 8,
In the case of $10 No 5 or 9:
(1) Place $5 for partial hedge
    (a) You're in position to risk $3 to win $5 and odds are 3 to 2 in your favor to win the five bucks.
(2) Place full Hedge of $10,
    (a) You're now in position where there is zero loss factor versus possible $4 profit.
With a $10 Don't bet and 4 or 10 shows:
(1) Partial hedge of $5 place bet.

    (a) You'll either lose $1 or win $5, not a bad spot to be in, especially with odds 2 to 1 in your favor.

(2) Full hedge of $10 means you'll lose $0 or win $8, again you're in perfect position.

    (a) No loss possibility versus chance of winning the amount of the place on the 4 or 10.

Go over these full and partial moves and note that they put you into positions of higher wins versus lesser losses while still keeping the 7 as the hammer in your favor.

Let's go to the $15 Don't bet that gets established and work the hedge possibilities, but just remember that since there are so many variations, these examples may differ from ones in my first book.

SIX or EIGHT (Options)

(a) $12 Place.

(b) $2 Hard Way.

(c) $6 Place and $1 Hard Way.

FIVE OR NINE (Options)

(a) $5 Partial hedge.

(b) $10 Partial hedge.

(c) $15 Full hedge.

FOUR OR TEN (Options)

(a) $10 Partial hedge.

(b) $5 Partial and $1 Hard Way.

(c) $15 Full hedge.

You know, there are guys who make a living with full hedges against these Don't numbers and while it is an intense grind to squeeze out these small returns, I know of many people who do.

The next chapter will focus on these moves as we increase the amount of the No bet.

108

Hedging Grind

You don't need me to show all the possible moves off of the $20 and higher bets 'cause you already got the drift.

But I'd just like to spend a moment touching on the full hedges against the $25 bet.

Whether you bet straight Don't Pass or establish your Don't wager with hedging lay bets is your choice. Say you got $25 established and go for the grind. You'll always take the full hedge of $25 versus the 5 and 9 with place bets, the 6 and 8 calls for $24 place bets and the 4 and 10 gets $25 buys. Here's the breakdown:

SIX OR EIGHT

(a) You're either gonna win $1 or $3.

FIVE OR NINE

(a) You're either gonna break even or win $10.

FOUR OR TEN

(a) You either break even or win $25 (minus buy charge).

In all situations you're trying to grab a profit with no chance of loss. There is zero chance of loss once that Don't number is set and you go for the full hedge.

Just to give you one more look at the full hedge angle, let's make the Don't number that established a $50 wager. You can work out partials but these are all full moves which means that after the number is established, there is no loss factor at all.

SIX OR EIGHT (Place $48)

(a) You'll win $2 or $6.

FIVE OR NINE (Place $50)

(a) You'll break even or win $20.

FOUR OR TEN (Buy $50)

(a) You'll break even or win $50 (Minus 5 percent buy charge).

The only one of the above that I'll show a partial hedge will be versus the 4 or 10. Since there is a lot of leeway in the payoffs, you can put yourself in a position on winning whether the 7 or 4 or 10 shows. All the other full hedges kick off a profit only if the place or buy shows:

FOUR OR TEN (Buy $35)

(a) If 7 shows you win $15.

b) If point shows, you win $20.

FOUR OR TEN (Buy $30)

(a) If 7 shows, you win $20.

(b) If point shows, you win $10.

The partial move against the 4 or 10 wraps up a profit no matter what side shows and the 5 percent for the buy is based on the amount you got on the buy side.

If you wanna shoot for higher hedging amounts, that's your choice, but just be aware that they are there for the Don't bettor.

109

The Martingale

You all know what this method entails so I'm not gonna bore
you with eight dozen reasons why you shouldn't use it. You
better already realize that it's the biggest drain on your
pocketbook since Jesse James hung up his guns.

At least Jesse would take your money, then put a slug in your
gut and relieve you of having to worry about the fact that you
were broke. You had no worries at all.

But the Martingale smacks you in the mouth, grabs your
money in giant gulps and leaves you bleeding and beat.

The stupid analogy is that when you lose a bet, all you gotta
do is keep doubling up subsequent wagers, until you recoup all
past bets and show a profit. Let's say you play Don't Pass with
the Martingale.

So what that you lose your first bet of $5, then the double up
to $10, then $20, then $40, then $80, then $160, then $320. All
you gotta do is bet $640 and if you win you got it all back, plus a
$5 profit—and if you lose that bet of $640, the next bet of $1280
will bring you back a $5 nest egg.

The fact that you're risking a total of $2,555 to win $5 doesn't
seem to faze the backers of Martingale. They feel that eventually you're due to win a hand.

Garbage!

The Martingale is a farce and any of those dorks that believe in something being "due" to happen will also tell you that:

(a) It's due to snow in July in California.

(b) It's due for man to be able to walk on water.

(c) It's due for a cow to learn how to lay an egg.

(d) It's due for me to get an obscene call from the Playboy Bunny of the year.

There ain't no way three of those things are due to happen. However, I expect a phone call any day now from a farmer friend of mine who probably has a cow that'll squat out a dozen or so large white eggs.

The other things are just not "due," and putting your money on those stupid thoughts is just plain, well... stupid.

Don't play the Martingale. Never, never, never, ever, never, ever, never, never, never!

110

Mini Martingale

I've just finished blasting the Martingale system and now I'm gonna give you the green light to use the Mini Martingale.

The reason for the partial pull back on my part is to appease the more aggressive player who believes in a theory whereby an opposite can occur on a fairly regular basis.

Since I won't dispute a person's theory, at least let me put a ceiling on the amount of your Martingale series.

That ceiling has a high of three rolls, and not a single solitary roll more.

Since we're going over Wrong betting right now, it's safer to apply this approach to the Don't Pass or Don't Come boxes. That's because you can apply this move on straight Don't bets and not lay odds. Following is an accepted Mini series:

(1) Bet $5 Don't Pass.
(2) No other bets are made, either the laying of odds, placing any numbers or coming through the Don't Come.
(3) Sit and wait for a decision.
(4) If shooter makes the point, bet $10 Don't Pass.
(5) Sit and wait for decision.
(6) If shooter makes the point, bet $20 Don't Pass.
(7) If shooter makes the point *stop*, the series is over.

The total risk is $35 and you are looking for a seven out anywhere along the way that will kick off a $5 profit.

If a craps or a 7 or 11 shows on any Come-Out roll and produces a decision, then that series is over and you start again.

For instance if you bet $5 and shooter pops an 11, that's a loss and you follow up with another Don't Pass bet. He bangs a 7, knocking down your $10 wager.

You then bet $20 and he pops another 7 right back. You're out $35 and that series is over.

Now you either leave that table or wait until that particular shooter finishes his roll by sevening out. Then you may start another series.

I think a few personal comments are in order here, so as to clarify my feelings on this type of play. I neither condemn it nor condone it. That's because it has some good points and some bad points.

A couple of weeks ago I watched a man use a variation of this method at a choppy table and he was doing tremendous. However, his maximum exposure was two bets.

He'd bet $25 Don't Pass with no additional moves, just waiting for a decision on that wager.

If he won, he'd come back with another $25 Don't Pass. If he lost that first wager at $25, he'd go for $50 on next Come-Out. If that went down, his series was over and he'd wait for the next shooter.

His total risk was $75, the theory being he was looking for a bust out at least once in every two points. He was doing quite well and I especially liked his discipline.

If this is to be your play, you'd need ten times the amount of your total series. That means a series of $5, $10, $20 has total loss potential of $35. You'd need $350 per session and naturally a loss limit of 50 percent.

The win goal is 20 percent, and then you slide into guarantees and excesses, staying at that table as long as it stayed cold.

Along with that loss limit of 50 percent is the fact that three straight losing series in a row is an absolute wrap-up of that session.

The next few chapters will look into variations of this approach.

111

Sleepers

You don't have to be a rocket scientist to understand what a sleeper bet is. It's a decision on a happening without money being wagered.

I want you to use the sleeper as a tool in adopting the approach to the Mini Martingale betting series.

If in fact you believe in the theory that something will occur in three rolls, then I'm giving you a tool to stretch that theory to four or five rolls.

You've probably already figured out where I'm coming from, but I'll explain it for people like Frank Blank who's looking at me with a blank look on his kisser.

Let's suppose you're deep into the belief that a shooter "can't" make five points, or sevens, or elevens on the Come-Out roll.

Don't you dare have the audacity to tell me this can't happen, but let's suppose you believe it can't happen consistently.

Instead of jumping right into the shooter and betting $5, $10 and $20 on subsequent Come-Outs, you wait for him to make two winning wagers.

The two wagers you wait for, without a bet being made, are called "sleepers." There is no money involved.

When a shooter makes two points or two winning Come-Out rolls in a row, you then jump in with your betting series of 1–2–2 or 1–2–3 or 1–2–4. You now have increased the odds in

273

your favor that such a thing "can't" happen in five rolls instead of three.

It simply calls for you to wait out a shooter with no money in action, and hold back all wagers until he has had two successes in a row, and it ain't going to cost you a nickel.

If you want, you could just incorporate one sleeper before jumping in. For you safe conservative players, you could wait for three sleepers, but now you're getting to a point where the casino may charge you rent and electric.

But there's nothing wrong with this method as long as you believe in the theory. Of course your total loss potential is still the total of your predetermined series and that's control.

Frank Blank just smiled. The blank look as disappeared so it means one of three things:

(1) He got the message and understands.

(2) He forgot what the question was in the first place.

(3) His wife called him for supper.

Knowing the probable capacity of Frank Blank's mind, I'd say number 2 or number 3 occurred.

Then of course we have the super conservative player like Connie Cerv who wets her pants every time she loses even a quarter in the slot machines.

She loves the idea of the sleeper cause she sees a way to cut her losses way down to the bone.

She waits for the shooter to make twenty-three passes and then starts her betting series.

She hasn't made a bet in four years, but the good part is that it's been easy on her underwear.

Take a look at the theory of sleepers and its use with the Mini Martingale. My suggestion would be two sleepers and then 1–2–4.

There'll be a lot of days when you'll do a lot of standing around, but I think you'll see the power in this approach.

112

Hedge Betting

I've already touched on hedge betting, so you know what it is. So now we swing through a couple of chapters that emphasize this style of play—and it's super conservative.

Hedging is only used to reduce your losses, but not everyone is equipped to handle the stares of the casino people or other players, so even though they may like to hedge, they don't got the guts.

A couple of chapters back I explained a system employed by Les Scally called the Richochet method.

You wait for a point to be established and then lay against that point while coming through the Don't Come with a $15 bet and a buck on the 11.

The only thing that can hurt you on this system is the point bouncing back. But once you get that Don't Come number established and it only costs you that buck on the Yo, you've put yourself in a position to book the house.

I've explained it before but the reasons for going over it again is to lead into the next system and I want you fully cognizant of what hedging is all about.

The conservative player can now take a partial or full hedge versus that $15 Don't Come number, after he removes his bet from behind the point.

Notice that now you become a hedge player, with the seven working for you if you go partial hedge, or if you go full hedge.

And the 7 was always kept at bay. The hedge may be a grind but it does allow a ton of offshoots, 'cause it reduces total wipeouts per series, while giving you the chance to grind out small returns.

Since the hedge is usually used to offset a Don't number, it is the Wrong way player who gets the most use from it.

And get that nonsense out of your head that everyone is looking at you and you feel funny doing this. Don't be intimidated!

The other day my friend B. N. Kautious was hedging his bets at a craps table and called me over. "You know these people keep looking at me. I don't think they like the fact I'm so cautious by hedging all my Don't numbers."

I looked at B. N. Kautious and tried to reassure him that they weren't really looking at his play and not to worry about it.

I had to leave the table before discretion became the better part of valor and I would tell him why they were staring at him.

B. N. Kautious weighs about 380 pounds, give or take a ton. He had on a ten-gallon cowboy hat with a feather that was two feet long. A bright red t-shirt was trying its best to restrain a gut that looked like it hadn't missed a ten-course meal in fifteen years. The shirt was losing the battle.

To say B. N. was a little fat was like saying Dolly was a tad developed. Putting it bluntly, B. N. would make a whale look like a goldfish.

B. N. had on a pair of purple shorts that had already given up and was straining to find a resting place on the floor and hang the fact that B. N. would be bare ashen by embarrassment.

Holding up this hulk of a man were two legs that would have trouble passing for straws capped off with black hightop sneakers with no socks.

And B. N. was worried that people would stare at him for hedge betting.

Put all that crap out of your head. Sure you're gonna get stares if you hedge and comments and even ridicule. So be it!

If you got the guts to gamble, then have the guts to follow the ways that cost you the least worry.

The next system will test your intestinal fortitude.

113

A Story About Reality

Before we go deeper into the world of Don't betting, let's go a little deeper into the world of reality and see if one or two of you can grasp the true meaning of what you're fighting when you gamble: reality!

I've written enough chapters on the subject for you to begin to get the drift, but there are still some of you who still believe gambling is the way to untold riches. Garbage!

My friend D. R. Reamer is an intelligent chap with a degree in electronics, a good job, a bright future, but a dim insight into how to handle himself at the craps table.

He thinks if he doesn't double his starting bankroll, he's had a bad day. So does D. R. Reamer accept percentage returns? Of course he doesn't.

He'll get ahead $100 on a starting bankroll of $500 and shout, "Hey, this is peanuts. If I can get ahead $100, I can get ahead $500."

He then proceeds to bang away, eventually giving back the $100 profit and the $500 he came with.

D. R. Reamer is a dreamer. The times he hits that jackpot return is more than made up for by the days he blew his $500 stake.

I was at a table one day with D. R. Reamer, playing the

Richochet system. He was also betting Wrong that day, in more ways than one.

All I did was wait for a point to be established and then lay against the point. Then I'd put $15 in the Don't Come, a buck on the Yo and sit.

When that Don't Come number was set, I'd remove my lay and wait for the 7. On this day I was not going for the extra Don't Come numbers because the pattern was so strong in that every shooter seemed to bang that 7 right back and I was grinding out some healthy returns.

D. R. Reamer was right there with me, grinding out good returns but every once in a while he'd tap my arm and say, "Come on, let's get a little heavier. Let's go for the kill."

I managed to keep him under control for awhile, but then we were joined by another acquaintance, a nervous, anxious-type guy who also wanted to "make a score." His name was Ed G. Pantts and his idea of gambling was to have every chip in his rack in action on every roll.

He got D. R. Reamer's ear and together they started to escalate their bets, and they won.

Then they won some more. All of a sudden a funny thing happened to Ed G. Pantts and D. R. Reamer. The table started to turn. Not drastically mind you, but ever so slightly.

I caught the message and backed off with about a $900 profit with a $3,000 buy-in.

The other two guys were up well into the thousands, due to their aggressive play when the table was ice cold.

I told them that things were changing, that they were starting to lose. Did this register with them? No way. They increased their bets and started laying double odds against the Don't Pass and the Don't Come numbers.

I will spare you the gory details cause you already know the result. In exactly twenty minutes they were broke and I mean flat out broke, including kicking back the profits plus their starting bankroll.

This is a true story. It happened yesterday, Friday February Ninth, and was probably repeated in many casinos all over the world.

I stood there and watched two dorks chase the impossible dream, refusing to accept the reality of gambling: that trends last for only so long and when they go against you, you can't buy a turn-around.

Ed G. Pantts, with his stupid illogical, let-it-all-hand-out type of play and his dreams of gigantic returns got clobbered—again.

The story is not only true, but sad. They walked away crushed, cursing their rotten luck, blaming everyone but themselves.

How many times have you played the same way, and don't be too proud to admit that you also may have rejected reality!

I walked away from the table with a small percentage return, happy that it was not a losing session.

The Richochet worked yesterday and I'll be back there again today hoping to find another cold table, praying I got the guts to quit if I start to lose.

Poor D. R. Reamer. He's probably home right now dreaming of what could have been. He's a dreamer! And so are you if you don't realize that gambling is *not* the road to gigantic riches.

114

The Patrick System

Here is a system that I threw out to the world several years ago, a super-grinding but strong effective method of beating the 7 on the Come-Out roll. In fact the 7 will never be a factor against you.

It is a simple method that you will grasp in a matter of chapters, but one that you will be scared to use, because of the intimidation factor.

Let's start with the theory. As every craps shooter knows, the 7 is the crusher whether you bet Right or Wrong.

From the Don't side, you gotta beat the 7 on the Come-Out in order to get your point established.

As soon as your point is set, you got the edge in your favor, 'cause the odds of winning has now swung over to where you are now "booking the house," 'cause the chances of your winning are now in your favor by odds of 6 to 3 or 6 to 4 or 6 to 5.

That depends on whether your point is 4, 10, 5, 9, 6, or 8. But the odds now favor you. It doesn't necessarily mean you are going to win, 'cause the shooter can bang that point back.

But you have put yourself into the position of having the odds in your favor.

One tiny little problem with getting to that position. You gotta get your point number established.

And standing in your way is that rotten, lousy 7 or 11 on the Come-Out roll.

Betting the "any seven" is a stupid move, so throw that theory out. Here's what your chances are:

There are eight ways to make a 7 or 11 and three ways to bang a craps, leaving the 12 alone cause that's a wash. So there are five times out of thirty-six that absolutely crush the Don't player.

Here's what the Patrick system suggests: Bet Do and Don't at the same time. This way the 7 or 11 cannot hurt you. After the point is established, lay odds against the Don't Pass bet and place a wager in the Don't Come.

When the Don't Come number is set, remove the odds off the Don't Pass and now the Don't Come number is your dominant.

The bets on the Pass Line and Don't Pass remain a wash. All you've done is make the second number become your point instead of the first.

But the 7 or 11 was never in a position to beat you, 'cause if it showed on the Come-Out while you were betting Do and Don't, you'd lose on the Don't Pass and win on the Pass.

If the 2 or 3 craps showed, you'd lose on the Pass Line and win on the Don't Pass, again for a wash.

If the 12 shows, you push on the Don't and lose on the Do side. But since the 12 can only be made one out of thirty-six ways, you've reduced the chance of losing from five down to one, and we'll take care of that 12 later.

Before we go on, look back over this chapter and understand the basic premise: beat the 7 and 11 on the Come-Out.

This does it!

115

Theory of the Patrick System

You know by now what this system is focused on doing, but let's explain it for the purpose of X.P. Lane who's already wondering what the purpose is:

It's to get a number on the Don't side established without worrying about the 7 or 11 on the Come-Out. The whole theory is in that sentence and now I'll explain it.

Starting with a $5 wager, this is how you would play it:

(a) Bet $5 Do and Don't.
(b) Leave 12 naked.
(c) After point is established, lay single odds against the Don't and put $5 in Don't Come.
(d) The number that shows now will be your dominant Don't.
(e) When Don't Come is established, remove odds from Don't Pass and now you have your don't number. The 7 was never your enemy.

When you had that Don't Come bet in action, the 11 could beat you, but the three craps is an offset with Snake Eyes a plus in your favor.

All you've done is make that Don't Come number become your dominant. Now you can swing into variations.

Some of you will complain that maybe the 4 or 10 became the

283

point on the initial Come-Out and when you laid your odds versus the number and came through the Don't Come, you then got an 8.

By removing your odds off the Don't Pass (4 or 10) you give up a hard number to make in exchange for the easy 8. Sure these situations are gonna pop up. But they'll also work the other way around.

This system never has the 7 as your enemy and as you increase your bets, you'll also use the Yo to offset the 11.

The only thing you're fighting is the number to repeat immediately after the initial Come-Out.

At that time you are vulnerable because of the odds lay. But if you were betting straight Don't, you'd be vulnerable anyway, so I'm not exactly asking you to stick your head in the lion's mouth.

If the 7 shows on the first roll after the Come-Out, you'll lose your Don't Come bet, but win the odds lay against the point. The Do and Don't bet becomes a wash.

But if you were trying to establish a Don't Come number with your basic play, the whole thing would occur the same way anyhow. Which brings us back to the intent of this move—beat the 7 on the Come-Out. Or have I said that before?

If you bet $10 Do and Don't and the 9 becomes the point, lay your odds of $15 to $10 versus the Don't and now your option is to come through the Don't Come with either a $5 or $10 wager.

My suggestion would be $10. A 7 gives you a wash, but a 4, 5, 6, 8, or 10 gives you a $10 Don't and now you can protect subsequent Don't Comes by betting smaller.

Suppose you pop a 5 with that first Don't Come. Immediately take down odds as the $10 moves behind the 5. Now you can put $5 in the Don't Come and the 7 is working for you, with no worry about laying odds.

Now a 6 shows and the $5 Don't Come moves behind the 6 and you have $15 in Don't numbers working. To establish a third Don't, you can now go up to a $10 Don't Come.

Suppose the 8 shows. Right away I'd hedge the 8 for $6 and sit on my three Dont's.

You have $10 Don't 5, $5 Don't 6 and $10 Don't 8 which is hedged for $6. You only replace twice and that is for the same amount as the hit.

Suppose the 8 shows. You win $7, lose $10 for a net loss of $3 and now come through the Don't Come with a $10 wager.

X.P. Lane should now understand the theory, so let's get to higher bets.

116

Saving the Eleven

Let's move into betting of $15 Do and Don't. At this stage, the
bets on the Come-Out still protect you against the 11, so you
don't have to worry about dropping a dollar on the Yo.

But let's move to the Don't Come bet. After the point is
established and you lay your odds, the $15 you bet in the Don't
Come gives you an option of hedging that buck on the Yo.

In fact every Don't Come bet from $15 through $25 offers you
that option. It's not a bad move because you still have 2 and 3
craps kicking off a $15 return and the 7 is covered by the odds
lay on the Don't Pass.

When you reach a Don't Come of $15 thru $25, I'd take the
Yo.

When your Don't Come wager hits an amount of $30, you
should definitely take a buck Yo and seriously consider $2. Since
payoff is 15 to 1, you wanna protect those wagers. Here is a
guideline for your Don't Come plays:

Don't Come	BET ON 11
$5 or $10	NO BET
$15	Option of $1
$20 or $25	$1
$30	Option of $2
$35 or $40	$2

286

$45	Option of $3
$50 or $55	$3

On these option bets from $30 and higher, at least put something on that Yo. I don't like leaving that Don't Come wager naked. Take a look at these suggestions and make your decision now.

117

Handling the 12

The only thing that stands between the Come-Out roll either being a wash or giving you a point is the 12, but then you're talking about a number that can only be made one out of thirty-six rolls.

So when I have a bet of either $5, $10, $15, or $20 Do and Don't, I don't concern myself with the 12.

When I reach the level of $25 and more, I start thinking of the hedge. That's done by tossing a buck on the two sixes, which pays 30 to 1.

At this point you've absolutely guaranteed yourself a no-loss on the Come-Out:

(a) A 12 will eat up your $25 Pass Line but kick off a payoff of $30, for plus $5,

(b) 7 or 11 is a wash, minus the buck on the 12,

(c) 2 or 3 is a wash, minus the buck on the 12,

(d) 4, 5, 6, 8, 9, 10 gives you a point and now lay odds and get into your play.

The three percent vig I lose by playing that hedge on the 12 is worth the risk because of the intended results. I use that hedge on $25 or higher 'cause my purpose is to bypass that Come-Out and give me a number that now puts the 7 working for me.

You decide on your use of the $1 on the 12, but at the $25 bet and higher, I'd definitely do it. When you reach $50, go for $2 hedge.

The same rate of hedge should be used at every $30 interval. Even you high rollers that go $100 Do and $100 Don't could drop $3 on the 12. It'll get you out, and once you're out, the odds are in your favor.

Think about it.

118

Patrick System Hedging

Hedging is a direct spinoff of Wrong betting and once you get a Don't number established, a world of options has now opened up.

The only threat is a repeat of the point, but again you *must* realize that the house always has some hidden edge and my intent is to lessen its whack against you.

Even though you're risking odds on that roll after the Come-Out, at least it is lessened by the odds being in your favor.

It's the Don't Come number that I'm attempting to reach. If it becomes a 4, 5, 9, or 10, you can go into two types of hedging:

(1) Direct hedge against that particular Don't Come.
· (2) Placing the 6 and 8 and using established Don't Come number as the protection.

Let's go into the direct hedge against the established Don't Come. That means you are forsaking the setting of another Don't Come and concentrating on a sure pop profit versus that number.

Naturally this can be done versus any betting amount, but the system is stronger versus higher bets, due to the small vig on the 6 and 8.

Suppose you bet in increments of $20 and eventually get a Don't Come wager of $20 established. We'll say it is a 5. You can swing into partial or full hedges directly against that number. $15 is your hedge.

(1) Place $15 partial hedge directly against that number.

(2) If 7 shows, you win $20, lose $15 for a profit of $5.

(3) If 5 shows, you win $21, lose $20 for profit of $1.

(4) You win either $1 or $5.

This partial hedge can be adjusted down to $10, which strengthens the 7 but weakens the place payoff. In other words a 7 would be a profit of $10, while your loss potential would be $6. You are risking $6 to win $10 but the odds are 6 to 4 in your favor for a 7.

Either way is giving you an edge on the house. Let's look at a full hedge, still using $20 as the betting increment and again 5 (or 9) is the Don't Come number.

(1) Place full hedge of $20.

(2) If 7 comes it is a wash.

(3) If 5 shows, you lose $20 and win $28 for a profit of $8.

(4) You either break even or win $8.

You can work out your own partial and full hedges versus the other numbers but remember that the 4 and 10 give you great opportunities of payoffs on both sides, while the 6 and 8 show up as a wash.

Let's move into the $50 bets and you now get a $50 No 10 established. Look at a partial hedge of buying the ten for $35:

(1) If 7 shows, you lose $35, win $50 for profit of $15.

(2) If 10 shows, you lose $50, win $70 for profit of $20.

(3) You win either way.

Staying with the $50 bet, let's say the 6 becomes the Don't Come. A partial hedge leaves the 7 giving you a profit, while a full hedge is practically a wash.

(1) Place six for $42.

(2) If 7 shows, you win $50, lose $42 for profit of $8.

(3) If 6 shows, you win $49, lose $50 for loss of $1.

(4) You are risking $1 to win $8 and odds are 6 to 5 in your favor.

There are a ton of offsets in full and partial hedging techniques versus direct Don't Come, so before you go further, decide if this is the way you like.

Next chapter we'll touch on number 2 of your option after a Don't Come is established.

119

Hedging Strong Don't

This ain't gonna be long, and it ain't gonna be complicated cause you already understand the concept.

Once you use the Patrick System to establish a number and work your way through the Don't Come, the number you get signals your moves.

If 4, 5, 9, or 10 becomes the Don't Come, you can use the direct hedge versus that number itself, or you can use that Don't Come to protect a place bet on the 6 and 8.

Suppose Don't Come 10 showed for an amount of $20. Place the 6 and 8 for $6 each and put $10 in the Don't Come.

If 4, 5, or 9 shows, you now have two strong Don'ts and you can now go through Don't Come with a $10 wager and either leave the place 6 and 8 at $6 each or raise to $12 each.

Since at this point you have $30 in strong Don'ts working for you, go ahead and increase place bets to $12 each.

If the 5 comes as that second Don't Come at $10 and you raised Place bets to $12 each, the next roll will establish a third Don't for $10.

If the 6 or 8 shows, you'll pick up a $14 payoff. Immediately regress the place on the number that showed to $6 and remove the other Place bet.

You have three Don'ts working and you only replace twice.

Personally I like having the 6 and 8 working when I have

293

strong Don't numbers established. It gives me a chance of collecting a profit while looking to establish additional Don'ts.

You decide how you wanna handle these moves through the Don't Come.

120

Variations of Patrick System

This method gets you out without worrying about the 7. But let's go all the way back to that first Come-Out roll and offer you a spinoff.

I told you that whatever number becomes the point should then be used to work towards protecting the Don't Come.

But let's say the 6 or 8 becomes that initial point. Instead of betting Wrong, you now swing over and bet Right.

Suppose 8 shows as the initial point. Take double odds on the Pass Line bet and Place the 6 for $6 and the nine for $5, or Place the 6 for $12, whichever you choose.

Notice that you have become a Right bettor when the 6 or 8 was the point and a Wrong bettor when the 4, 5, 9, 10 showed.

That means that you're always with the shooter when the "easy" numbers of 6 or 8 is the point and against the shooter when the tough 4, 5, 9, 10 is the point.

In essence you are throwing out the Patrick system when 6 or 8 is the initial point and don't worry about the loss of the 7 or 11 on the Come-Out. The Craps is also a nonfactor and look into the pickup of payoffs.

A $5 player puts $5 on the Pass Line and 6 shows. He takes $5 odds and if the 6 is made, he wins $11.

You take double odds behind the Pass Line bet when 6 or 8 shows as the point in the Patrick System. If that 6 shows, your original Do and Don't bets are a wash, but you get paid $12 for your double odds. It's a buck higher than the guy with the Pass Line and single odds, and makes up for the loss of the 7 and 11 minus the craps on the standard betting method.

Some of you decided Don't bettors will not worry about what number becomes the point and will want to lay against the point, regardless of what shows and that's fine.

For you people with an aversion towards laying against the 6 or 8, I give you the option.

121

Synopsis of Patrick System

Let's put the whole system in a nutshell and list good and bad parts plus some of the Hedges.

(a) Beats 7 and 11 on the Come-Out.

(b) Bet equal amounts on Do and Don't.

(c) At $25 level, take buck on 12.

(d) After point number is established, lay odds versus Don't Pass and put bet in Don't Come, equal to or less than amount of potential profit.

(e) When bet in Don't Come reaches $15 put buck on Yo.

(f) When Don't Come is established, remove odds on Don't Pass.

(g) Option is to sit with that Don't Come without odds or establish additional Don't Come.

(h) Make sure additional Don't Come bets are equal to or lower than the protection afforded by the established Don't Come.

(i) Be sure you understand (h)

(j) Only 12 can beat you on Come-Out.

(k) The bad part I hate is the roll where you can lose the laying of odds if shooter repeats number.

(l) The good part is 7 is offset on Come-Out and from then on it always works for you.

(m) You've controlled the number that the house always uses as its hammer.

(n) After Don't Comes are established, you can use full or partial hedges.

(o) You can Place 6 and 8 versus strong established Don't Comes.

(p) If 6 or 8 becomes the initial point, you have option of becoming a Right Bettor.

(q) When Don't Comes are established, only replace twice.

(r) There are a ton of variations of moves to be made after first Don't Come is established.

(s) The Don't bettor has eliminated the biggest obstacle to his getting established. (The 7!)

Finally, understand one thing about this method. It gets you out!

Naturally, it doesn't prohibit the shooter from banging his number right back nor prevent him from popping off your Don't Come bets.

But that's where hedge betting comes in and where you finally learn to accept small consistent returns.

Several years ago I held up my Basic Craps book and video tapes and said that there was a system that the casinos would complain about and give you some heat.

The prophecy came true. Yes, there are certain casinos that will tell you they don't like or don't want your action.

There will be dealers who will question your intentions. Players will comment on your stupidity and make jokes.

It's because they don't understand the theory. One casino in Atlantic City, who shall remain nameless, called me in and flatly told me to stop giving out this system and that they will refuse comps to anyone playing it.

Their assessment is that the player takes up space, offers the house practically very little chance at him, except for the 12 on the Come-Out, and is not in the "true spirit of craps."

Yes, you will run into occasional distractions but theory is very strong. If you are a Don't bettor, why in heaven's name would you not want to play this way?

All I am doing is making your second number your dominant Don't instead of the first, and offsetting the 7 while I'm doing it.

What's the difference if the first number becomes your dominant or the second! The trick is beating that 7.

The Patrick system does that!

122

Patrick vs. Richochet

Before we wrap up Don't betting, let's put a comparison of the two strongest Don't methods up for a vote.

You've just trudged through some rough theories on the Patrick system so you are aware of all of the good and bad parts and are probably weighing your decision as to how or if you will use it.

I just wanna remind you of the Richochet system so you can compare.

The Richochet waits for a point to be established, so you don't have to concern yourself about the 7.

After the point is established, whichever number shows, you now lay against that number for an amount high enough to allow for a Don't Come bet to be made in the amount of $15 or $10.

Suppose you played the Patrick system with a bet of $10 and $10. Nine shows as the point. You lay $30 to win $20 and put $10 in the Don't Come.

Notice you are laying the true odds of 3 to 2 or $30 to $20. Now swing over the Richochet system which calls for a lay bet of $31 to $19 versus that 9.

In that instance you pay 5 percent or $1, whether you win or lose. It's a 5 percent bit but since I'm not totally scared off by the word vig, I don't believe it is all that damaging to pay that $1 to establish a Don't Come, which is the object of the move in the first place.

Also take this into consideration. You lay the $31 No 9 and put $10 in the Don't Come, let's say a 5 shows. You immediately take down that $31 No 9 so it hasn't cost you anything.

So you'll only pay that buck if a 9 or 7 shows. That No bet is strictly protection.

It is my very humble opinion that there is really not that much difference in either the use of the Patrick or the Richochet systems, even though the Patrick system saves you a buck on occasion.

You make your own decision on which method you'll adopt, since there is minimal difference and you do not give up any hedging possibilities either.

Now let me throw another monkey wrench into your thinking. You could throw both of these systems out the window and use a little of both to form a method that we went over way back in the early look at Don't.

(a) Bypass Come-Out.

(b) Whatever number shows as the point, lay $41 No 4 or No 10, and go through Don't Come.

(c) This way you always have the hardest number protecting your Don't Come.

(d) Or you could always lay $31 No 5 or No 9 to cut down the probable loss from $41 to $31.

(e) This way you never have to worry about the 6 or 8 beating you.

Have I confused you? No way! I'm just giving you options on how to bet Don't by avoiding fighting that 7. All of those approaches are powerful.

Whichever one you choose will go a long way towards making you a strong Don't player.

And don't let the possibility of paying the buck for the right to buy against a number be the biggest distraction. Sometimes you gotta pay a little extra to get what you want.

I'd sure pay extra to get chicken over tuna fish or steak over hamburger or ice cream over milk or Sophia over anybody.

It's all in what you want!

123

Sayonara Bet

Lets go back to my good friend Howie G., a guy blessed with the ability to show discipline at every game he plays.

One of his pet moves is a thing he calls the Sayonara bet in craps. For you people who have mastered the art of talking only in Italian, Polish or Brooklynese, *sayonara* means good-bye.

Obviously it is a bet he makes just before he leaves the table. Most of all it is only performed when he has shown a profit of at least $100 for the session.

As soon as his win goal is reached and his plateaus have gone cold, Howie makes his Sayonara move:

(a) $41 No 10
(b) $41 No 4
(c) Both at the same time.

Naturally the shooter cannot make both numbers at the same time, so the worst he can do is lose one of those bets for a loss of $41. He'd then remove the other No bet and still leave the table a winner.

If the all-powerful 7 shows, he wins both No bets and adds the $38 to his excess, plus, he already has a locked in profit even if he should lose.

Naturally Howie does this *only* at the conclusion of a winning session. That still leaves him a walking profit regardless of the results.

124

Wrapping up Don't

You've got enough approaches to Wrong betting to give you a foothold on establishing the method you'll use.

Remember, I don't give a rat's tail whether you play Do or Don't, only that you choose one side, set up a system, and master that method before you play.

Here are some tidbits to remember about playing Don't and this is strictly my conservative approach. You adjust it if you want, but someday you'll realize that "white man does not speak with forked tongue":

(1) I despise laying odds.

(2) But I will lay them *only* to protect future bets in the Don't Come and then quickly remove odds.

(3) You *must* chart the tables to find a cold game.

(4) Optional whether you go for additional Don't Comes or stick just with single Don't Pass.

(5) I go for two additional Don't Comes.

(6) Only replace twice.

(7) Hard Way offshoots are suggested on even number Don'ts.

(8) Always hedge your No 6 or 8, at least for a partial Place at $10 level and up.

(9) *Never* say "No Action" on a No 6 or No 8. Hedge it for full

amount if you want, but let those chips move behind the number.

(10) You *must* chart the tables, oops, I already said that.

(11) I like coming through Don't Come for amount less than the Don't Pass bet. Eliminates my laying odds.

(12) $41 No 10 or No 4 is O.K. but you're out a lot of bread if it hits.

(13) Using the $41 No 4 or 10 to protect inside bets is OK if you come down quickly, like after two or three hits.

(14) Hedging full amounts on high Don't bets is a powerful move: boring, yes! But powerful, yes!

(15) If you play Don't Pass and get beat three times at a table, move.

(16) If you're losing on Don't Pass but winning on Don't Come, just bet Don't Come.

(17) If you're winning on Don't Pass but losing on Don't Come, stop playing the Don't Come. (Did I really have to tell you that at this stage of the book?)

(18) I'll O.K. the Mini Martingale of 1-2-4 but that's all.

(19) I'll also give stamp of approval to 1-2-2 or 1-2-3.

(20) I'll also give nod of approval to sleepers. It's a slow process but effective. Two sleepers. It's enough and then you can start your three series bets.

(21) The Patrick system is strong, as it beats that 7 AND 11 on the Come-Out. Why in heaven's name should you fight those two numbers?

(22) The Richochet is also strong if you have the bread to lay against the point.

(23) As soon as you lay against the point, put that Don't Come $15 bet and $1 Yo in action. Then remove your lay when a Don't Come is set.

(24) Be sure you chart those tables before you play. Oh, I apologize—I think I've already said that.

Way off in the distance I can see Watt E. Cey turn to his friend E. Sawatt and ask "What's charting?" and E. Sawatt will shrug his shoulders and say, "I dunno. It must have something to do with the dice sailing across the table." (Dorks!)

    (25) Laying against the No 4 or No 10 on the Come-Out is O.K. to protect against the 7, but at least Hedge with a Hard Way bet.

    (26) Be sure you have ten times the amount of your total exposure bet to play at any session.

If you're a Don't bettor, go over these methods until you zero in on your favorite and master it.

Start slowly, build up a profit and then increase your bets. There are some chapters on plateaus coming up that will enlighten you on the secret of smart progressions.

It must be a secret, cause looking over the table play in Vegas and Atlantic City, I see very few people using smart money control.

I Do know this much! The Don't section is Done and you'll Do yourself a big favor by Doing the Don't things I recommend. Cause if you Don't, you Don't stand a chance of Doing Good at the tables! But if you Don't you Do stand a chance of Doing bad at the table!

125

Wrapping up Systems

We've about come to the end of systems to use, and now we'll begin the countdown to the end of this section with the true meaning of money management.

But first I want you to understand what a system really is.

A system is a disciplined, pre-determined method of play that you must use at every session.

Most people who play craps haven't the foggiest idea of what approach they will use until they get to the table.

Ena Fogg is a typical craps shooter. She loves to be a part of the game with all the shouting and yelling and fast pace of the table. But Ena Fogg is in a fog when it comes to explaining exactly how she will play.

'Oh, I just go with the flow," she smiles. "If the guy next to me is betting the 4 and 10 I'll go with him and hope I get lucky."

She is no different than most people who pop into a Casino, walk up and down the aisles looking for an opening at a table and squeeze in as they reach for their wallet.

There is no plan of attack and that's why I give you systems to set and stick with. If they're not working, leave that session and go to another. Chart the table and if it is running the way you predetermined to play, then buy in and go to work.

This incident happened just two days ago but I have seen it many many times.

I was in the Claridge in Atlantic City charting the tables, looking for one that was kicking off numbers, as I wanted to bet Right. One particular table I was watching was ice cold, as shooter after shooter established a point and after one or two rolls, banged a 7.

The table was ice cold and I kicked myself for predetermining to bet Right, cause this would have been a terrific cold game.

Anyhow, the table was so cold all the Right bettors eventually stormed away cursing, after getting clobbered. There were only four Wrong bettors left at the table.

The stickman swung the dice from player to player, looking for a shooter. No one wanted to shoot, they wanted to stay betting wrong.

"Well, that's the game, gentlemen, we have no shooter," explained the dealer.

One dork spoke up and said he'd shoot the dice. Remember now, he had been betting Wrong all along and now, for some unbelievably stupid reason, he agreed to bet Right just to keep the game going.

The dice were shoved to him and he placed $10 on the Pass Line. He threw a 12 craps, loser. Again he bet $10 and this time popped 1–2 craps, loser.

A few curse words, a look to heaven in an attempt to either ask God for help or to blame Him for his rotten luck and then a defiant fling of the dice across the table. Snake Eyes! Loser!

This is a true story cause it was too unbelievable to be believable.

I glanced at the other three shooters who were playing Don't, 'cause the shooter was now belting out curse words that even I had never heard before. I made a mental note to check and see if they were legal.

The other three shooters tried to look unconcerned, keeping their heads bowed. They didn't dare look over to their benefactor.

The dealers were very sharp and tried not to show any emotion.

One blew his nose, trying to stifle a grin. Everyone knew they were observing the back end of a horse.

Anyhow, the shooter regained his poise, popped $10 on the Pass Line and banged out an 8. He took single odds and placed the 5 and 9 (not the 6). The other players made their moves and our hero proceeded to continue his roll.

Now you probably already know the end of the story, so I ain't got any big bang-up finish for you. You know dog-gone well he threw a 7. I won't describe this cat's actions, but I will tell you he again looked to heaven and this time there was no mistake about it.

He was blaming God!

He finally grabbed the remainder of his chips and stormed away, the classic "jerk of the day" award a cinch to be his—if they awarded such a prize.

The game broke up, but you knew everyone else knew what a jackass that guy was. They build stalls for animals that have more brains than him. He belongs in one.

Why would anyone swing away from the system that got him ahead? Yet it happens all the time.

And you do it yourself!

That's why I give you systems and ask you to choose one, master it, chart the tables, 'til you find a game going that way and jump in. Nothing hard about that. Except you won't do it.

126

Reviewing Win Goals

These next two chapters are the absolute keys to your day but you still get ding-dongs who think that the time you spend in a casino should be controlled by a watch.

The truth is that your bankroll and your preset win goal percentage is the clock that counts.

I tell you 20 percent win goal, but that's because you won't accept the true figure of 10 percent. Shorty Shortkash agrees that 20 percent is an acceptable percentage, but then brings $80 to the casinos.

He wins his $16, figures out it cost him $23 to get there, so he goes for more. He ends up getting whacked.

The players with the larger bankrolls of $5000 and higher scoff at a $500 profit and refuse to quit when they get ahead a decent amount and so the pitiful blunders of mismanagement go on.

I ain't gonna repeat a hundred things about the importance of setting a goal, but the day will come when you'll realize this is the area where 95 percent of all people who gamble screw up: setting win goals.

A couple of chapters ahead you're gonna see plateaus explained in detail. It'll be a method to show you how to go for bigger returns. But the first step is setting your initial win goal. The more you bring, the less percentage you go for.

You can bring $300 and set a 20 percent win goal of $60. Maybe that don't sound like a big score but it is.

If you took $3000 and won 20 percent you'd have $600. Now you're getting interested.

If you took $30,000 and won 20 percent, you'd have $6000 profit. I think you could struggle along with a kick-off like that, yet it's still "only" 20 percent win goal percentage.

Even cutting it in half and accepting a 10 percent win goal of $3000 is a fantastic profit. Yet it's 50 percent of the percentage that you scoffed at a few paragraphs ago.

Let's get ridiculous and say you brought $30,000 to the casino and played for a 5 percent return. That's $1500 a day. Don't laugh until you grasp the logical example I'm trying to convey.

A lot of people take $400 to a casino and laugh if I ask them if it's easy to win $10. Their heads bob up and down like a yo-yo, "Of course it's easy to win $10, which is 2.5 percent of what they took with them. But they can't quit 'cause the dollar amount is too small. So all I ask is for you to understand that winning $10 with $400 is the exact percentage of winning $100 with $4000. There is absolutely no difference, except in the dollar amount. So even go down to 2 percent and take $80 a day.

That's a decent payday, five days a week, with a percentage that's way lower than the 2.5 percent that they already admitted was very easy to reach.

It comes down to having the money, setting that goal, and accepting a logical return. The more you take, the more you'll win from a dollar amount and the less percentage win goal you'll have to set.

But hear me, oh ye of little faith: you absolutely, positively gotta set that win goal and make it your primary function for the day.

The more you bring, the less percentage you go for. Or have I said that before?

127

Reviewing the Loss Limits

Here's where I lose most of you. For some stupid, unexplained reasoning, the majority of people at a table have a loss limit of zero.

That means that when they reach zippo status, they figure it's time to go. That's another pitiful example of the height of ignorance.

I ask people what their loss limit at a table would be if they bought in with $200. They answer: "When I lose the $200."

Then they laugh! Can you imagine? They stand there and laugh as if this were the universal acceptance figure. The sad truth is that it is!

Most people play 'til they lose it all. What a devastating feeling to leave a table with absolutely nothing to start another session with.

And to compound this crime, take a look at I.M. Madork when he happens to be playing at a crap table and observe his action as he winds down a session.

I.M. Madork bought in for $200 and caught an unusually cold table that ate up most of his money. In fact he's down to $17 as the only thing standing between him and total wipeout.

He pops $5 on the Pass Line and when 9 becomes the point,

he takes $6 odds. He doesn't have enough to place on the 6 and 8 which he has been doing all along, but do you think he'll put that other $6 in his pocket? No way, José.

He's gotta play to his last chip: "Gimme a dollar each Hard Way and a dollar Yo," he yells. He still has a buck left and it's burning a hole in his hand. Since I. M. Madork doesn't believe in tipping, he is sweating as he struggles to find a way to spend that chip.

Too late, the dice screeches to a halt and up pops the 7. "Out 7, line away" shouts the dealer and down come all of I. M. Madork's bets. He winces, curses and screams out: "Darn it, I was just gonna play the Big Red!" He flings the chip on the floor and walks away broke.

His loss limit is the last chip in his rack, and he's not alone in that childish thinking.

If he had cut his losses, he'd have at least left the table with some money, instead of a washed out, wiped out frustrating empty feeling—and empty wallet. Well, at least they match his empty head.

I want you to set a loss limit at every session. In craps that loss limit is 50 percent. It doesn't mean you have to bet to exactly that loss limit, but it does mean you cannot lose a dollar more than 50 percent of what you started with.

If you had a $450 bankroll and broke it into three sessions of $150 each, then the most you can lose per session is $75. The other $75 is put in your pocket not to be touched again that day. The absolute worse you can do that day is lose $225.

The other $225 you bring home with you, and no, you may *not* use any of that money that's left to start another session. You bring it home.

You'll come up with your own thoughts and percentages on this, but please don't make it more than 50 percent per table. If you can't win with 50 percent of your stake, there's nothing written in stone that the other half will bail out your day.

Take what's left and run. Believe me, this is so important. You just gotta realize how imperative it is for you to set and follow these loss limit rules.

Set win goals.

Set loss limits.

If you do just five things I ask you to do, put these two at the top of your list.

128

Guarantee and Excess

Before I explain to you the reasoning behind Guarantee and Excess, let's go over the fact that you don't have to use this method at all.

Let's look at the three things that you could do as soon as your win goal is reached.

(1) Stay there and give it all back.

(2) Leave the table with the whole profit.

(3) Employ the Guarantee and Excess theory.

Most of you are familiar with number one because that's how most of you play. Don't even dream of using number one.

Number two is naturally acceptable and I ain't gonna find fault with anyone who grabs a profit and runs. That's what gambling is supposed to be all about.

Many people tell me they are now in the habit of leaving the table as soon as they reach a predetermined win goal of 10 percent or 20 percent or whatever.

I love to hear that, and will definitely not try to change that thinking. If that's your style—great!

But if there is a method that I'd like you to look at, number three is that third option.

By immediately rat-holing your session money, you now destroy all possibilities of turning that table into a losing proposition.

Then comes the important part of splitting that win goal in half and stuffing half of it away. You're guaranteed to end up with at least 50 percent profit of the session win goal.

By playing with the other half, called the Excess, you get to stay at a table that is obviously going in your favor.

Now you can stay at that table until you lose a percentage of that Excess, approximately 60 percent, still cognizant of the fact that you already have a guaranteed profit salted away. The Excess gives you a chance to stay with that hot table and take further advantage of the trend.

I like this system and use it all the time. The next chapter gives you some variations, so wait until you finish it before making your decision.

129

Handling the Excess

As soon as you swing into your Excess betting, I want you to adopt a conservative move as soon as a series is completed.

Suppose you complete a series that had you bang out several numbers in a row and show a profit of $56. Immediately break that $56 in half. Half goes with the Guarantee and half stays with the Excess. This is done as soon as a loss occurs, ending the series.

By immediately splitting that profit in half, you increase your Guarantee and increase the amount of your Excess, giving you more money to work with.

Continue splitting every subsequent winning series. Your Guarantee keeps increasing and so does your Excess.

You can stay there as long as that Excess is alive, but continue with your splitting. The chapters on plateaus will allow you to increase your future bets. That's coming up pretty soon.

Even though you learned how to handle your winning series, don't go forgetting that you may swing into a losing streak, so you gotta be prepared for that to happen.

It's not necessary to lose the entire Excess amount back, even though your Guarantee will give you a profit.

Set an amount of losing shooters in a row that you will allow, and then run. Or at least set a loss limit on your Excess and when you reach that loss limit, put the balance of chips with your Guarantee and head for greener pastures.

I hope you'll give this approach a good long look. I've had times that my Excess was a quick three losses in a row, so I just grabbed the balance, put it with my guarantee and ran.

And then there were the days when the Excess plodded along for awhile and then exploded for a good hot run.

The fact that you split all subsequent winning series keeps you constantly re-enforcing your eventual profits. But if you are still intent on reaching your win goal and running, beautiful, I won't try to change you.

The important thing is that you have a win goal and know exactly what you're gonna do when it is reached.

In all honesty, I like this method and use it constantly.

130

Plateaus

We're winding down the Money Management section but even though it's coming to an end, I want you to zero in on the power of this approach. It is called plateaus.

Let's go over exactly what the purpose is: plateaus are a point in your money management approach whereby once you reach the fantastic accomplishment of hitting your win goal, you have the opportunity of increasing your bets in designated amounts as you continue to win. Each of these stages are called plateaus.

My friend Shea Agen doesn't understand English too well, (or Green or Italian or German or jive), so he wants me to say it again, in a tongue he grasps—so here we go:

When you set a win goal and reach it, you now can increase your wagers, safe in the knowledge that you have a guaranteed win set aside, and you continue to increase your bets as you continue to win.

Shea Agen doesn't need me to say it again. He's grinning so I think he gets the message. I hope you do too.

To bring you up to date, let's say you bought into a session and set a win goal of 20 percent. When that win goal was reached, you broke the profit in half, putting the Guarantee in your pocket and setting the excess on the table, in order to go for bigger scores.

The guarantee in your pocket is proof positive that the session will now depend on how long you can sustain the winning streak.

This is the part that guys like Imus Pressit at least get a chance to increase their bets. Even though they reached their goal by betting conservatively, they still wanna let it all hang out. OK, I'm gonna let you.

The next chapter shows you how to handle those increases. This chapter just wants to get the message across to you that there are times when you can go for the shot.

Shea Agen should now read again the purpose of this move. Then go on and see how to set up your plateaus.

131

Setting the Plateaus

Now we'll go over how to set your plateaus and as you continue to climb the profit ladder, you continue to alter your bets.

It doesn't matter what method you use cause the theory is always the same. Let's say you were playing the $44 Inside method, whereby you bypassed the Come-Out, placed $44 Inside, regressed to $22 Inside after one hit and then came off after the second hit.

Eventually you hit your win goal and go through the process of splitting that profit into Guarantee and Excess. Here's where the Plateaus take over.

At that point you set up goals or plateaus that you want to reach. We'll say your next plateau is $50 and now you also want to increase your bets.

Instead of coming off after that second hit at $22 Inside, you can remain up for one or two additional scores. When that second hit comes, just drop $5 on the table to add to the $7 payoff on one of those inside numbers.

You press the 6 and 8 to $12 each. Take one more hit on either of those four inside numbers and then come off.

When you reach the plateau you set, you again make a change and this time it is in the amount of your starting series.

Instead of starting with $44 Inside, you begin with $66 Inside. After the first hit, regress to $22 Inside and then get into

320

the process of pressing the 6 and 8 if you get another hit.

Since you are now increasing the size of your bets, the $50 plateaus will be easier to reach, so you again stretch the amount of the next plateau to $100.

As long as you stayed hot, the changes in your series went from two hits to four and your starting series from $44 Inside to $66 Inside.

If you continue to win, then your starting series will be upgraded to begin at $88 Inside. After the first hit, regress to $44 Inside, next hit same bet, next hit $22 Inside and after the fourth hit—all off.

Notice I've restricted your hits to four but have allowed the starting series to escalate as you continued to win.

I use $150 as my next plateau, and look to start my series off at $110 Inside ($25 5 and 9, $30 6 and 8).

Before we start analyzing the variations of moves that are available, just get to understand the purpose of plateaus and how to handle them intelligently.

I always stop with four hits and as I climb higher and higher in my starting series, I'll come back down to three hits.

I *hate*, absolutely *detest,* leaving money on that table for the 7 to gobble up. So I wanna get down as quick as possible.

There are three word sentences that I can rattle off in my head.

(a) I hate losing!

(b) I love Racquel!

(c) Take me down!

—and they all have merit.

You can set your own advanced standards as you move through the plateaus, but try not to get too cocky. Four hits is plenty and you can use different spinoffs from your opening series bet, and even a double regression move wouldn't be all that bad.

I think you have the theory down pat, so next we'll straighten out the loose ends and give you a couple of restrictions so as not to have you playing like a boob in a boat who just dropped both oars.

132

Handling the Plateaus

It's one thing to reach the pinnacle of our dreams, it's another to know how to handle them once we get there.

Since the plateaus are handled after we reach our win goal, you can see that it comes after we have accomplished our primary objective: the win goal!

Now we gotta be smart to handle this next step in our play and don't make a fool of ourselves. Knowing how to act when we finally reach Utopia is something a lot of us lack.

I.M. Madork gets a date with a girl he's been chasing for six years, Lotta Chesterfield. Lotta has a lotta, well, anyway Lotta was well worth the chase.

But I.M. Madork shows up an hour late for his date, runs over a skunk on the way to the restaurant, sticks his elbow in his soup, forgets his wallet, and overall, makes enough mistakes in one night to cause Lotta to put an end to any advanced engagements.

So let's lay out some ground rules so you don't make mistakes when you finally accomplish your goal of getting to the plateaus.

  (a) At every plateau, be sure and split the winnings between the Guarantee and Excess.
      (1) You gotta keep putting money aside as you reach the subsequent plateaus.
  (b) Keep the plateaus at an intelligent level, starting low and

then increasing as you continue to win. Start with $50 plateau goals.

(c) If you lose a predetermined specific amount, even in the plateaus, don't be afraid to wrap up that session and walk.

Believe me, using the plateau approach will give you the chance of getting good scores, but be sure you set your guidelines ahead of time. Some advice:

(a) First plateau should be no higher than $100 level.

(b) Second plateau could be $150 higher than the first, then each subsequent plateau set at $200 intervals.

(c) Restrict the number of hits you look for to a logical amount, so as not to get whacked by that 7 (four is safe).

(d) Use the plateaus to increase the amount of your series, as long as the series increases you set don't get out of hand.

Most players walk up to a table as soon as they roll into a casino and get right into playing heavy.

I ask you to build up a stockpile of chips before getting aggressive. So what's so wrong with that request?

If you play conservative you'll still be winning, even if the returns are not gigantic in the beginning. The main thing is that an early losing streak won't put you in a defensive position, praying for a couple of scores.

The plateaus should be used by both aggressive players and conservative players when the win goal is reached and not before.

This is a strong way to play. If you give plateaus a good look from a logical approach, you'll see a lot of opportunities to go for the kill.

But keep pulling back profits as each plateau is reached and using the next plateau to upgrade your starting series.

Two losses in a row at two successive plateau levels mean it's time to wrap it up for that day.

There's always tomorrow and besides, you already hit your win goal.

Plateaus—a big, big, strong point in your play.

133

Imus Pressit

My friend Imus Pressit really get around. You'll see him at many craps tables in every casino in the world. He usually goes under an alias as he feels people will copy his style of play and want to elect him governor for his being so smart.

The lousy thing about Imus Pressit is that he usually loses. I've discussed his aggressive style of play and while he admittedly has a terrific knowledge of the game and he always has plenty of money, the bottom line is he ends up giving back all his profits.

One particular day I stood at the table with him and observed his style of play. The first four shooters had good runs, whereby they made three point numbers, plus about eight to nine inside numbers, which Imus was playing.

I asked him how much he was ahead and he said: "I'm out about $200 but the table's cold."

I told him "Are you crazy, if the dice get much hotter, you'll burn your fingers. How can you be behind?"

He wasn't only behind, he was a behind and the next shooter solidified that fact.

A lady picked up the dice and Imus popped a quarter on the Pass Line. She banged a 7 and Imus left the fifty ride. Again she banged a 7 and again he let the $100 ride.

You could see the smile of contentment cross his face as the dice again flew out and up popped 11. The dealer slid a black chip to Imus and he popped it on top of the other one, letting the $200 ride.

The lady established a 10 as the point and Imus took $400 double odds, place the 5 and 9 for $100 each and the 6 and 8 for $120 each. Then he put $50 on the hard 10 and winked at me: "My man, here's where the casino goes belly-up."

Before the words were out of his mouth, the shooter popped two fives on the table and the dealer sung the song that's music to every Right bettor.

"Winnah, Winnah on the front line! Come hard. Pay the Do's and take the Don'ts."

This surely was Imus Pressit's day. The dealer paid him $1000 for his Pass Line bet with odds and $350 for his hard 10.

Imus grabbed the money and in the same breath said, "You see my man, everything comes to he who bets big."

At that he popped $1000 on the Pass Line and the shooter re-established the 10 as the point. Imus reached into his pocket, pulled out the remainder of his bankroll and took $2000 odds.

Then he turned to me with his saintly words of wisdom, "You see, my man, you gotta know when to press up your bet. I can tell that this shooter will throw for a long time. It's all in knowing the game."

I tried a little reasoning with him, "Don't you think you ought to pull back just a little profit?", I pleaded. He gave me an all-knowing wink.

"Tut, tut, my man, this is my day." He had that stupid grin on his face that reminds me of a dumb dog ready to pounce on a black and white cat, only the cat was a skunk.

In the dog's case it was dark and hard to see. In Imus Pressit's case he didn't *want* to see!!

Well, even if he couldn't see the dice on the far side of the table, he sure as heck could hear the dealer's shrill cry: "Out 7, line away, take the Do's and pay the Don'ts."

Imus Pressit was shot down again. Why does he press his bets? Why won't he pull back a profit? Why won't he come down after a few hits? Why must he think every shooter is a possible key to the greatest roll of all time? Why does he and 90 percent of all the dorks that go to a craps table leave more money on the felt than they've pulled in as a profit?

There are answers to all these questions and the same retort could be given to all of them:

Because they're dorks!!

Imus Pressit cannot help himself, still chasing his dream. So are you, if you refuse to say these three little words: "Take me down."

This story, or at least one like it, is repeated in this book for one reason. It is of such great importance. It is the reason Imus Pressit loses, and why you lose.

Memorize these words and use them.

Poor Imus! As soon as he lost, he turned and looked at me with the face of a guy who had $5000 handed to him and stuck the money in his pocket, walked three blocks and found out he had a hole in his pants pocket.

The hurt, the frustration, the bewilderment, the anger, and the despair of that loss has no explanation and no remedy. It's just a stupid move.

Imus Pressit! (Does he really have to?)

134

Aggressive Place Moves

You know doggone well I don't bet the Pass Line unless I throw the dice or else the table is absolutely scorching on the Pass Line bets.

But I do use the Place bets and I handle them like my good friend X. Bert Peeanno masters the keyboard.

X. Bert Peeanno wouldn't bet you Dolly Parton couldn't pass for a boy, cause he's not an expert in things like stacking cards or growing watermelons or anything other than the piano.

But boy can he play the piano, so he stays with it, and boy can I play craps. So I stay with that. You don't see me trying to play a piano.

I wanna clue you in on being a maestro at playing those place numbers. You all know I pull down after two hits, with three my maximum per shooter.

But there are times when I climb right up to my win goal, break it into Guarantees and Excess and lay out my plateaus.

You gotta have a game plan and so I'll simulate a roll, based strictly on the shooter popping off a scorching roll.

Naturally there are examples back in the other chapters but we'll just rehash a roll now and I want you to make decisions on how you will increase, decrease or stay with your bets.

We start off with $18 6, $18 8, $15 5 and $15 9. It's called $66 Inside.

You need $660 per session and $1980 bankroll. Notice that this example is for the higher-heeled player and is not designed for a "take me down" after two or three scores.

Shooter establishes 8 as his point and since you were not betting the Pass Line, you now take $66 Inside.

You may not like the first move cause it's a regression but that's the key move in your series. You should drop to $22 Inside, leaving yourself in Fat City, cause now a 7 causes you only a buck loss.

But let's say you regress to $44 Inside after that first hit. Your loss potential is now only $23.

Shooter pops a 6 and you get paid $14. Since you have already regressed your bet, there are a few options.

(1) Same bet.

(2) Press the 6.

(3) Press 6 and 8.

You make your choice, but I suggest (1) Same bet. Shooter rolls again and pops a 5. You're paid $14 and now you press both the 6 and 8 and pull back $2.

Next number is a 6 and you're paid $21. Increase all bets by one unit. You now have:

(a) $15 5

(b) $24 6

(c) $24 8

(d) $15 9

Shooter pops his point 8 and you are paid $28. This time say same bet: take $28 payoff.

Place bets are off on Come-Out and shooter establishes 9 as his point.

You have option of keeping the bets the same or regressing to $44 Inside.

I'd keep them the same, due to the fact that your regression move and same bet play has already wrapped up a profit for this series and even a loss would have you holding a profit.

Shooter is scorching and bangs a 5. You have a ton of options, but my suggestion is to press the 5 and 9 for one unit each and pull back $11. (Up-and-Pull).

Again a 6 is thrown and you are paid $28. A couple of options:

(a) Same bet.

(b) Press 6 and 8 one unit each.

(c) Press all four numbers.

(d) Regress to $44 Inside.

My suggestion is (b), press 6 and 8 one unit each and rat-hole $16. You make your decision.

Again the shooter pops an 8 and you have $30 on both the 6 and 8, so you got $35 coming. Again a ton of options are open, but here is where I toss a big bucket of ice water on your dreams.

Once you reached the $30 level with any of your bets, which was two units higher than the starting bets of $66 Inside, the light goes on for a definite regress.

Take the $35 profit and regress back down to $66 Inside. At this point you have your original starting bet of $66 tucked away plus a healthy profit.

Now every subsequent winning score is used to increase two numbers at a time, with the numbers coupled as 6 and 8 being both increased by one unit on the next hit. Then the 5 and 9 gets increased together on the following hit.

This is done regardless of what place number scores. When the point is made, leave place bets at same amount for the duration of that point roll. If the shooter makes that particular point, then when next point is established, regress your place bets to $88 Inside.

Every subsequent winning point calls for an alternate move of leaving your Place bets intact and then the next point calling for one unit increases.

Please and I mean *please* go back over the past two paragraphs to zero in on the correct plays for these extended hot rolls.

You absolutely must guard against having the 7 show, with you having a ton of money on the table.

This method I showed you has locked in Up-and-Pull moves,

regressions and aggressive but controlled bets, all put together.

Place betting and the availability of manipulating your wagers is right there for the Place bettor. Why the deuce don't you take advantage of it, instead of banging up your bets in such a way that you never take back a profit.

Then the 7 ends your world of dreams. You deserve to get whacked.

X. Bert Peeanno is banging away on his piano, wrapped in his own world and making a ton of money, concentrating on what he does best... playing the piano.

You wanna play the piano? Listen to X. Bert Peeanno and learn. You wanna play craps? Listen to me and learn.

You wanna bet me Dolly can pose as a boy and get away with it? I'll take all the action you want.

No wonder you lose at craps. You don't know how to stack your chips, and you don't know a stacked chick from a.... but that's another story.

135

Take Me Down

There's a song that goes "take me back to old Virginia." Well, I ain't aiming to take you anywhere but to the cashiers window in the casino, in hopes that you'll be cashing in some winnings.

The three words that you should write on your sleeve, paste to your eye-balls and repeat two-thousand times on the way to the casino "take me down."

It is a request that you make to the dealer to get him to remove your Place bets. A simple little statement that requires about two seconds to say. Two seconds that will guarantee that for that particular shooter, you have eliminated any chance of losing any of your bets.

The statement is made after you have made two or three scores with your Place bets and now want to wrap up that series with a guaranteed profit. Yet only a handful of players has the guts or intelligence to say "take me down."

The biggest argument is gonna come from people like Imus Pressit who still believe that every single shooter at the table is gonna hold the dice for three hours.

They feel if they take their bets down, they'll miss out on a few good rolls that will pop up. I can see their point and heartily agree that I am asking you to sacrifice those possible rolls.

But if you won't adhere to my theory of grabbing two hits per shooter and coming down, at least take a look at some options:

(a) Take two hits until you reach your win goal.

(b) Take three hits until you reach your win goal.

(c) At least wrap up a profit per shooter, before leaving your bets working.

(d) Have enough of a bankroll to allow your series to be high enough where you can incorporate regressions that give you a profit and still allow some bets to remain.

Read (d) over again because that may be your answer. Of course the key to that option would be that if you leave your bets working, after picking up two hits, the amount of your profit is not blown when a 7 wipes out your remaining Place bets.

Man, you better read that last sentence over. It has to do with getting a profit on a certain shooter and still leaving some bets up there but in an amount that will allow a profit when the 7 shows.

Every day, in every casino, there are crap rolls where a shooter bangs out 6, 7, 8, 9 numbers and one stinking rotten 7 wipes out all the gains.

And the reason is because the money is still on the table. You gotta pull back, you can't just sit there, waiting to be whacked!

Which brings us right back to square one. What should you do?

Come down, my friend, come down! If you got the guts.

The next section goes deep into discipline, but it's all gonna revert back to the message in this chapter: "Take me down."

136

You and Money Management

A true story! Couple of days ago I was playing at the Claridge in Atlantic City and a sharp looking dude came up to me. A little cocky perhaps but very well spoken and he obviously wanted to get across the fact that he was an expert at money management.

He told me he liked my theories but that he had his own money management method and it worked for him 'cause he had been using it for years.

I was interested 'cause maybe this guy had really come up with something that was usable. I asked him what his system was.

"I take $1000 to the casino, walk up to a table and play until that $1000 is gone. If I win $3000, I quit. When I lose $1000 I quit. That's my system."

I stood there waiting for more, hoping there was more.

Finally I asked, "Where's the money management?"

His words of wisdom were: "It's in the fact that I don't lose more than $1000 'cause when that's gone, I don't have any more money. I don't take credit or markers. I just lose everything I started with and don't have to worry about losing more."

I was hoping some guy would come and shoot me or else a

train would wander by and run me over. I was wondering how to get away from this dork gracefully.

I finally left him, but his words still hung on. This poor guy figured money management was not losing more than you brought. But he honestly felt that he had discovered another wheel.

I don't know what your definition of money management is. I hope it isn't the stupid analogy that this guy followed.

Don't you dare play down to that last dollar. Do you honestly think that if you brought $500 to the casino and you lost $495, that that last $5 chip would bring you back?

If you believe that, you'll also believe that you could leap off the Empire State Building and sprout wings around the forty-fourth floor.

In fact you gonna better chance of sprouting those wings than you do of re-couping your stake with a lousy $5. Yet people play that way every day, and continue to lose.

The way you handle your bankroll is your own business and the way you bet is also your own affair. But I'll tell you what money management is and you can decide yourself if you wanna swallow it:

Money management is the art of knowing what to bet when you win and what to bet when you lose.

That's it in a nutshell. You can flip back through these pages and pick up the theory or you can flounder through the casinos with illogical fantasies of making big killings at the sacrifice of your entire bankroll.

137

Wrapping up Money
Management

Finally we bid adieu to the section on money management, leaving most of you bothered, disenchanted, wary, skeptical, agreeable, or enlightened.

Maybe you learned something about gambling. I hope you did. My theory is very conservative but it works. We'll tie the whole package together and then you can review the chapters that you still haven't perfected.

(1) Set aside your bankroll.

(2) Divide bankroll into sessions.

(3) Predetermine whether you'll bet Right or Wrong.

(4) Predetermine your system.

(5) Chart the tables.

(6) Chart the tables again!

(7) Be perfect in the knowledge of the system you'll play.

(8) Predetermine your series.

(9) Set win goals.

(10) Set loss limits.

(11) When loss limit is reached, leave the table.

(12) When win goal is reached: divide into Guarantee and Excess.

(13) Put guarantee in pocket and play with excess.

(14) Set plateaus.

(15) Readjust series.

(16) Continue breaking subsequent winning series in half.

(17) Stay at that table as long as excess stays alive.

(18) Leave the table when the excess starts to dwindle.

(19) You don't have to give back all of the excess.

(20) When session is completed, decide if you want another session.

(21) If win goal for that day is reached, based on your starting bankroll, no more sessions are needed.

(22) Wrap up that day's play if win goal reached in prior session.

Will you do it? Will you adhere to this restricting, although powerful approach to gambling? I doubt it! I really doubt that the majority of people will realize what is needed to win consistently. You went to all the trouble of buying and reading this book for a purpose: to learn *how to win!!* Well I've just given you the paths to take. It's up to you to decide if you really do *want to win!!* Next we go into discipline. There we'll separate the men from the boys.

Discipline

138

Now we come to the section that wraps up all the knowledge, all the systems, all the money management, and lays the cards on the table with the burning question: "Have you got the guts to use discipline?"

Naturally a boob like D. C. Plinn nods his head and screams to the world that he surely does not have Discipline and what right do I have to question his control.

D. C. Plinn claims that he only brings an amount of money that he "can afford to lose." He stubbornly insists that the money he brings to battle won't affect is lifestyle and that it won't bother him to lose it.

Naturally my first question to this ding-dong is, "Are you independently rich that you can afford to lose money without it bothering you?"

He almost snaps his neck nodding his agreement that he goes with the intent of doubling his money and that he sets a certain time period for him to gamble, like three hours per trip.

He claims he starts with $300 at a table and sets two hours as his "discipline" time period. He then quits when the two hours are up.

337

I ask him: "Suppose you lost eight of the first nine rolls and were down $165. Would you still play even though your time wasn't up and you were getting whacked?"

"Well, er, gee, I dunno, maybe I'd think about, er, I never thought about that."

So I asked him another question: "Suppose your two hours were up and you were at a scorching hot table, ahead $3,740 and shooter after shooter was banging out numbers. Would you leave that scorching table?"

"Well, gosh, gee, golly, er, maybe I'd, well I dunno."

You see what a dope D. C. Plinn is? He doesn't have discipline 'cause he doesn't even know what it is.

But I'll tell you what it ain't.

(1) It ain't playing with a clock.

(2) It ain't taking money to the casino and playing 'til it's all gone.

(3) And it sure ain't playing for amounts that don't have a logical or realistic percentage.

Discipline is an art. It is the ability to quit when you lose a certain part of your bankroll and the ability to rat hole a small percentage profit when you get ahead and not give the money back to the house.

Discipline! It's the key to winning, yet only a handful of players have it.

139

A Percentage Return

Man, are you gonna hate this chapter. In fact 90 percent of you won't even finish it.

You'll scream, curse, laugh, disapprove, mock and disagree with the true percentage of what you should shoot for at the tables.

A tremendously fantastic super colossal return of 10 percent.

Go ahead—laugh, get it outta your system. Throw the book against the wall, call me a dope, count to ten very slowly.

Then when you've got your composure back, continue. We've probably lost a large majority of readers, but that's the way the tick tocks.

And to break your chops a little more, for you people who haven't slammed the book closed, let me tell you that the amount I gave you was a little high and that I hope you can cut it back a little.

(A short pause for the people who were on the fence about accepting a 10 percent return. Let them finish their ranting and raving.)

Okay, let's analyze my so-called restriction on your fun!

We're playing a game (craps) whereby the house always has a slight edge on us, regardless of what system we play.

For the sake of making my point, let's go a step further and say we're playing at a game where we have no better than a

50–50 chance of winning.

You all gotta agree with that, so let's put our shot at a 50–50 chance of winning or losing.

Then how the deuce can you expect or even think that you should play until you double or triple your stake? It's illogical. It's like asking a pint container to hold a quart of milk. It can't!

It's like asking one of Twiggy's bras to hold Dolly's... but that's another story.

If you really get down to a real honest assumption of your chances of winning, you oughta be happy to break even—'cause you're going in with only a 50–50 chance.

And the way most of you play, with a gigantic lack of knowledge, it's like going on an elephant hunt with a water pistol.

Most of you leave your knowledge at home and those same people would probably forget to load the water pistol, but there again that's another story 'cause I don't wanna get into knowledge of the game again.

Just stop and think about what I'm asking you to do: Accept a 10 percent return, from a game that offers you about a 50–50 chance of winning.

What you are looking for is a trend, or streak so that your money management moves can help you take advantage of that run, show a profit, and quit a winner.

The same people who disagree with me about trends being dominant in a casino are now nodding in unison. Do you think a light is starting to get into their closed thinking?

My friend Lee Till Moore has taken a look at the 10 percent and asked if I could raise it a little more.

He agrees wholeheartedly with accepting a small profit, but he is operating with such a small bankroll that 10 percent of the $100 that he brings to battle is hardly worth the effort of going.

Lee Till Moore is right. Most people don't have the proper bankroll and play short, which leads to playing scared, which leads to playing stupid.

I told Lee Till Moore to go back to the story where I showed him that 10 percent of $10,000 would be a nice payday and he agreed.

I also told him that if he liked 10% of $10,000, why does he balk at 10 percent of $100—it's the same percentage.

Again he agrees but is quick to point out that he doesn't have $10,000 and can only scrape together $100 to gamble.

He is right, because most of you fall into the category of lacking bankroll, so you think it's OK to change the rules to coincide with your short amount of money.

So I have to go all the way back to the beginning of the book and remind you that you need four things to have a 50–50 chance of winning:

(1) Bankroll.
(2) Knowledge of the game.
(3) Money management.
(4) Discipline.

You gotta have all four and the lack of number (1) doesn't give you the right to infringe on the necessity of number (4).

Lee Till Moore is crushed. He wants to play, he wants to win, but he doesn't wanna do the things that will help him win.

10 percent is the true percentage return, but I realize there are circumstances that prevent people from getting the proper Bankroll, so the next chapter reluctantly offers an offshoot.

140

Discipline on Winning Days

Hey, there are days when you're gonna get a hot streak and bring home a beautiful return.

My intent is to make your winning days happen more often. The way to do that is to curb your play on the days you get off to a quick hot streak and within a few hours have a healthy profit.

You look at your watch, figure you've got another three hours to kill and decide to take a shot.

Up go your bets, down go your profits, up goes your blood pressure, down goes your level of intelligence.

You give back all the profits 'cause you didn't set any disciplined stop gaps to offset your chances of blowing everything back to the casino.

And now we gotta hear from Noah Little, who knows very little about a lot of things, mostly gambling. Noah knows little or nothing about systems, money management, odds or anything pertaining to the things you need to have a chance to win.

All Noah knows is that you pick up the dice and hope to hold them for three hours. He goes to the casino every two months, plays craps the entire time the tables are open and usually leaves his $3000 bankroll behind.

Sometimes he gets ahead, but never knows enough to quit. The casinos are jammed with people like Noah Little. They never know when to quit.

Gene E. Yuss is a rocket scientist who can throw a hair from his head in the air in the middle of a wind-blown field, and by calculating all of the wind currents, sun rays, moon beams, and cauliflowers, tell you exactly where that hair will land.

Gene E. Yuss is a genius in his field but like a fish out of water in the casino. He can spell discipline backwards, forward, sideways, and in fourteen different languages.

But he can't practice it at a table. He has been ahead on seventeen straight trips to the casino. He has lost seventeen straight trips, 'cause he never had the discipline to quit.

In fact his discipline is so bad he is now completely bald because he showed that trick with his hair too many times. (Be sure you ain't standing close to him when he goes into his spiel.)

The first thing to realize about discipline is there will be days when you get ahead and even if you have six more hours to go before heading home, you gotta stick your starting bankroll in your pocket, plus a profit.

Maybe that profit is only 10 percent or 20 percent or maybe even 5 percent. But it's a profit just the same.

Next time you get ahead the win goal you set, be sure you don't give it back.

Sure it's gonna be hard to quit—real hard. But it's a start. By the time you get home, that profit will look a whole lot better.

Psychologically you'll look forward to your next trip to the tables with a better outlook.

When you lose, it's almost as if you dread the next trip, afraid that you'll again get whacked. But even if your prior trip resulted in just a small profit, you're more apt to look forward to another winning day, rather than a long dreary frustrating ride home after getting whacked.

First thing I want you to do on days you get ahead is sock away a profit along with your starting bankroll.

Play with the excess and keep dividing subsequent winning series in half. You'll be increasing your guarantee, at the same time you are increasing the excess that you're working with.

When the excess is in remission, grab what's left, add it to your guarantee and head home a winner.

Don't be a ding-dong by getting ahead and blowing it back. Learn how to handle your winning days.

Learn how to win.

141

Discipline on Losing Days.

Just as you practice discipline on winning days, by leaving with a profit, you also gotta know how to handle the days when things are going bad.

The biggest drawback for most players is the reluctance to set a loss limit. I've written chapters about the importance of this move, so if you don't understand it, go back and re-read them.

Penny Down is a good craps player but a lousy handler of money. When Penny Down is on a hot roll, she knows how to incorporate the Up-and-Pull and reap in the profits.

On the other hand, when things are going bad, Penny Down bets down to her last penny. She'll turn her pocketbook inside out looking for enough change to make one more bet, then run through eight toll plazas on the way home 'cause she doesn't even have change for the tolls. Handling your money on losing days is just as important as knowing how to manage money on winning days.

It takes guts to quit when you're in a bad run but forcing the bets ain't gonna make things change. You gotta accept the fact that there will be days when things are going against you.

You're not gonna believe this next paragraph but it's true.

When I run up against cold tables and losing days, and it does happen, I pull back and don't even make a bet. That means I drive two and a half hours to a casino, chart the tables, find nothing going my way, then drive two and a half hours back home—without making a bet.

This is not an isolated instance and I don't tell the story to fill space. There are many days when I don't risk one single nickel at the tables.

Those days are usually in the middle of dry runs and admittedly it's because I wanna cut my losses and play only when trends are tilted sharply in my favor.

I realize you won't do this and that's your choice. But at least give it some thought, at least pull back to where you reduce your playing time on days when things are going bad.

That's Discipline... and you gotta practice it on those sure to happen cold days.

142

Understanding Discipline

Don't go telling me that you've read five or six chapters and have now become an expert on the subject.

It'll take you hundreds of trips to the tables to find out if you really got the guts to be able to walk when things are going bad. I want you to realize the different facets of discipline.

(1) It takes discipline to avoid the casinos until you have the proper bankroll.

(2) It takes discipline to chart the tables until you find one going the way you predetermined to bet.

(3) It takes super discipline to pre-set a strong money management method and stick to it.

(4) It takes discipline to hold your bets down when you're dying to go for the juglar.

(5) It takes discipline to walk around the casino without making any bets on the days that either your win goal or loss limit has not been reached.

(6) It takes discipline not to make a pass at the good looking dealers while you're playing.

   (a) It also takes brains, cause your wife has probably got you pegged and keeps a wary eye on you.

All of the above takes discipline and you'll be tested time and time again. Just because you master a few of the restrictions doesn't mean you've conquered the art of complete control.

Discipline is hard to understand, hard to put into practice and harder to maintain.

The key is in realizing how important it is to your chances of winning. If you could but understand that trends don't last forever, you'd realize that quitting before you kick back all your profits takes a real strong person.

The other players will give you looks when you pull your bets down after two hits. They don't understand discipline.

The dealers will comment that you're giving them extra work. They don't understand discipline.

Your friends will call you chicken for quitting with only a 10 percent or 20 percent profit. They have a lot of time to watch you play 'cause they're usually wiped out after an hour or so of dumb play. They don't understand discipline.

To repeat: discipline is hard to acquire, doubly hard to maintain. But it'll help you become a winner. You can understand that word.

143

The Last Chip

You've heard of the "Last Supper", the "Last Straw", the "Last of the Mohicans", the "Last Hurrah", the "Last Tango", and the "Last Guy Standing Picks up the Check."

All of these "Lasts" represent kind of a final ending to something, and none of them really turn out good.

Add to that list the dork who bets down to the last chip. Does he really think that bet is gonna recoup all his prior losses?

You bet your ding-dong that's exactly what he's thinking. How the deuce can he believe that a rotten lousy $5 chip will all of a sudden ignite a seventy-four hand winning streak and put him in Fat City?

But that famous craps player Stu Pidd jumps up and proclaims, "the race to victory starts with the first step." Then he sits down right on his hat.

I try to explain to him that he is not in a race, and even if it was a race, you don't start out seventy-four lengths behind.

Stu Pidd jumps up and again spits out his words of wisdom: "Nothing ventured, nothing gained." Then he sits down and attempts to avoid sitting on his hat. He misses his chair and lands on the floor.

I try to tell Stu Pidd that nothing is gained by throwing money down the drain, bucking a cold trend. I ask him what is wrong with taking money home with him, instead of betting 'til he's broke.

Again Stu Pidd jumps up and crows: "I ain't used to bringing money home, I always lose everything I bring." Then he breaks into a hearty laugh, and again opens his mouth to probably give us some more words of wisdom.

But just as he is about to give us his thoughts, he accidentally spits out his false teeth. In his attempt to bend over and pick them up, he loses his balance, steps on his teeth and crushes them. He is unable to speak.

I'm crushed cause now I can no longer listen to his reasons for betting down to his last chip.

If you agree with any of his ideas, I think you better have the fuel gauge in your brain fluid checked. Betting down to the last chip or even the last handful of chips is not a smart move. In fact, it's a stupid move.

Speaking of stupid, I see Stu Pidd reaching for a pen and pencil so before we're subjected to more nonsense, let me wrap up this chapter.

Use my all important loss limit approach, and don't bet down to that last chip. Never, never, never, ever, never, ever, never.

144

The Author and Discipline

Maybe some of you are thinking: If this guy is so smart, why ain't he rich? The answer of course is that you don't get rich in gambling, but you can make a decent living if you have all parts of the Big Four.

But go back to that question again about being so smart. That part I gotta take exception to. I am smart when it comes to gambling. In fact I'm a genius.

But I didn't get borned a genius. I got born a dork and I gambled like one for years and years and years and years... and, well, you get the point.

The rotten part is that it took me so long to realize that I was so stupid. I always thought that with all my knowledge about the game, that it was only a matter of time before I became rich.

How wrong can you be! Well I was 100 percent wrong. On the days when things were going wrong, I compounded the losses by betting higher and higher, figuring things were due to change.

I'd bet down to my last chip, then go around checking the trays of all the slot machines, hoping to find a few left over quarters.

Then I'd check the phone slots to try and find some loose nickels and dimes. You think I'm kidding?

I used to go through the garbage bins in the yards of pizza

parlors and candy stores, looking for bottles that could be turned in for deposits. We're talking 2¢ Coke, Pepsi and Royal Crown. Bet you never heard of Royal Crown.

On big days I'd be lucky enough to find five-cent refund bottles of Hoffman Cocoa Creme and Sasparella. I was in clover then.

When I got enough for a $20 stake, I got into fifty cent roulette games or a dollar seven-card stud game. You only had to ante a nickel to get three cards.

I'd squeeze and crimp my play until I reached a hot roll. Many times I'd run my $20 stake into a thousand dollar bankroll. I'd leave my $2 a day boarding house palace and take up residence in one of the upscale casinos on the strip, like the Riviera or Sahara.

Then I'd play like a big shot in a $5–$10 poker game or try to break the bank in a $25 crap game. Like a boob I'd give it all back and crawl back to my one room flat, where the only window gave me a bird's eye view of Harry's Hamburger Haven's garbage bin, where come nightfall I'd be picking through the rubbish, searching for my next bankroll.

I learned how to lose because I did so much of it, and I hated it, but it never dawned on me that the key was in money management and discipline.

The revelation didn't come until I had sunk so low that I considered getting an (ugh) honest job, making a regular salary.

Since I was too dumb or too lazy to go that route, the only alternative was stop losing so much.

That meant quitting with a tiny profit, a tough pill to swallow. But when you are so low that you gotta look up to look down, you realize that discretion is the better part of valor.

So I pushed aside my illusion of grandeur, swallowed my pride, and got down to the business of winning, and the big thing was winning and walking with a profit.

I mastered the Regression system, which kept me in the game, but most of all I set and stayed with my win goals and loss limits. There were no more big paydays, but no more wipe outs.

I had acquired discipline and just in time. Shortly thereafter the soda companies went to disposable bottles. I'd have had no way of raising a stake to get into action.

So don't go thinking I just fell across these methods or read them in a book somewhere. I learned them through the school of hard knocks but it all didn't come together overnight.

Remember that old saying that your parents used to hang on you: "If I only knew then, what I know now, I'd be a genius."

Well, I now pop it on my daughters. But it's true: If I knew how important money management and discipline was, way back in my dopey playing days, maybe I would be close to being rich.

I sure did leave a lot of money on the table in those days, but then I was walking on my brains, so my thinking was all disoriented.

But you have the chance to learn from my mistakes. Hear my words, O ye of Little Faith.

Discipline is the key!

145

Who Gambles?

My mother likes to gamble, she loves the thrill of the chase.

She is eighty-three years old. For fifty years she was married to the greatest guy who ever breathed—my Dad, my best friend. They raised three kids, one of which turned out to be a gambler.

When my Dad died, I needed something to keep my mother happy. Today she is completely happy going to bingo, playing gin rummy with my daughters Lori and Colleen, and going to Atlantic City every week, sometimes twice a week.

She plays the slots, video poker, and roulette and enjoys it. I drive her to the casinos every week and she goes off and plays for four hours.

Right now it is 11:15 on a Sunday morning and as soon as Mass is over, I'll pick her up and whisk her to Atlantic City.

She doesn't have a lot of money, in fact her bankroll is about $170. How can she go to Atlantic City every week, play bingo and gin rummy, take a shot on the lottery and not go broke?

The answer is discipline. When she gets ahead, she stops and plays video poker, a game that can give you two hours of play on a handful of quarters.

When she loses, she keeps the losses down, walking the Boardwalk or listening to the band in the cocktail lounge.

My mother is just like hundreds of thousands of people who

love to gamble, love the excitement, love the involvement, love the chase, love the fact that it is an outlet for their dreams and helps pass the time in a relaxing manner.

But you gotta have discipline, or else you ain't gonna be back three times a week.

There are millions of people who love the thrill of the casinos but haven't a clue as to how to manage their money in such a way that they can stay alive for hours with a short bankroll.

It is my humble opinion that 70 percent of the people who enter a casino get ahead a decent (10 percent) percentage of what they brought with them and 90 percent of that 70 percent give it back. How stupid.

That's the second time I've given you that figure—memorize it. Maybe it'll help you realize why people lose. They have no discipline.

Gambling ain't something that's gonna go away, but it ain't something that's gonna make you rich. On the other hand you don't have to play like a dork, just because you get to visit the casinos only once every two or three months.

If you gamble (and why else would you be reading this book except to see the pictures) get to realize the necessity of having control.

Millions of people gamble every day and they love it. But they lose for one reason: they gamble stupidly. They are *not* stupid people, they just don't know how to gamble. It's all money management and discipline.

Time to pick up my passenger for our trip to Atlantic City. There'll be a basketball game on the radio and I'll have a few quid on the outcome.

My mother has a running $5 wager on every game I'm on. She finds it hard to keep up with the running account of the game on the radio, so she spends the time saying the Rosary, or chattering about her last bingo encounter where she needed just one number for the jackpot—last week it was B-14.

The stories remain the same, the numbers that got away change.

As soon as the game on the radio is over she hits me with the stock question: "Did we win?" She loves to gamble, and so do you.

So do most of the people who plop two feet on the floor every morning. But they lack discipline, or have I said that before?

Incidentally, look around, you may have a spare Mom or Dad who'd love to have an outlet. It could be a trip to the casinos with a couple of rolls of quarters, a nice lunch and a nice change from their everyday routine.

Maybe you're rotten company on the way home because you played like a dope and got whacked, but perhaps they'd like to do something different.

It doesn't have to be gambling, but at least do something *for* them, so they can be involved.

Who likes to gamble? Thousands of people my friend. Thousands and thousands and thousands and....

146

The Loud Mouth

I love the Casino life, the world of gambling, the thrill of the chase and the people I meet day after day at the track, in the Casinos, and at card games. It's quite a life.

But since that life brings me into contact with so many people, there's gonna be some that rub me a little wrong.

One of these the Loud Mouth. You can probably see him at every gambling endeavor and you can be sure to hear him.

The Loud Mouth makes it a point to be noticed, working overtime to impress people who have the rotten misfortune to be at his table.

His enormous ego has to be fed constantly and the first bite comes with his buy-in. He likes to buy-in with a thousand dollars at a five dollar table, well aware that most of the players at that table are competing with a handful of chips.

"Well, I guess you dealers are glad to see old Bubba at this table. Give you a chance to handle some big bets!"

Big deal sees some poor guy squeezing the remainder of his chips, obviously trying desperately to stay in the game. Big Bubba tosses him a $5 chip and then makes sure that the world knows of his generosity.

"Here you are fellow, start your second million, and you got good natured Bubba to thank!" Then he looks around to make sure everyone is tuned into his display of good will.

When it's his turn to roll the dice, he holds up the game by positioning and repositioning the dice as everyone steams. The floor people bit their tongues trying not to antagonize this pest, but aware that everyone else is furious.

Big Boob Bubba completely disrupts the game, insults the other players when they bet small, makes a play for every attractive lady that happens to come to the table and hands his business cards to players that would like to stuff them up his ear.

He orders three drinks at a time from the cocktail waitress and when she returns he makes a big noise out of dropping his chips into that piece of no man's land this is politely referred to as "The Cleavage."

The waitress attempts to pass it off as part of the price you pay and tries to smile and walk away.

Old Bubba takes one last shot. "Hey, beautiful, you looked like you needed a little help up there, so old Bubba was just trying to lend a hand."

Then he roars at his sadistic humor as the girl walks away in total embarrassment.

The Loud Mouth continues his attempt to control the table, but you'll notice his so-called forced bravado is only apparent while he is winning. The more he wins, the louder and more obnoxious he gets.

But let him run into a cold spell. In a flash he becomes sullen and downright nasty. He asks for the dice to be changed in the middle of a roll.

He blames the other players for casting shadows on the table by having their hands hanging over the edge.

He challenges the floor people to give him a comp, then bad mouths the casino he happens to be in.

If things start to turn right again, he switches back to a low class loud mouth and stays that way only as long as he is winning.

The Loud Mouth cannot be avoided. He seems to find your table and no one is safe from his self-centered banter.

The other players hate him, the dealers try to avoid him, the floor people try to ignore him.

Everyone gives him plenty of space, hoping he'll blow away. The Loud Mouth brings his own windbag!

147

Setting an Amount

The reason people lose in a casino is because they won't set their win goals and loss limits. Those amounts should be set ahead of time and not when you get to the table.

A couple of chapters ago I told you that 10 percent of your starting bankroll was a fabulous return. It is!

I also gave you an alternative amount of 20 percent, due to the fact that most of you don't have the proper bankroll to follow my correct percentage return of 10 percent.

As you grow wiser in the business of gambling, you'll soon be ready and willing to accept 10 percent and even 5 percent profits.

If you already have reached that point, you'll see that the times you grind out a 10 percent return will happen more frequently. That's because you're asking for realistic profits and if you do proper charting and money management moves, you'll see an enormous upswing in the number of times you reach that 10 percent.

In fact, the feelings of winning will so engulf you that you'll start to drop the percentage return lower and lower, but your starting bankroll will be getting higher. Which means the amount of percentage return that you set will be easier to acquire, even though the figures will be the same.

Here, suppose you took $300 to the table and set a 10 percent return or $30 profit. That's not asking for a lot. In fact if you placed $22 Inside, you're asking for just a tiny amount of five hits and you've got $35.

Now let's say you take $440 to that table. You can increase your bets to $44 Inside. Now you need only three hits and you have a $42 profit.

You see ow the higher bankroll allows higher bets, less hits, and lower percentage returns, but the same amount of profit return—or, sometimes higher.

It's all discipline and *wanting to win*. Next time you go into a casino, set the amount you want to win, based on your Bankroll.

... But don't be a dork by weakening your disciplined approach by giving it back to the house.

148

Accepting Your Goal

This is really a continuation of the previous chapter, but it is the icing on the cake.

What's the use of setting your amount and then when you get it, not use the discipline to accept that profit?

It's like you spending six months trying to get the private number of Miss World and when you finally get it, not having the brains to use it.

My friend Hope Liss is a hopeless case when it comes to Discipline. She goes to the casino three times a month, plays craps and loves the method of $44 Inside. Bankroll is no problem, but setting a win goal is her stumbling block.

She has lost twenty-seven times in a row, not because she didn't get ahead, but because she doesn't quit when she reaches her goal. The last time she went, she swore up and down that this would be the day she would set her win goal amount and quit when it was reached.

Glory be! Hope Liss was finally gonna quit a winner. Sure enough she set her percentage amount and settled in on 10 percent of her bankroll.

She charted the tables, eventually finding a table that was going the way she predetermined to play and bought in. Within twenty minutes she had a $120 profit and true to her word, she grabbed her chips and walked.

Then she located her boyfriend, Les Hope, who had just blown $150 on the big wheel, and dragged him towards the door. I couldn't believe what I was seeing. It restored my faith in Hope.

As Hope Liss was dragging Les Hope to the door, he asked for a minute to go to the john.

While she waited, Hope Liss stood watching another craps game that was in progress. She glanced at her watch, noticed that less than an hour was used, and decided to pad her winnings, just until Les joined her.

She bought in and started to play. By the time her better half returned, Hope Liss was hopelessly entrenched in a losing streak. It was all over but the shouting.

And the shouting continued all the way home. Hope Liss blamed every shooter at that second table, the dealers who were probably rooting against her, the guy who invented craps and the fact that Les Hope's weak kidneys had led to her weak discipline.

A timeworn story. Hope Liss and Les Hope haven't got a prayer of a chance of changing their style. They haven't a clue as to what it takes to win.

If you can't accept you win goal then it's obvious you don't know how to win.

Don't laugh at or scoff at this example. We've all been guilty of this scenario, and the crusher is that we never learn from the mistakes!

149

Why Do You Gamble?

You'll give me one thousand reasons, ranging from thrill, outlet, excitement, pasttime, to the most popular retort of all: "I dunno!"

I already explained that the reasons fall into the category of need. If that need is money, then I wish you'd learn to satisfy that need by accepting logical percentage returns.

I love to win money. I am on a high every time I wrap up a session and have a profit to rat-hole. I ain't no smarter than any person at that table.

I just play smarter. That means I quit with a profit, even if it is only a tiny return. The reason I go to that table is to win money, so that when the feat is accomplished, the feet start walking.

I don't know why you gamble, but methinks the underlying reason for most of you is like the reason I do things:

(a) I eat because I'm hungry.
(b) I sleep because I'm tired.
(c) I drink because I'm thirsty.
(d) I play softball because I'm good.
(e) I read because I'm curious.
(f) I drive because I'm lazy.
(g) I run because I'm late.
(h) I laugh because I'm happy.
(i) I cry because I probably lost a bet.

(j) I gamble because I want money.

(k) I don't date Racquel Welch because she won't say yes.

(l) I dream about it because I'm a dirty old man, but that's another story.

You notice how all of the above actions are positive fulfillments of a desire (except k). All of these things in me can be fulfilled by just satisfying the need (except k).

Since we're talking about gambling, go to (j) and notice that the reason I gamble is for money. That is a logical reason, and I want that money bad enough to accept small consistent returns.

(a) I wish you'd feel the same way.

(b) I wish you'd realize how great it is to win.

(c) I wish you'd realize how horrible a feeling it is to lose.

(d) I wish you'd grasp the theory of accepting percentage returns.

(e) I wish you would learn how to win.

(f) I wish you could get me a date with Racquel.

All of the above is within your grasp...well, all but (f).

150

The Shot

My friend Tyne Gole is my idea of a great player. She has mastered the game of craps, follows the Big Four, and keeps a wary eye on the Little Three.

Most of all she sets win goals and loss limits and the goals that Tyne Gole sets are very tiny goals. In fact she is more than content to accept 10 percent returns.

But alas and alack, she longs for the day to go for "The Shot."

Every day that feeling creeps into my mind. People come up and ask if I ever get the urge to go for the shot. My answer is a resounding yes. But I suppress the feelings and revert to the Regression System and incorporate a strict Up-and-Pull series with double and triple regressions.

There are days when my first bet is $20 and a win calls for a regression to $10 and then subsequent wagers of $15, $20, $25, $35, $20, $25 etc. as the wins continue. These eight winning bets kick off a nice return and I'm deeply gratified.

But the hindsight of parlaying those eight wins would have given me a profit of $5110. Hey man, that's some return. But I push the thought from my mind and try to concentrate on other things, like the fact that after the first Win, the Regression locked up a profit for me, while the parley demands a constant winning pattern and a loss gobbles up everything.

The temptation is always there to go for "The Shot" and I'm

sure that Tyne Gole has a lot of second thoughts on her way home, wishing that some day she'll stuff her pocketbook with that seven or eight thousand dollar profit.

Tyne Gole is not without feelings. She starts at a table, grinding out small series returns, pulling down her bets after one or two place numbers have been banged, while glancing jealously at the other players who suddenly catch a hot shooter and reap in chip after chip.

She stands there with her locked-in profit, trying to ignore the scorching roll, but secretly wishing that some day she will succumb to temptation and go for that "Shot."

You've probably suffered through those times and I'd be lying if I didn't also admit to that feeling.

But that's where they separate the men from the boys. It takes guts to maintain the discipline that's needed to be a consistent winner.

Your bonanza days will come because of the use of the plateaus. If you master the approach, you'll get your kill. But as for taking "The Shot" on a constant basis, I vehemently disagree.

I like Tyne Gole and love her style. She sometimes goes home a small loser, but most times it's as a steady winner.

She sometimes goes home with a thought of going for "The Shot." But the next time down, she goes back to the approach that taught her how to win.

As the saying goes, "You always stay with the gal you brought to the dance."

I ask you, I bet you, I implore you: put the dreams of "The Shot" on the back burner. It don't take discipline to go for the kill, it only takes a careless disregard for money.

People have been going for "The Shot" for years. How many really make it?

Find Tyne Gole in the casino and do as she does. Go for the tiny goal and go hope happy.

151

Wanting to Win

We're winding down the section on discipline but I think the whole message can be wrapped into three little words: "Wanting to win."

You gotta wanna win so bad that it becomes an obsession. In the previous chapter I alluded to the fact that Tyne Gole sometimes goes home with a headache, due to the pressure. That ain't a fallacy.

There are times I go home with everything aching but my left pinky, both kneecaps and my right big toe.

Standing for seven hours at a craps table has me seeing dice jumping off the wall and numbers flying through my mind: 38–23–37!!!

Seems those numbers are always on my mind—but that's another story.

There are guys who *say* they wanna Win, but when they do get ahead, they give you that stupid grin and that stupider analogy: "Well, I don't go to the casinos too often, so when I get to the tables I like to get in a lot of action."

So the dork plays for three more hours, screams himself hoarse, spills four drinks down his shirt, splits his pants bending over for a dollar chip, gets into an argument with the box man for throwing the dice off the table six times, gets poked in the ribs by the guy next to him for inadvertently taking his neighbor's chips, blows back the $200 he was ahead, gets to his car and finds he lost his keys and wallet when his pants ripped, can't prove to the cops whose car it is, and gets cited for indecent exposure because of the slashed pants.

When he finally gets home, his wife asks him how he did. Again he flashes that half baked smile and says, "Well, I didn't win, but I sure did get in a lot of action."

People like this say they wanna win but I rather doubt it. I believe they'd rather play.

They lack the burning, driving, fanatical, obsessive desire to win. Now you can disagree with my priorities when it comes to gambling, but I believe if you really don't wanna win, then you shouldn't play.

So even on the days when everything aches, my feelings are soothed by the added paper in my wallet.

You just gotta win. How bad do you wanna win? Tell the truth.

152

The Professional Gambler

You don't have to be Fred Astaire to dance, you don't have to be Larry Bird to play basketball, you don't have to be Frank Sinatra to sing, you don't have to be a kid to like Christmas, you don't have to be Irish to wear green, but you gotta be good to win at gambling.

So despite the millions and millions of people who gamble, only a handful can make a living at it. They are professional gamblers.

I ain't trying to say you should be a professional gambler but at least you should use the discipline that they exhibit.

After all, you use your feet like Fred Astaire, your shooting hand like Larry Bird, your voice like Frank Sinatra, you approach Christmas with the same outlook as a kid and you even lie about your Irish heritage. (Believe it or not I'm writing this chapter on March seventeenth and so far today I was greeted by several guys decked in green from head to foot. Their names were Tony, Nick, Angelo, and Roberto.)

So why is it that when you gamble, you emulate one of the seven dwarfs, Dopey.

I've been gambling since bread was eleven cents a loaf and I know how to lose. In fact I was so dumb that it was the only thing I was good at.

My gut feeling about gambling was that everybody lost. I was living proof that a fool and his money are soon parted.

There were weeks when I'd win on Monday, Tuesday and Wednesday, be broke on Thursday, pull ahead Friday and Saturday, and give it all back on Sunday.

My initial trips to Vegas allowed me to come in contact with guys who made a living gambling. These pros played at the tables where I dealt when I was broke, which was most of the time.

They didn't win all the time but their losses were small.

They played poker like rocks, blackjack with impeccable decisions, and craps with unbelievable control. From them I learned how to win. I think the biggest thing these pros showed me was that smart gamblers weren't always the high rollers.

Somewhere in the back of my mind I always pictured the professional gambler as driving a black convertible, wearing a black hat, escorting two gorgeous blondes and tossing money around like Imus Pressit tosses advice.

How wrong can you be? I spend two-and-one-half hours every day driving to Atlantic City and two-and-one-half hours back. It takes me two to three hours a day to handicap all of the football, baseball, or basketball games to come up with one or two lousy decisions.

A poker game offers the thought that it is a happy exercise, where seven or eight guys get together and stuff their guts with goodies while the players take turns telling stories of big wins at other games and tell tales of big nights with beautiful women.

Let me clue you in on a typical poker game where I attempt to pick up a few dollars. The other players don't make jokes and don't make mistakes.

If you stay too long, or get out too soon, or play scared, or play stupid, these wolves will gobble your money quicker than a blink.

Talk is minimal, mercy is absent, good hands are scarce and skill is a necessity. Mistakes are expensive and losing nights are very discouraging.

What I am trying to say is that the life of a professional

gambler isn't the fun and games that Maverick would lead you to believe.

Being a professional gambler calls for you to have all facets of the Big Four, especially discipline, and even then, the pro has only a 50--50 chance of winning.

You don't have to be a professional gambler to win but at least take the time to learn the game where you risk your money. Approach gambling the way the pro does.

If you risk your money at any form of gambling, be sure you're perfect at that game, be sure you have enough money to compete, be sure you know what to bet after a win and what to bet after a loss.

Finally, be sure you have the driving desire to win, just like the professional does. What the heck to you think I'm asking you to do?

(a) Go without eating for 7 days?

(b) Walk on hot coals?

(c) Not watch TV for three weeks?

(d) Talk nice to your wife?

(e) Throw away the back issues of Playboy you have hidden in the garage?

I ain't asking you to do any of these things that will cause you grief! I'm asking you to have the guts to practice discipline like the professional gambler and the brains to realize that it's more fun to win small amounts than be entertained for five hours and lose like a jerk.

If the pro can master discipline, so can you.

153

Wrapping Up Discipline

We finally wind down the section on discipline. Maybe it was just words to you but those words contain the message that will get you to understand what gambling is all about.

The characters who appeared in this book, D. C. Plinn, Watt E. Cey, Hope Liss, Shorty Shortkash, Buck D. Trenn, The Loud Mouth, Les Hope, Y. R. Kash, Buck D. House, Lou N. Shirt, Stu Pidd, I. M. Madork, Imus Pressit, and all the rest are not fictitious characters.

They are real people, people that you'll see every day in the world of gambling. They are oblivious to the mistakes they make. They could read this book from cover to cover, nod and agree with the theory, swear to correct their mistakes and then go to the casino and revert to their controlless idiotic style of play.

You can make all the resolves you want about changing your approach to gambling. Let's see what you do when it's time to pay the fiddler.

Let's see if you got the intestinal fortitude to follow these strict rules of discipline:

(a) Chart the tables.
(b) Set win goals.
(c) Set loss limits.
(d) Have a predetermined method of play.

(e) Use the regression system.
(f) Incorporate plateaus.
(g) Utilize Up-and-Pull method.
(h) Divide win goal into Guarantee and Excess.
(i) Quit a winner.

I've given you a ton of systems but in my heart I know you won't or can't adopt my conservative approach.

Go back and look over the money management chapters and zero in on the "$22 Inside" or the "$44 Inside" or the "$66 Inside" or the "Richochet System" or the "Patrick System."

They're all effective, but they do require discipline. Only you can decide how much you'll accept these theories.

The answers are all on these pages, but it's gonna be hard to change your approach to gambling and adopt the conservative style that's necessary to win consistently.

The next time you're in the casino, look for my friend Dyann Tuplay. She needs money but is dying to play, mostly for the thrill it gives her.

As much as she needs a decent return to offset prior losses, Dyann Tuplay cannot push herself away from the tables. People like her will never swing over cause they're more wrapped up in their chase for the golden goose and the fun that they get out of making that chase.

Discipline is the final part of the Big Four and the one that causes most people to slip.

A lot of you can raise the proper bankroll, and many others spend enough time picking up all the knowledge that's required.

Some of you even master the strict rules of money management and even go so far as setting win goals and loss limits, and believe it or not, you even adopt the Regression System.

But then the time for discipline comes and your resolves to quit melt from your repertoire like a soggy pound of butter melts in a red hot oven.

You laugh at Imus Pressit, who presses his bets at a craps table faster than a three-hundred pound food junkie shovels a seven-course meal into his oversized belly.

You scoff at Shorty Shortkash who enters a game with a roll of quarters, his penny-filled piggy bank, and a clammy hand wrapped around a set of Rosary beads.

You smile at Les Hope, who never played craps, but brings a set of instructions to the table and tries to copy the different players at the table but in reality lacking any hope of winning.

All these people lack a part of the Big Four. You're proud that you have the first three parts of the Big Four, but you crumble like a straw building in a windstorm as soon as it's time to exercise some discipline.

Maybe you gotta be compared to I. M. Madork and be ranked number one on the Ding-Dong List of Losers but that list is so long, you'll probably feel comfortable being with all your friends.

I think what has to happen to you is just what happened to me. You gotta wake up one morning and realize that losing is a rotten feeling and a one way road to disaster.

You'll realize that discipline is the key to winning and all of these messages of control that you skipped over and ignored will now have a different meaning. You'll start to pick up things that will reduce losses and kick off consistent profits.

You'll finally realize that I do not speak with forked tongue and the money management and discipline *are* the key to gambling.

You'll think I walk on water—I do, but that's another story!

Right now just swallow the one on discipline. It'll make you a winner.

Odds and Ends

154

Comps

Let's get right to this subject 'cause there are a cluster of people waiting for me to tell them how to get comped. The word is derived from the term complimentary, and there are people who believe that being comped is more important than winning.

I. M. Loudd has a mouth that is in continuous motion and he never talks in less than a holler. Besides being a loud mouth, he numbers a lot of other attributes such as trouble maker, bore, griper, and beggar.

I. M. Loudd is constantly begging for meals, rooms, show tickets, anything he can weasel out of the floor people. He does it in a loud, obnoxious, almost demeaning manner, attempting to shame the hosts into fulfilling his wishes.

The loud one is not a heavy player although he does bet in the range of $10 to $15 a number, a decent play but not in the category of the green and black chip players that the casinos try to appease.

It puts the Casino people in a touchy position. They want to take care of their patrons, but at the same time they can't give away the store.

Let's put the comps in their proper perspective. First of all the casinos offer free drinks, coffee, and soda all day long to anyone who desires them.

The right to give out meal comps falls on the shoulders of the pit bosses and floor people who keep a close watch on the betting amounts of the players at the table.

If your play falls in the predetermined category that is set by the casino, then these floor people will reward you. But they can't comp everyone. Not because they don't want to. They can't. The meal lines would be fourteen miles long.

Nick L. Bett is a weekend player, visits the casino three times a year, bets nickels at the tables but has heard all about comps. He doesn't have a mouth like I. M. Loudd, but he plays at a table for long periods, even through his losing times, hoping he'll be comped.

He blows $150 hoping for a $15 comp at the deli. When he doesn't get it, his world is shattered. He is more upset about not being comped than he is over the money he lost.

On the slow days when a kind-hearted floor person will offer Nick L. Bett a pass to the food kitchen, the poor guy wets his pants he's so happy. I feel sorry for the poor guy or anybody who lives and dies by the fact that he receives a comp.

Speaking of feeling sorry, my sympathies go out for the poor pit people who have to deal with I. M. Loudd. He begs for comps in loud screeching exhibitions of tasteless prodding and many times gets one, just so he'll keep his trap shut.

Try to understand that it is not important that you get comped. I'd rather see you follow the loss limits and win goal theories and buy your own dinner from the profits.

When the day comes that you are betting amounts that warrant a comp, you'll be taken care of. Don't beg and don't worry if your play is overlooked. You're not there to eat, you're there to win.

155

Tipping

Here's a subject that comes into our lives every day and in most cases is an abused undertaking. People don't know how to deal with it. They either tip too much or too little, depending on whether you are the tipper or the tippee.

My oldest daughter Lori works part time as a waitress while she goes to college. Her whole day is made by the tips she receives, as there is no base salary.

The stories she tells are truly unbelievable. I asked her to give me a couple of examples and these happened in the past two weeks:

(1) Six men tied up a table for four hours, ran up a bill of $140 and left a $12 tip.
(2) A family of four had dinner and drinks totalling $62 and left a $5 bill.
(3) Two women had lunch, the bill was $26. They left $2.
(4) A husband and wife duo had dinner, a couple of drinks, talked all night to Lori, ran up a bill of $43 and had "just enough money to cover the bill." They asked for her address so they could send her a tip. That was over a week ago.

The above examples are true. There are eight million stories in the world of tipping. These have been four of them.

It's a crime how stupid people are when it comes to tipping. Maybe I should say cheap. Lori also says there are people who are overly generous and many people fall into that category.

But in the casinos you don't have the unwritten rule of 15 percent or 20 percent of your bill to guide your tip, so you have to use other barometers.

The dealers do not make a big base pay, so they rely heavily on the generosity of the players. When they do get a big tipper at the table, you'll notice the stick man will thank the tipper and then the dealer on his side of the table will also acknowledge the gratuity.

Rather than just give the dealers the chips, I suggest making a play for them. This way they have a chance of getting a bigger return. Here are some methods to use:

(a) Dollar any craps.
(b) Dollar Yo.
(c) Hard Way bet.
(d) Bet on Don't Pass.
(e) Bet on Pass Line.

You don't have to overtip, either in dollar amounts or number of times. My suggestion is a tip every five or six shooters, depending on whether you are winning.

I tip when I'm winning, usually every fourth shooter and my play is the Hard Way bet. I'll throw $4 on the table and state "Two Way Hard Six and Hard Eight."

That merely means a dollar on the hard six and a hard eight for me and one each for the dealer. They're now in action and have a potential for a 9 to 1 return. I like these plays better than the one roll action bets like the Yo or any craps.

If you bet in green and black chips, you can either use this method in higher amounts, or else give them a $5 bet on the Pass Line or Don't Pass Line.

However, it you get a couple of wise guy dealers or surly people who act like they're totally bored with your play, don't tip. There is absolutely no reason to tip a cranky, uncooperative, irritating person.

Read into these next two paragraphs as I ain't gonna draw a picture for you.

When you tip, the dealers are aware of your generosity and let their fellow dealers know of your action. In fact some of them use so much energy thanking you and alerting their co-workers that they get a little sloppy and end up making mistakes. In fact, some of those mistakes result in bonanzas in your favor.

Also, these dealers hit lapses when they get tired and make errors in payoffs and usually in favor of their benefactors, human errors, but these things tend to happen.

Watt E. Cey has a typical blank look plastered across his mug as he attempts to decipher the previous two paragraphs. But then Watt E. Cey can't see the lawn for the grass and wouldn't know a "hidden message" even if it was written in blood and plastered across his eyeballs.

Should you tip? Yeah, it ain't a bad idea.

Word spreads and soon all the dealers are zeroed in on who's apt to give them a tip—and a lot will reciprocate.

Should you tip? I already told you... Affirmative!

156

Attitude

You may think this has no bearing on your gambling forays, but attitude has a big input into the way you approach gambling. A lot of people firmly believe that it is impossible to win and that it is only a matter of time before they are whacked at the table.

Ken Twinn is the ultimate pessimist when it comes to gambling. Ken Twinn believes he can't win no matter how he plays. His attitude is one of surrender, before he even gets to the table.

You've heard Ken Twinn talk to his wife as he enters the Casino: "I ain't won a bet in six weeks, there's no way I can hold my losses under $2000!"

With an attitude like that, how can this morbid moron hope to compete? He's beat before he even makes his first bet.

You ain't gonna win every time you play, and that's not a guess. It's a truism that you better swallow, and it's even based on the fact that you're a perfect player. But you don't have to go to battle with your tail between your legs.

Get the proper winning attitude or stay clear of the tables. A lot of people like Ken Twinn honestly believe they can't win. So they end up losing.

If you have the proper bankroll, a complete knowledge of the game, a strong money management method and the ability to practice strict discipline, you'll get your share of winnings.

But if you don't have the proper attitude, if you don't believe you have a chance at gambling, then don't gamble.

157

Luck in Gambling

There is no such thing as luck in gambling. Yet you hear people moan and groan about their rotten "luck" when they lose.

They didn't lose because they were unlucky. They probably lost because they played like dopes. Yet people still refer to their outcome as being the direct result of either bad luck or good luck.

My friend Horace Minure has no concept of gambling and every system he tries stinks. In fact Horace Minure plays like. . . . well, like horse manure. No wonder he loses. Yet the first thing out of his mouth is "Boy, if bad luck was a sneeze I'd have pneumonia. The only luck I got is bad."

The poor guy plays blackjack but never heard of surrender or insurance. He splits tens against everything, stands with a soft (A-3) fourteen versus dealer's nine, doubles a ten versus dealer's queen, splits sevens versus dealer's Ace and hits hard thirteen versus dealer's four.

Then cries about God hating him and wishing all this bad luck on him.

My idea of good luck is calling the dentist, getting a wrong number and ending up with Loni Anderson on the other end, in a talking mood, and eventually making plans to meet her that night.

My idea of bad luck is to show up and find Burt Reynolds waiting for me and popping a few short rights to the jaw for having the audacity to call his wife.

Thinking back, maybe the fact I didn't get the dentist was bad luck and not good luck.

But in the casino, luck doesn't even enter my mind. I've lost a ton of sports bets in the last two seconds, when somebody hits a trey with time running out and I lose by a point.

In baseball, a .212 hitting utility infielder, who hasn't had an extra base hit in four years, pinch hits in the bottom of the ninth and bangs a tape measure shot into the third tier.

These things happen but they also even out over the course of time. I feel rotten but surely don't blame it on luck. It has nothing whatsoever to do with luck.

I walk on cracks and my mother doesn't have broken back, walk under ladders, bet on a pitcher who wears thirteen and wouldn't know a four-leaf clover from a handful of spinach. So much for "unlucky" symptoms.

If you lose in a Casino and attribute it to "bad luck," look over the Big Four and see if you weren't playing with a short bankroll, a lack of knowledge, no money management system or else got ahead and didn't have the discipline to quit. That's probably why you lost.

If you won, it wasn't luck, it could have been you caught a hot table and landed on a scorching trend. That, coupled with the Big Four, gave you a good return.

I hope you don't rely on luck in a casino and I hope you don't have the rotten misfortune to foul up your dentist's phone number and get stuck with Loni's number. That Burt sure can hit.

If I'd have had any luck, it would have been that I ran out of gas on my way to the meeting. But as bad luck would have it, I won a contest that morning and first prize was a full tank of gas, free for the next six months.

Now that's bad luck!

158

Etiquette in a Casino

Man, you don't have to shake the trees to find the loony birds in this world. Just walk through the Casino and watch some of the actions that people go through.

Some act like they never had a meal as they pull out all the stops in trying to get a floor person to issue a comp.

Porter House weights 280 pounds and looks like he just finished off a dozen porter house steaks. Yet there he is, leaning over the velvet ropes, harassing a pit boss for a meal.

"Hey Mac, my brother was one of the electricians who wired this place, and now you're telling me one of his relatives ain't worth a meal?"

At the same time in the roulette section, some guy is attempting to reach over three lays of people to get down a bet. This dope doesn't realize you have to be seated at the table or at least be standing right at the table to make a bet.

But he has the classless taste to bump innocent bystanders in an attempt to get down his action. Then he'll swear at some poor lady who had the misfortune to be standing there and blocking his view.

At the blackjack table, O. B. Noxtious is giving instructions to all the other players as to when to hit, stand, split or double. This obnoxious boob doesn't have the brains to realize he is an irritating jerk and doesn't even see the dirty looks from other patrons.

You've already been introduced to the Loud Mouth at the craps table, also the superstitious characters that take three minutes to "set the dice" a certain way when they are shooting. These people ruffle the feathers of the other players.

The guy who gets me is the loud mouthed Right bettor who has just picked up a score when the shooter makes his point. He yells over at the guy betting Wrong and proclaims, "Let's get all the Don't bettors. Let's show them they can't beat us." Then he screams and claps his hands in an obvious intent to harass the poor guy betting Don't, who just takes his loss and stares down at the table.

I could fill fifteen pages of stories about people who unwittingly or intentionally act like they should be in a pen somewhere. Their manners are crude, their actions unacceptable and only result in other people looking at them in disgust.

It don't take much effort to handle yourself with class in a casino, and in the long run you'll be treated to the things you're striving for in the first place.

My youngest daughter Colleen has more brains in her pinky than I have in my whole body. My graduation from high school was not only a minor miracle but a big assist from a handful of teachers who figured it was a waste of time to inject blood into a stone and perhaps this rock would gather more moss in the outside world.

Colleen has been on the Dean's List the last three semesters, and no, the brains didn't come from my part of the union. But the other day she made a classic revelation in one of our talks, where naturally, I am the listener.

"You know Dad, I notice that in most of my classes, it's the quiet retiring people who are noticed the most. The teachers respect them the most, and they're usually the best liked."

Then she finished with, "I guess you don't have to *force* people to notice you to be seen."

No wonder she's on the Dean's List. But even a dope like me

could add to her insight.

"Colleen, as my old pappy used to say to me, 'If you wanna be seen, stand up. If you wanna be heard, speak up. If you wanna be liked, shut up.'" She liked that.

Eddikit, you don't have to be able to spell it to use it.

159

Intimidation

Don't skip this chapter, especially if you have never played a table game in a casino. Especially if you have never played craps.

Most women who are dying to play this game tell me they are flat-out intimidated by the noise at the tables. They think these crap players know the game and a newcomer would look bad in front of them.

Let me tell you something about those so-called geniuses at the table. They may yell loud, but their knowledge of the game and the proper betting methods is as foreign to them as it is for me to bake a cake.

But I admit to being lost in a kitchen. These guys cover their lack of smarts by yelling, and letting people think they know what they're doing.

So, newcomers are intimidated by the noise and stay away in droves. Yet the game is snap city to play, as shown to you in the basic betting methods.

Betty Stares has been trying to get I. M. Madork to look at her for the past three years with little success. I. M. Madork couldn't see the forest for the trees but still Betty Stares hopes to get him to stare at her.

She is blessed with a 44-inch bust that she stuffs into a size small sweater and puts on a pair of jeans that won't make it through the day.

She heads to the casino with I. M. Madork, completely unaffected by the stares of three thousand boobs like myself who have just witnessed the ninth wonder of the world. Yet Betty Stares can't get a look from the dorky one.

He asks her to play craps and all of a sudden this knock-out who has stopped traffic all day without even a hint of nervousness, becomes petrified at the thought of walking up to that table.

What is that scares people away? What is it they see at that table that forces them to be intimidated?

Maybe you fall into that category. Maybe you think other people are looking at you and you get scared to become involved in the game. So you run off and hide in the slot machine section where you won't be noticed and nobody can judge your play.

Don't scoff at this chapter. Don't think it hasn't crossed your mind that people are looking at you. Don't think you are above intimidation.

I'm asking you not to be worried about what you *think* people may be *thinking* about you at all. You only *think* they are. (I know exactly what I said in that paragraph and I *think* you ought to *think* about it).

Speaking about thinking, I spoke to I. M. Madork about what he thought about Betty Stares.

Nudging me with his elbow, looking around to make sure he wasn't overheard, and giving me an all-knowing wink, he whispers to me in his infinite wisdom, "Man, has she got nice hair."

I walked away in amazement. I must have been intimidated by her attributes. I didn't even notice if she had hair.

160

Reality III

We're down to the last chapter of the book and it is only fitting that I write one more chapter on reality. That's because 99 percent of all the people who gamble don't grasp the true reality of what they're up against. They don't got the insight to see that they're fighting games that only offers them about a 50–50 chance of winning.

So even if you know that your chances of winning or losing are only 50–50, how can you logically expect to double and triple your money?

The answer is in that part of the Little Three called Trends. There are trends all day long in every form of gambling. I try to get you to understand that these trends are there and that all you gotta do is:

a) Chart the tables.
b) Find the trend.
c) Apply your pre-determined system.
d) Follow the money management moves.
e) Quit when you get ahead.
f) Never leave the table a loser when you get ahead at least 20 percent.
g) The amount of the win is unimportant, only the fact you leave the table with more money than you started with.

The day that you grasp the true reality of how tough it is to win at gambling is the day you turn your sessions into winning endeavors.

The day you learn to accept small percentage returns is the start of your being a successful player.

Guys like Imus Pressit will never listen. They can't. They can't see the hopelessness of their super-aggressive, crazy, unpatterned, undisciplined style of play.

They are truly chasing the impossible dream of becoming rich at gambling. That is unrealistic. Reality is accepting what is logically applicable to the endeavors you are undertaking.

In my life I have dreams that are simply false hopes. Things I wish would happen but realize the reality of those things happening and being smart enough to accept less:

 a) I'd like to pitch a no-hitter every night in my fast-pitch softball league.
 b) I'd like to hold the dice for four hours every time I shoot craps.
 c) I'd like to win $5,000 every time I gamble.
 d) I'd like to date Dolly and Racquel and Sophia on alternate nights the rest of my life.

All of the above are dreams. They're unrealistic and in the true world of reality they can't happen:

 a) So when I win a game 9 to 8, after getting whacked for twenty-three hits, I'm ecstatic.
 b) So when I get two hits per shooter and pull down my bets, I'm completely satisfied,
 c) So when I win a beautiful 6 percent or 7 percent or 8 percent, or even 10 percent of my starting bankroll, I'm in seventh heaven,
 d) So when I get a wrong number and the lady on the other line talks for ten minutes, my day is made.

All of the above is reality. It is what I should expect and accept from each undertaking. It is the reality of realizing that you don't get upset when you don't get the super colossal things you think you should.

I want you to realize the reality of gambling. Realize that it is possible to win at gambling. But winning is also small percentage returns.

Make your own list of priorities and see if they are not just a bit unrealistic: like trying to double your starting bankroll at a gambling table.

It'll happen occasionally but *never* enough times to make it a realistic dream.

Reality... It is gonna change your gambling forays if you accept logical realistic returns.

Gambling Books Ordering Information

Ask for any of the books listed below at your bookstore. Or to order direct from the publisher, call 1-800-447-BOOK (MasterCard or Visa), or send a check or money order for the books purchased (plus $4.00 shipping and handling for the first book ordered and $1.00 for each additional book) to Carol Publishing Group, 120 Enterprise Avenue, Dept. 40577, Secaucus, NJ 07094.

Beating the Wheel: The System That's Won More Than $6 Million, From Las Vegas to Monte Carlo by Russell T. Barnhart
$14.95 paper   0-8184-0553-8   (CAN $19.95)

Beat the House: Sixteen Ways to Win at Blackjack, Craps, Roulette, Baccarat and Other Table Games by Frederick Lembeck
$12.95 paper   0-8065-1607-0   (CAN $17.95)

Blackjack Your Way to Riches by Richard Albert Canfield
$12.95 paper   0-8184-0498-1   (CAN $17.95)

The Body Language of Poker: Mike Caro's Book of Tells by Mike Caro
$18.95 paper   0-89746-100-2   (CAN $26.95)

The Cheapskate's Guide to Las Vegas: Hotels, Gambling, Food, Entertainment, and Much More by Connie Emerson
$9.95 paper   0-8065-1530-9   (CAN $13.95)

The Complete Book of Sports Betting: A New, No Nonsense Approach to Sports Betting by Jack Moore
$14.95 paper   0-8184-0579-1   (CAN $20.95)

Darwin Ortiz on Casino Gambling: The Complete Guide to Playing and Winning by Darwin Ortiz
$14.95 paper   0-8184-0525-2   (CAN $20.95)

For Winners Only: The Only Casino Gambling Guide You'll Ever Need by Peter J. Andrews
$18.95 paper   0-8065-1728-X   (CAN $26.95)

Gambling Scams: How They Work, How to Detect Them, How to Protect Yourself by Darwin Ortiz
$11.95 paper   0-8184-0529-5   (CAN $15.95)

Gambling Times Guide to Blackjack by Stanley Roberts
$12.95 paper   0-89746-015-4   (CAN $17.95)

Gambling Times Guide to Craps by N.B. Winkless
$9.95 paper   0-89746-013-8   (CAN $13.95)

How to be Treated Like a High Roller by Robert Renneisen
$8.95 paper   0-8184-0580-4   (CAN $12.95)

John Patrick's Advanced Blackjack
$19.95 paper   0-8184-0582-1   (CAN $27.95)

John Patrick's Advanced Craps
$18.95 paper   0-8184-0577-5   (CAN $26.95)

John Patrick's Blackjack
$14.95 paper   0-8184-0555-4   (CAN $19.95)

John Patrick's Craps
$16.95 paper   0-8184-0554-6   (CAN $20.95)

John Patrick's Roulette
$16.95 paper   0-8184-0587-2   (CAN $22.95)

John Patrick's Slots
$12.95 paper   0-8184-0574-0   (CAN $17.95)

Million Dollar Blackjack by Ken Uston
$16.95 paper   0-89746-068-5   (CAN $23.95)

New Poker Games by Mike Caro
$5.95 paper   0-89746-040-5   (CAN $7.95)

Playing Blackjack as a Business by Lawrence Revere
$15.95 paper   0-8184-0064-1   (CAN $21.95)

Progression Blackjack: Exposing the Cardcounting Myth by Donald Dahl
$11.95 paper   0-8065-1396-9   (CAN $16.95)

Win at Video Poker: The Guide to Beating the Poker Machines by Roger Fleming
$9.95 paper   0-8065-1605-4   (CAN $13.95)

Winning at Slot Machines by Jim Regan
$6.95 paper   0-8065-0973-2   (CAN $7.95)

Winning Blackjack in Atlantic City and Around the World by Thomas Gaffney
$7.95 paper   0-8065-1178-8   (CAN $10.95)

Winning Blackjack Without Counting Cards by David S. Popik
$9.95 paper   0-8065-0963-5   (CAN $13.95)

(Prices subject to change; books subject to availability)